Sense and Finitude

SUNY series in Contemporary Continental Philosophy

Dennis J. Schmidt, editor

Sense and Finitude

*Encounters at the Limits of
Language, Art, and the Political*

ALEJANDRO A. VALLEGA

Published by
State University of New York Press, Albany

© 2009 State University of New York

All rights reserved

Printed in the United States of America

For information, contact State University of New York Press, Albany, NY
www.sunypress.edu

Production by Eileen Meehan
Marketing by Fran Keneston

Library of Congress Cataloging-in-Publication Data

Vallega, Alejandro A.
    Sense and finitude : encounters at the limits of language, art, and the political /
Alejandro A. Vallega.
        p. cm. — (SUNY series in contemporary continental philosophy)
    Includes bibliographical references and index.
    ISBN 978-1-4384-2509-2 (hardcover : alk. paper)
    ISBN 978-1-4384-2510-8 (pbk. : alk. paper)
    1. Continental philosophy.   I. Title.

    B805.V35 2009
    199'.83—dc22   2008025085

10 9 8 7 6 5 4 3 2 1

For Daniela

Contents

Part III: Unbounded Finitudes:
Thought's Sensibility in Art and the Political

Illustrations

Acknowledgments

Those who have sustained my work are many, and they have done so in so many wonderful and unexpected ways. Here I can only mention a few: I thank Omar Rivera, James Risser, Jason Winfree, Ben Pryor, Marcelo Caracoche, Christian Amigo, Roberto Alperoli, Gregor Neu, Mark Brown, Eva Mo, Susan Schoenbohm, Charles Scott, Walter Brogan, John Sallis, and Jerry Sallis. I also thank John Felstiner for allowing me to reproduce the two works by Gisèle Celan-Lestrange that appear in chapter 7. I offer my strongest gratitude to those who worked directly on the project: Claudia Baracchi for her friendship and generous and insightful reading of the manuscript; Jane Bunker and Dennis Schmidt for their support; Patrick Williams for his close editing of the manuscript; and, Daniela Vallega-Neu for her insightful and constant reading at the various stages of the manuscript and for her patient support. I should also note the generosity of the participants and faculty of the Collegium Phänomenologicum over the last six years.

Introduction

Words are the gestures that remain and expose us to the tacit language of being in its many passing senses. This experience of language and thought requires a sensibility that opens for us through contemporary thought: Once conceptual thought, sustained by the metaphysical tradition in the history of the West, encounters its finitude face to face, at that point a sensibility in thought begins to become explicit, a thinking beyond the rational-irrational divide that traditionally frames all determinations of being. The point is not to discover a new faculty or capacity in thought, but to bring forth and highlight a certain disposition towards experience and sense, one that opens when one thinks in light of the singularity and incommensurability of experiences such as the coming to presence of things, their value and meaning, images, words, ideas, desires, memories, sense experiences, and our selves as rational subjects; to mention a few of those moments that we encounter under that slippery word "being," and to which we make claims through language, art, politics, and philosophy. To say it in another register, the aim of this book is to engage a fundamental shift in conceptual philosophical understanding—an epistemic shift.[1] In this sense, for example, the discussion of Heidegger in chapters one through four marks a border that limits his thought as well as an opening in that delimitation towards other ways of undergoing temporality in thought. It is this diversified and diversifying experience of conceptual thought at the limit of its determinations and always already on the way to unbounded configurations beyond its tradition(s) that is sought in various manners in this book. As such, this book does not pretend to have an all encompassing and final interpretation of the many figures and encounters it discusses. My aim is to introduce a sensibility operative in thought in various ways that may encourage the reader to go further into the spaces explored.

A brief mention and explanation about the original and untranslatable title of this book gives a further idea of its focus. The original title was *El Pensamiento Sentido*. Although the phrase "sense and finitude" seems appropriate, sense, as equated with reason on the one hand, and the five senses or faculties on the other, falls short of a certain connotation in the single word, *sentido*. In Spanish, the word "*sentido*," (from the verb *sentir*) refers to the

1

understanding of the senses of experience as simultaneously rooted in ideas or conceptual meaning as well as in sensible experience (hearing, seeing), and ultimately in sensing with heart and soul. Therefore, in speaking of this *pensamiento sentido* under the title *Sense and Finitude*, this book attempts a thought explicitly engaged in the dense interplays between these various registers in which we undergo configurations of being and come to experience them. The interplay is purposeful, and aims for thinking in ways that overflow the traditional divisions between mind-body, reason-passion, objective calculation-feeling, sense perception-intelligible knowledge, contingency-soul, et cetera. In this sense, one might also say that this work engages the concreteness of thought. Furthermore, this thinking between registers particularly concerns the way language, the basic requirement for Western culture and philosophy, can be undergone in relation to nonlinguistic passages, passages that may be uncovered as they situate linguistic meaning in its representational and logical frameworks. For example, I am speaking of the way the senses intermix in the sense of poetic words (synesthesia), such as when a color is understood as a texture and scent; or the way a nonrepresentational graphic image may have sense and call for a title-word, as in the paintings of Paul Klee; or, that tacit sense I experience of the world beyond words already shaping them when a cat sits next to me as I write. Indeed, throughout this book thought arises in relation to elements often thought of as the other of the rational (the irrational, nature, the non-Western, the artistic, the foreign, the fantastic, the ephemeral, the animal, and the forgotten), and, for this reason, as the other of language. In these chapters a resistance to this separation becomes apparent. Furthermore, each chapter calls for a continuous recognition of a certain otherness operative in the very configuration of what we call language (the representational system of significations and logical rules), as well as in what we call philosophy.

A second aspect of the original title takes us a little further into this last statement: *el pensamiento sentido* is meant as a thinking (in words) that is *sentido*, that is, a thinking that is felt, undergone, and withstood in its singular, ephemeral, and concrete finite passages. The book engages the senses of words and ideas in their coming to pass. In this sense, words, ideas, and language do not aim to represent, order, explain, or justify being: my aim is neither ontological nor analytical. Here, words and ideas, images, marks, gestures, absences, and silences function as sites that open and expose us to the singular and transformative undergoing and unexpected possibilities underlying the orderings, logic, definitions, and representations that compose and sustain our senses of truth and reality. Each discussion entails an encounter that exposes the reader to singular sensibilities in thought's engagement of its finitude (most chapters play out the double encounter of a philosopher with a writer or artist and vice versa). These sensibilities occur in the exposure of a philosophical thought to that which it attempts to articulate. In this sense, a determination of thought finds itself exposed to that which informs the thought in its attempt to articulate it. Thus, in its encounter with its object, thought is exposed to that which remains beyond it: in this sense the already self-determined meaning configured by thought suffers a rift as it is situated in its insurmountable otherness, difference, and singularity. Thus, in the unsettling of thought's configuration of sense in its encounter with what cannot be subsumed by it but inspires it, I find a transformative or abyssal, but most importantly, a fecund moment for thought. The way of encountering such moment is perhaps best indicated in my case by the word "exposure" as I have learned to understand it from the poetry of Paul Celan. While composing the various chapters, one line Paul Celan wrote in 1969 often came to mind: "*La poésie ne s'impose plus, elle s'expose.*" "Poetry no longer imposes itself, it exposes itself."[2] It is this turn in language and thought towards its exposure to its concrete and ephemeral finitude that I seek in the following work. This means that ultimately each chapter strives for undergoing the fecund arising of senses of beings through words informed by sensibilities that expose us to the fragile, ephemeral, and concrete movement and figurations that release us to senses of beings. In the following discussion the terms dis-position, sensibility, flesh, abyss, fecund, overflowing, transformative, and unbounded indicate the movement of concrete and ephemeral unfoldings of sense. This is not to forget the ethical-political dimension of such task. In this sense, the point of exposure is that of setting out towards a thought that in exposing itself to its finitude situates our sense of humanity in its open and unbounded possibilities.

In light of this task, it is not enough to follow each philosopher's thought in what they say and intend. If the aim is thought's exposure to its singularity, then we must seek not only what the philosophers say but also how they say it. We will have to pay particular attention to the internal movement of thought, to how the argument is held forth and also transgressed in its very passage. Only then can one begin to understand in what manner and to what extent a thought does expose itself to its very transformative openings. Thus, for the most part, in each chapter I read a philosopher's text closely, and mark the performative character of the thought, that is, the way dispositions, hesitations, silences, differences, and what cannot be said inform the various discourses. For reasons of space, although crucial to my arguments and to the unfolding of thought's sensibility beyond them, I have kept most of the secondary literature off the page. A reader who wants to follow through those important strands should read along with the footnotes. Finally (although for readers less sympathetic to hermeneutics at times the discussions in the various chapters may seem a mere recounting of a philosopher's thought), each discussion is interpretative, that is, the thought is often developed through close interpretative reading of the main original texts discussed.

The structure of this book is simple and straightforward: the first part introduces the central theme and some of the main issues around it; the other two parts unfold these out of specific encounters between artists, philosophers, and writers.

Part 1 is composed of five chapters. The first four form an extensive meditation on one of the most violent encounters of conceptual philosophy and its metaphysical tradition with its temporality or finitude, namely Heidegger's attempt at a "beyng-historical thinking" in his most intimate and second major work, *Contributions to Philosophy*. Each of the four chapters introduces a central theme concerning the opening of the sensibility and exposure in finitude that our book engages. Chapter 1 discusses thought in its singular situation in our times, that is, life under the rule of the strongest form of metaphysical rationalism, that which Heidegger calls machination (*Machenschaft*). The discussion focuses particularly on the overpowering and infinite formulation and production of the senses of all human experience and its contexts (in its present, past, and future) as dominated and determined by reason's quantification, calculation, and production. Chapter 2 points out the emptiness of this manner of understanding existence, and explains how in such exposure to its emptiness rational production encounters a limit. The meditation goes on to indicate how, in the marking of this limit, thought encounters an opening beyond the product of the rational, and towards thinking in the arising of unbounded, fecund, or overflowing senses of beings. This opening leads towards understandings of sense that may be engaged out of other traditions, histories, concerns, and experiences than those framed by the history of the rational metaphysical tradition and machination. Chapter 3 takes chapter 2 further, and explores the specific sensibility or disposition of thought in its unbounded undergoing of senses of being. This chapter articulates thought in its undergoing exposure to its finitude, specifically as a thinking that arises in and through undergoing its overflowing diversifying singularity. The theme is developed by showing how this thought's disposition takes concrete form in its unfolding in a language that exposes us to the emptiness and overflowing passage of sense beyond the confines and domination of rational quantification and production, and in a manner that is transformative for the senses configured as well as for the tradition. Chapter 4 turns back to look at Heidegger's specific engagement with such fecund abyssal exposure. The discussion shows that Heidegger's thought is caught between two visions: the overflowing of being, and the task of leading the Western philosophical tradition to its justification and thought to its single destiny. This double vision leads Heidegger to a certain indecision, or immobility, with respect to a direct engagement with the fecund opening beyond the tradition his thought undergoes: as a result he does not take up the task his thought opens for philosophy, that is, the task of thinking sense in and from its overflowing. Chapter 5 introduces the work of the American philosopher Charles Scott. In his work on memory, Scott takes a decisive step (in departure from Heidegger) and begins to think sense out of and through its emptiness and fecund overflowing, without burdening or justifying this exposed thinking by assigning it to the task of the destiny of thought in the Western philosophical tradition. Indeed, Scott takes the tradition as the site for the undergoing of the unbounded overflowing of sense.

Part 2 explores the sense of language in light of the task of configuring senses of being out of and in fecund finitude. In diverse ways the chapters discuss the play of nonlinguistic experience in the configuration of language and its sense. Chapter 6 discusses the arising of language out of *physis* in Plato's *Phaidros*, particularly the way logos arises in *physis* not above or as other to it, as is the case in the modern juxtaposition of language and nature. At the same time, the discussion also develops a sense of logos as a medium in which sense is configured and articulated. The chapter closes with a reflection on the transformative character of sense in its coming to presence in language. Chapter 7 explores Gadamer's elegant and rich reading of Paul Celan's poetry in *Who am I, Who are You?* The analysis takes its departure from Gadamer's exposure of thought to Celan's poetry, then goes on to discuss the limits of his reading in his inscription of Celan's poetry in a continuous uninterrupted linguistic sense of language. The chapter then suggests a more radical reading of the sense of language in hermeneutics by exploring Celan's unfolding of his poetic language out of his relation and sense of the nonfigurative and nonlinguistic graphic works of his wife Giséle Celan-Lestrange. The next and final chapter in the section takes up Derrida's lifelong engagement with the works of Antonin Artaud. The piece points out the opening as well as the limit of Derrida's strategic reading of Artaud's work as a site for the deconstruction of transcendental signification. This strategy is then confronted with the radical character of Artaud's language as it figures the undergoing of words in the flesh rather than in terms of signifying.

The three chapters that make up part 3 unfold senses of the political out of the sensibility of thought developed through the book, that is, in light of thought in the undergoing of its singularity and fecundity of sense and as a being exposed in language. Chapter 9 discusses Benjamin's idea of a politics of art in "The Work of Art in the Age of Mechanical Representation" as a nonideological thinking which ultimately exposes us to the bodily experience of the political. The second part of the chapter discusses a concrete example of such politics in Marguerite Duras and Alain Resnais' film, *Hiroshima Mon Amour.* The penultimate chapter explores three ways of understanding ethics and the possibilities of human community out of experiences of the overflowing of sense. The three figures of "Spirit" I discuss, come from close readings of Hegel, Frantz Fanon, and Gabriel García Márquez. The closing chapter is a short study on Italo Calvino's *American Lectures*. This is a reading of this work as an opening towards a politics arisen out of a sense of diversity found in thinking through the ephemeral singularity and lightness of the fragile relations between individuals, experiences which underscore signification in language and political ideologies.

Milano, January 2008

PART 1

Unbounded Thoughts: Fecund Overflowing in Philosophy's Finitude

Finally, it must not have been
Easy to be there, as now, in its hours,
In language's very unreality or ocean,
Swimming, from the shock of the wreckage,
$\qquad$ Toward uncertain islands
That no map, up to then, had made known.

$\qquad\qquad\qquad$ ("Segovia," Juan José Saer)

CHAPTER 1

Four Meditations on Heidegger's Undergoing of Thought's Finitude

One of the most direct encounters of conceptual thought with its finitude, and perhaps the most violent, occurs in the work of Martin Heidegger. In his early work, *Being and Time*, time appears as the transcendental horizon of all determinations of senses of being, be they conceptual or physical. Indeed, already in this work, Heidegger seeks to think towards temporality in order to think the ground of the ontological difference, between entities and ideas, that serves as the foundation for the history of metaphysics, and Western thought in general. Thus, in *Being and Time* and thereafter, Heidegger seeks a thought that occurs in light of its (thought's) finitude or temporality. In his second major work, *Contributions to Philosophy*, Heidegger's project continues through a shift in the way of his project. This refers to a shift in the very situation of thought in relation to the issue of temporality. In *Contributions*, Heidegger seeks to think in light of the temporality and finitude of thought in its coming to pass, rather than thinking towards time as the horizon of thought. In other words, the task of *Contributions* is to begin to think thought in its finite situatedness, that is, to think in and with the temporality of thought. However, this cannot mean engaging in either a purely conceptual nor in a pragmatic or historiographical explication and analysis of thought; already since *Being and Time* such ontological difference would not serve us to understand Heidegger's work. Thus, in Heidegger's *Contributions* we find an attempt to engage thought's temporality through the specific undergoing of the temporality of thought as such, and to do so in a manner that will not simply re-inscribe the undergoing of philosophical thought within either side of metaphysics. Heidegger calls this thinking beyng-historical thinking (*seynsgeschichtliches Denken*).[1] The abstruse terminology in English requires an immediate clarification: the archaic spelling of being that uses the "y" (*Seyn* rather than *Sein*), indicates a move underneath or back to the undergoing of thought that remains beyond, yet underlying, the history of metaphysics. The term "historical" (*geschichtliches*) points to a specific concern with thinking as the undergoing of the very dynamic situatedness of thought. As von Herrman puts it, the thought of *Contributions* "is a phenomenological and then a hermeneutical thinking," that is, its way is found in undergoing the concrete temporality of thought.[2] As my discussion in the next five chapters, and the book's orientation as a whole make evident, I take this insight as a point of departure, that is, we will go beyond von Herrman's formulation, because we will take this phenomenological accent in Heidegger as the opening of a sensibility, or disposition, in which thought goes beyond its delimitation, into an unbounded fecund opening diversifying of the sense of time and being in Heidegger.[3] Thus, the next four meditations focus on Heidegger's attempt in *Contributions* to engage philosophical thought in its temporality or finitude through this beyng-historical-thinking. The discussion delineates Heidegger's opening of spaces for such undergoing of philosophical thought and marks the limits that also occur in that thinking.

Before moving on to the four meditations, and in order to accentuate the intention and direction of my discussion, I mention some secondary literature crucial to my interpretation of Heidegger's *Contributions to Philosophy*. David Krell's *Intimations of Mortality, Lunar Voices,* and his work have been an inspiration for the development of this book.[4] The first book directly concerns Heidegger. In it, Krell makes clear that Heidegger's thought is not a matter of two separate periods of thought divided by a break in his thinking, or the turn (*die Kehre*), a divide often situated within the time frame of the composition of *Contributions to Philosophy* and "The Origin of the Work of Art."[5] Instead, Krell argues for a single thought that undergoes a thinking of mortality; "there is something particularly implacable about Heidegger's thinking of mortality, rooted in the experience he calls *oblivion of Being*."[6] Furthermore, this is "a thinking within anxiety . . . a descensional reflection determined to keep its feet on the earth."[7] Krell traces this thinking through its various undergoings of mortality, always relating Heidegger's later thought to *Being and Time*. The path of his discussion leads to Heidegger's later thought as poetic thought, to his concrete engagement with mortality through his discussions of Georg Trakl, and ultimately back to the thinking within anxiety already figured by Heidegger's analysis of *Dasein* in *Being and Time*.[8] The following discussion of Heidegger shares Krell's insight in situating Heidegger's thought within its mortal and concrete anxiety. Indeed, in the case of the following four meditations the issue is the explicit undergoing of mortality or finitude that occurs in Heidegger's thought in *Contributions to Philosophy*. The discussion closely follows the movement of Heidegger's thought with particular attentiveness to its attunement or dis-position (*Stimmung*), or the fundamental modality of the thought. Also, whereas Krell's reading turns to Heidegger's poietic thought as a way back to the concrete sense of mortality in the German philosopher, in my case, the discussion follows Heidegger's anxiety to its extreme. This extreme takes the form of his withdrawal from the thought he opens as he exposes the history of metaphysics to its mortality. This unbearable exposure culminates in his appeal to the destiny of the West, Hölderlin, and the last god as figures in which his thought finds an end or purpose, and hence a harbor, as it comes to be confronted with an unbounded sense of being. This exposure occurs on the one hand in Heidegger's furious engagement of our age of machination and forgetfulness of the forgetting of all senses of being, and on the other, in the unfathomable opening to a concrete diversified and diversifying arising to presence of beings that, in its exposure to concrete temporality, ultimately overwhelms the history of Western metaphysics and opens it to sheer difference. In this sense, I again sympathize with Krell's emphasis on Trakl as the figure of Heidegger's concrete exposure to mortality and difference, and yet, my discussion traces Heidegger's thought through its crisis. This tracing out of Heidegger's thought in attunement or dis-position (*Stimmung*) in *Contributions* does not lead back to *Being and Time*, but it serves as an introduction to the rest of this book's explorations, that is, to the discussion of instances of thought in which we may articulate the sensibility that unfolds through conceptual thought's exposure to its finitude.

Another fundamental moment for my reading is John Sallis's connection between Heidegger's "On the Essence of Truth" and *Contributions to Philosophy*. In this case the crucial point is the way he articulates the movement of Heidegger's thought with relation to the concept of truth. I agree with him that the transformation of the concept of truth in Heidegger's thought opens philosophy to another way of thinking:

> In the wake of this strangeness, a wake that has perhaps just begun, a wake in which we are to mourn nothing less than the passing of truth itself what is to become of the essentially other than truth? No longer is it the mere opposite that could be kept securely outside the essence of truth. Nor is it an other that truth could appropriate in such a way that the otherness would be retained within a new unity attesting the priority of truth. . . .[9]

Sallis's words point to the movement and space of thought opened by Heidegger, and in doing so, they also begin to give us a sense of the exposure undergone by Heidegger's thought. As Sallis explains, the essentially other than truth:

> It is even—as Heidegger would say in that perhaps most monstrous saying—something within the essence of truth that is older than

truth itself. . . . Thus, what is essentially other than truth belongs
to the essence of truth, even though within that essence its otherness is preserved, not just dialectically but as oppositional, even
older than truth.[10]

Sallis's interpretation opens Heidegger's thought in its unfolding through
a movement that does not operate in terms of the metaphysical difference
between beings and Being. Furthermore, the monstrosity of the essentially
other than truth figures the concrete unfolding of senses of beings in concealment and unconcealment or the movement of truth as *a-letheia*. Thus,
as does Krell's, Sallis's work points us to the mortal and concrete, the living
sense of Heidegger's thought.[11] More specifically, Sallis points us towards the
sense of truth in concrete ephemeral difference that arises in the exposure
of thought to temporality in Heidegger's work.[12] It is in the wake of this
pregnant transformative passage for philosophy that we undergo Heidegger's
thought in the next four chapters. At the same time, my discussion goes further as we take this insight as the introduction to the rest of the book. This
opening is then explored through the other sections of the book, that is, as
the sense of the other in the transformative movement of truth is explored
by way of diverse encounters, experiences, and thoughts often singular and
at times uncharted and impossible to inscribe under the history of Western
philosophy. My reading is always indebted to Daniela Vallega-Neu, from
whose reading of *Contributions to Philosophy* I continue to learn.[13] Finally, I
have learned much from the essays collected in the *Companion to Heidegger's
'Contributions to Philosophy.'*[14]

First Meditation

Abandonment: A Violent Encounter with Thought's Finitude

> The abandonment of being is the first dawning of beyng as self-sheltering-
> concealing from out of the night of metaphysics. . . .[15]
>
> (*Contributions to Philosophy*)

In *Contributions to Philosophy* thought is engaged in the specific finite situation in which it is undergone. This means for Heidegger that in our epoch
the task of thinking in its temporality requires that we think through the
highest point of metaphysics: Nihilism in its most extreme form. This is "the
abandonment of being" (*die Seinsverlassenheit*) that occurs in our era with
the forgetting of any question about the senses of being (*Seinsvergessenheit*).
This oblivious existence occurs through the expansion of rationalism into

a calculative technological appropriation of all senses of being. This is not an individual attitude but it refers to an epoch: the epoch of machination (*Machenschaft*). To begin to think in departure from thought's situation will be to think through this specific undergoing of the abandonment of being as *Machenschaft*. As our quote above indicates, the abandonment of being does not call for the abandonment of philosophical thought but, on the contrary, must be thought in order to find a path for thinking, a dim light out of the darkest night of metaphysic's rationalist abstractions and its calculation and production. In other words, we must think through, undergo, and withstand in an articulate manner this epoch by exposing thought to its situation, to that modality of forgetting of the forgetting of all senses of being that rules us and our time.

Forgetting or the Emptiness of Being

Heidegger's observations and warnings about machination are as clear as they are harsh, and it is worthwhile citing one of them. Heidegger writes about this epoch:

> One should speak of *the epoch of the total lack of questioning*, which extends its duration within time, beyond the present, far back and far ahead. In this epoch nothing essential—if this determination still has any meaning at all—is any longer impossible or inaccessible. Everything "is made" and "can be made" if one only musters the "will" for it. But that this "will" is precisely what has already placed and in advance reduced what might be possible and above all necessary—this is already mistaken ahead of time and left outside any questioning. For this will, which makes everything, has already subscribed to machination, that interpretation of beings as re-presentable and re-presented. In one respect re-presentable means "accessible to intention and calculation"; in another it means "advanceable through pro-duction and execution." But thought in a fundamental manner, all of this means that beings as such are re-presentable and that only the representable *is*. For machination, what apparently offers resistance and a limit to machination is only the material for further elaboration and the impulse for progress and an occasion for extension and enlargement. Within machination there is nothing question-worthy, nothing that could be esteemed through enactment of questioning as such, simply esteemed. . . .[16]

Speaking of the forgetting of being is not an abstract call for some other kind of being or experience beyond our existence. On the contrary, the forgetting of being is rooted in the fact that we exist in an epoch that concretely, literally in-deed, has abandoned questioning. According to Heidegger we come to the very configuration of our existence and thought out of a lack of questioning. We are without questioning, hence without dignity. But how do we make sense of this claim in a time when science and law seem to have conquered unsuspected frontiers to the point of our speaking of "global order" and "progress"?

The mechanism of forgetting under machination is simple and horrific. All senses of being, even being human, are defined in terms of the measurements and production fitting to rationalist calculative intentionality (*Machenschaft*). This means that not only any form of being can be quantified and manipulated but also determined and produced accordingly to the calculus of rational intentionality. Ultimately all senses of being are products, results, or effects of this powers of production; and, only that which can be quantified, catalogued, manipulated, or reproduced—only that which is made and dominated by reason, can be defined as being in any sense. Furthermore, what remains beyond this productive calculus appears as raw material or marketable natural goods, to be consumed or put to use by machination. Thus, reason is the executed desire that creates all senses of being, and that at the same time controls what has been created. This infinite chain of production and consumption appears as the product and object of all senses of being. This is why Heidegger concludes that in such economy of machination rational intentionality or will ends up being self-sufficient, since they continue to create themselves.[17] We should be clear here that this critique does not entail the rejection or abandonment of reason, logic, or mathematics. These are simply elements put to use by a specific manner of being that encounters all senses of being under a project of production and domination. Under machination rule the presence of entities at hand and the ideas fitting to things and their production through reason.[18] I don't believe a catalogue of contemporary analogies will do here, since such an attempt to give examples would never meet the expanses touched by machination in each reader's situation. However, I do not think it excessive to say that Heidegger's observations in the late nineteen-thirties and thereafter are already fitting introduction to our global economies today, to the conceptual and cultural poverty that accompany our new world "order and progress," when for example viewed in light of colonialism and Latin America.[19] Obviously, I step beyond Heidegger, and in doing so at least intimate a more radical and transgressive step along with his hope for a rethinking of the thought of the West. This will become explicit when we reach our third meditation.

To return to the analysis of *Machenschaft*, its three principle elements are quantitative calculation (*Berechnung*), velocity (*Schnelligkeit*), and the massive or gigantic (*das Massenhafte, das Riesenhafte*).[20] These elements together configure the horizon of our reality, as they situate us within a limitless projection of progress and expansion.[21] Today to be part of the project of humanity means for the self-appointed majority to be occupied with the construction of the future through the daily contribution to the development of technology that will shape all the sciences and human knowledge. The future depends on the urgent production of results and technological implements for shaping and making the future safe and secure through the expansion ad infinitum of rational quantitative productions of meanings and goods. Here appears Heidegger's point about the forgetting of the question of being and of questioning in such direction: We are so taken with the urgency for production that we do not have the time for remaining and undergoing the configurations of senses of being.[22] When all being is producing and producing is the infinite activity of being, there is not any time for questions, hesitations, doubts, pauses, or silences: what only counts, for now and for the future, if it is to be, is presence and production. In this urgency and fixation with the immediate presence of things and the securing of them in the future, we not only lose and forget being in other registers, but that very forgetting slips into oblivion. Even if one were to encounter questions, silences, and doubt, these are only referred to the need for more quantitative calculation and production, since any lack in the economy of machination can only mean that we must produce more and more effectively. In short, in light of Heidegger's observations, we can see that the quantitative and technological drive of machination and its velocity project us into a massive horizon of infinite progress that we follow with eye, body, heart, and reason; while in that infinite wave we recede towards a limitless emptiness marked only by our ever so close and almost imperceptible forgetting oblivion. To put it in another way, as Giorgio Agamben has indicated in *Homo Sacer* as well as other works, Heidegger already sees at this point the advent of biopolitics and the reduction of life to the material for the sustenance of sovereign systems of production and their blind quantitative expansion.[23]

The Impossible Language of Emptiness

I have just said heart and reason because machination's frantic production of being practically occupies every moment of existence. As Heidegger points out, the production of being under machination is accompanied by a certain rush, a certain feeling of adventure (*Erlebnis*) that is thoughtlessly called experience, and even real life experience. Next to quantification and production, and entangled with them, we find as an element of machination reason's fitting other, that most sexy of emotions, "the feeling of being alive."[24] We are alive when we produce, when we consume, when we surf along machination's fast wave, when we belong to the massive project actively, when we experience life as the adventure (*Erlebnis*) of being alive. When not assigned to calculative quantification, all questioning is covered over by the various appeals to life as adventure under words like "emotions," "feelings," "belief," and "power" (the force of the individual will).[25] The crucial point here is that reason and emotion correspond to the project of machination, and in their expansive doubling the questioning and pause that have been forgotten are simply closed down. In other words, what cannot be quantified can be lived.

As Heidegger points out in *Contributions* these two elements in their difference are situated by a single product and operational functionary of machination: the rational and emotional subject. As Michel Haar writes, along with calculation and production, machination requires a certain objectivity or pragmatism that may measure and resolve problems.[26] The rational subject is that objective point that ultimately performs the role of an impersonal will. We are speaking of a certain rational indifference that takes all undergoings of senses of being as problems that can at least be partially solved if logic and calculative quantification are applied (partially because of reason's supposed recognition of its own and self-produced limit). One could say that according to this impartial function, for the rational subject any undergoing of a sense of being has its value as a price or measurement. A simple example of this is the type of mechanism that runs most institutions, because their existence is determined by the impersonal application of calculations immediate and projected. I have yet to find an institution in which some one, rather than a functionary, would claim responsibility for what happens to those under its services at any level of decision. This reduction of one's existence to an impersonal functionary or customer becomes all the more uncomfortable when we consider to what extent institutions make decisions over every aspect of one's intimate existence; for example, as tools for education, health, and culture. What seals the functionary and the institution, and our being in them, is ultimately their discourse, or what the Argentine writer Julio Cortázar iderntified as the repetition of the same empty words in order to sustain putrefied ideas. I am speaking of that impersonal and semiformal language that attempts to recognize our use while saying nothing personal, thus securing the functionary's place, be it as customer or as sales representative, or what ever representing impersonal function the entity serves. Of course, the impersonal character of the institutional model and of each functionary has its limit in the rush of riding the wave of present and future progress and order. Along these lines, if the impartial rational subject deploys a language of indifference over every undergoing of being, it is the same subject that in its living the life of frantic production and projection spreads vacuous emotional discourses that seem to express what subjects feel and want (most of the time difficult to separate), all under the false impression of undergoing changes and of making a difference. How can there be change if the discourse sings that worn-out lullaby of the strongest form of living as experiencing machination's adventure? Here human experience is caught in a dualistic web: thinking has been reduced to reason and the intimate to a single intense sensation deceptively called adventure. Thus, the horizon of thought seems to entail this twofold possibility, or, the impossibility of a sensibility of thought.

Indeed, it is the danger of such empty double discourse that leads Heidegger to introduce *Contributions to Philosophy* by stating that language as the engagement of the senses of beings has become impossible: "all fundamental words have been used up and the genuine relation to the word has been destroyed."[27] One wonders how this situation can be sustained. Heidegger indicates that there is a third element added to reason and emotion, its most spectacular effect perhaps. This is enchantment (*Verzauberung*), that is, the illusion created in the frantic rush of productive consumption and emotion, an illusion that covers over the emptiness of life under machination with the impression of a grand future that is to be produced and, of course, protected.[28]

Heidegger identifies in machination four rules that secure its functioning and secure the oblivious forgetting of any diverse undergoing of configurations of being.[29] The stronger the development of machination the more it becomes hidden behind the enchanting promise of its great project. At the same time, with the strengthening of this economy life becomes more and more the fitting opposite to calculative productive reasoning, that is, it becomes the great indeterminate wave of irrational feeling and sensation opposed to the ordering of reason. As such, it is subsumed under machination as the adventure of life that can only be secured by reason's calculative production of present and future. With these two elements in full play, the possibility of recognizing and engaging machination as such, and therefore otherwise than from within its enchantment, becomes almost impossible. Eventually, without any other horizon than that of machination thought develops a simple indifference or aversion to any questioning beyond its frameworks. This is why Heidegger recognizes in our epoch nothing but the total absence of questioning.[30]

Conclusion

We have discussed the steps that according to Heidegger lead to the forgetting of being, and we have also developed them in order to engage that situation of thought in its epoch or finite situatedness. We encounter ourselves face to face with our situation of being in abandonment in the epoch of machination, or as Heidegger writes, in the epoch "of the forgetting of being and the decomposition of truth (*Zerfall der Wahrheit*)."[31] In this violent encounter with the situation of thought in our time we already begin to move towards the dim light Heidegger seeks out of the darkest night of metaphysics. According to Heidegger, this situation we have begun to articulate is what thought must come to engage if it is to set out in departure from its situation or very finitude. If in what we have said we seem to find naught but despair, hopelessness and emptiness, we should also be able to find a knot in our thoughts, in that situation where words have betrayed us, made us functionaries, or perhaps now, have left us. And in that knot, perhaps we begin to find the anger of being there under machination, the anger that at least insinuates and exposes us to the lack of words and the poverty of what we call reason, feeling, sensation, and experience. But perhaps Heidegger is right in thinking that it is precisely and decidedly in this encounter with our emptiness and aphasia, in light of even this brief look at the spectacle of machination, that we begin to find a path for the articulation of our undergoing of the configurations of being beyond the willful production of the self-fulfilling emptiness of *Machenschaft*. As he writes, ". . . not granting is not nothing but rather an outstanding originary manner of letting be unfulfilled, of letting be empty—thus an outstanding manner of opening."[32] If this is the case, it remains for us to seek the path and the words that will open our thought beyond the accounting of machination. This will be the task of our second and third meditation.

CHAPTER 2

Second Meditation

The Decomposition of an Illusion and the Fecundity of Thinking

Abandonment of being must be experienced as the basic event of our history and be elevated into a knowing awareness that shapes and guides.[1]

The Abandonment of being is the first dawning of beyng's self-sheltering-concealing from out of the night of metaphysics. . ."[2]

As we saw in the previous discussion, for Heidegger the face to face with the situation of our thought is the necessary step for moving beyond the forgetting of all senses of being under the spectacle or illusion of machination. This means facing the abandonment and forgetting of being, or thought's situation and possibility in our epoch.[3] But how does thinking pass from the decomposition of truth in machination to other ways of undergoing the configurations of senses of being? At stake is the possibility or impossibility of escaping the logic of machination. How may we reach for feelings, sensations, experiences outside machination? Can there be a way towards exchanges, affections, responses that are not always already caught in the double web of reason and adventure? Heidegger is clear that philosophical thought is not to be abandoned but recovered through the undergoing of this passage. He speaks of "a transformation of the cogitating attitude into a thinking comportment" (*eine Wandlung der denkenden Haltung zur denkerischen*).[4] As Dominique Janicaud points out, there is no reason to read Heidegger's thought in transition in *Contributions* as a call for the abandonment of reason.[5] Indeed, the contraposition of reason to thought would merely secure a place for reason as if above or objectively operative in relation to Heidegger's thought. Rather, the challenge is to understand how Heidegger's *Contributions* accomplish a broadening of the understanding of the task of thinking that may reconfigure reason by situating it in its temporality or concrete ground. This is part of the aim of the four meditations. In this one in particular, we must ask about the step from the darkest night of metaphysics towards the other beginning. The path is not so obscure if one keeps in mind that for Heidegger machination is a way of being, and the way of being in our epoch: then we can seek the transformation from within this movement, from within being's blind and violent configuration.

The Decomposition of Machination

> Abandonment of beyng is basically a decaying (Ver-wesung) of beyng.[6]

Heidegger's thinking through machination stands as a thinking that takes up the essence of metaphysics at its darkest hour, and in this sense it is a thought that attempts an overcoming of it (*Überwindung*).[7] Indeed, for Heidegger the direct undergoing of machination means the undergoing of that movement that underlies the most critical moment in modern philosophy, that is, Nietzsche's Nihilism.[8] As Heidegger writes in *Contribution's* first fugue, "Directed towards the other beginning, nihilism must be grasped more fundamentally as the essential consequence of the abandonment of being."[9] Nihilism, as the forgetting of being, is the last consequence of the abandonment of being. Heidegger writes in his Nietzsche lectures, "The grounding question remains as foreign to Nietzsche as it does to the history of thought prior to him."[10] Thus, in undergoing machination one would take up the ground question, the question of being in its abandonment, and thus, think essentially Nihilism and with it the Western tradition.[11] As we see in this chapter, Machination and Nihilism share in the decomposition of truth, they share that great emptiness, that lack of aims and sense of being behind the euphoria of rational quantitative production, that which must be undergone in order to begin to find an opening for thought.

That machination is the decomposition of truth has two meanings in Heidegger. On the one hand, as we already saw, machination figures the decomposition of truth (*Zerfall der Wahrheit*) through the forgetting of the forgetting of any question-worthiness in the configurations of being.[12] On the other hand, as the quote above indicates, the hermetic rationalist economy that figures the refutation and closing of senses of the undergoing of being carries its own deterioration or putrefaction (*Ver-wesung*): The quote begins to have since as an introduction to a leap beyond machination, that is, if we consider that every process of putrefaction can figure both the loss of a certain form as well as a coming forth of configurations excessive to what comes to pass.[13] In this sense, in the emptiness of machination that forgets the forgetting of all question-worthiness we may begin to engage a certain exuberance or overflow (*Überfluß*) of being that goes beyond machination's economy and its parameters in its appropriation of being. Here it is worthwhile noting that *Überfluß* takes the form of *Überwindung*: so that overcoming is thought fundamentally as overflow (this will be a crucial point through out the following chapters, and throughout the book).[14] But how does machination figure this overflow?

As Heidegger explains, ultimately machination cannot recognize a limit. "For machination, what apparently offers resistance and a limit to machination is only the material for further elaboration and the impulse for progress and an occasion for extension and progress."[15] Heidegger points to this incapacity for knowledge (and truth) when he indicates that one of machination's rules is its progressive ignorance of itself; an ignorance that augments with its growth and control over all production and senses of being. Heidegger writes, "the more powerfully it unfolds—for example in the Middle Ages and in modernity—the more stubbornly and more machinatingly it hides itself as such. . . ."[16] But here in this self-concealment, machination occurs in its incapacity; nothing may be decided or change without self-questioning and the view towards truth such activity affords.[17] It is at this point, in uncovering the incapacity for transformation or decision, that machination brings its very decomposition: "Undecidedness is the domain for the unboundedness of machination, where magnitude spreads out in the nonform of the gigantic and clarity spreads out as clarity of the empty."[18] Heidegger discovers the overflow and disintegration of machination precisely in the encounter with its non-form and clarity of emptiness, which are experience through the most immediate elements of machination. In order to undergo this we must look directly at machination.

In order to find release from machination we will have to recognize in the very mechanisms of machination something that overflows and goes beyond its frantic and infinite quantifying productivity and its claim of absolute control of all senses of being.

Let us take each of machination's elements briefly. Calculation and quantification (*Berechnung*) require that all undergoing of beings be quantifiable and logically coherent. What does not fit these needs is ascribed to the comfortable other of rational operations, to the subject's sentiments or psychology, that is, to emotion, to feeling; and in this way to luck, accident, or providence.[19] However, the problem is that the so-called irrational does not lack in the activities of calculation and the drive for more technology; and, as mathematics students know, they are inseparable from the accomplishment of any equation. They are inseparable not merely because they occur along with calculation but in that they are part of the very desire that sustains reason in its quantification, production, and domination. Thus, when machination claims its domain in terms of the quantifying and productive related operations of reason, it closes itself to part of the very undergoing of its configurations of being. In this sense, it secures its ignorance and reveals its ultimate lack of foundation and its emptiness.[20] When we see this, we can also begin to reinterpret velocity (*Schnelligkeit*) because now the frantic production can be seen as nothing more than a king of neurosis seeking to cover over the emptiness of the calculative production of technology and being. Machination's frantic production of senses or values of being cannot give us knowledge of it; it only sustains the empty illusion of infinite dominion over all configurations of being.[21] In the case of the gigantic, there is a projection of the massive (*der Aufbruch des Massenhaften*) with the gigantic that figures the expansive projection of machination, and this very projection (*Aufbruch*) towards infinite growth shows us that machination knows no limit, and in this lack of a sense of limit it already exposes us to the impossibility of its infinite and total domination of beings. In short, machination's infinite expansion will have always already taken itself beyond its determinations and limits. By virtue of its very claim, the gigantic illusion of infinite domination expands to lead us to the realization of its impossibility. This impossibility can only be repeated by the factors mentioned above, that is, the lack of self-understanding and the undergoing of calculation and the empty production of speedy sound bites, trinkets, and innocuous terminologies that sustain machination's sheer emptiness. As we look at the mechanism of machination we face its sheer emptiness, and, in this dissolution of its claim to absolute control or domination over being, we begin to engage its abyssal character.[22]

The conclusion that we may draw from this brief analysis in *Contributions* of the elements of machination is that in the very function of machination appears already a hint of something else, a certain overflow of being that its frantic calculative production might even sequester into oblivion, but that now begins to be heard. In the discovery that machination occurs in the absence of ground (*Bodenlosigkeit*), we can also catch a glimpse of something in the undergoing of its being beyond its economy. Thus, Heidegger himself asks: Why does the gigantic not know its overflow (*Überfluß*)?[23] Certainly part of the reply is in the emphasis on a culture of ignorance that works as part of the central mechanism of machination. But, this question leads us to a further issue: How do we understand that possible overflow of being that is already indicated once we have encountered machination face to face? To what senses of being in their movements of configuration might the hint of this overflow lead us?

Thinking in the Overflowing Fecundity of Beings

The dissolution of the illusion of total dominion or production of being that we have just discussed also means that the thinking of machination, that is, rationalist quantitative and productive logic and its irrational second, cannot lay claim to the determinations of the senses of beings. This means that the Western tradition of metaphysical and rational thought can not seek or claim dominion over the senses of being. Under the echo of the refusal of being in the epoch of machination, and its shattered hallucination, neither reason, production, nor the rush of their adventure suffice to fill the open horizon of the configuring of senses of beings. Once reason with its logic no longer has full claim to being, thought is open to be situated in its overflowing passing, which now is no longer to be concealed or shut down. Rather, this excess to rationality and emotion insinuates an opening towards a much broader and richer undergoing and withstanding of the configurations of beings and thought in their overflowing passages.[24] Heidegger finds the passage to thought in the most violent break in the homogeneous continuity of machination and thought in the overflowing movement of being.[25] It is this radical opening that Heidegger calls a thinking, *vom Ereignis*. This, in the sense that in encountering the dissolution of machination we find an opening, a space for the possible thinking of the senses of being of beings, humans, reason, and language out of their finite ephemeral and concrete temporal passage, and beyond the rule of machination. At this point, thinking cannot be a question of reason over or against emotions. But how do we understand this glimpse beyond machination towards thought's finitude or temporality at this point?

Heidegger's thought certainly does not intend to take over the role of machination. As we have seen, he exposes us to its darkest and harshest undergoing, to that violence and indifference that seem to flourish in our times. But here, we must be attentive to the effective movement of Heidegger's thought: If we gain a glimpse of light, this occurs by virtue of being exposed to our oblivious workings, to the forgetting of the forgetting of all question-worthiness in our undergoing of being, to the violent rule and demand of machination, and to the most fragile and difficult character of reason's workings under machination. We have begun to undergo the coming of thought through engaging our thought's situatedness, in its ephemeral, concrete, fragile, disquieting, and inviting passages. The opening for thought that Heidegger offers us occurs as we come to think philosophical thought in its finitude. This situated undergoing of thought is the opening that we may find, that is, in our being-thinking in abandonment in our epoch. Instead of the blind production of being by the reason and force of machination, instead of the hallucinating spectacle of a projected future always already delivered and secured, instead of the leaving to oblivion of the undergoing of all configurations of beings through the repetition of empty words, Heidegger offers us thought in its tremulous and singular temporality or finitude. If machination does not see its overflow, Heidegger's thought arises in engaging the overflowing movement of machination. He does so in the attempt to undergo in an articulate manner this being in overflowing movement. This also means thinking in openness to the uncertain figuration of the coming senses of beings. It is this sensibility of a thought in departure in the awareness of its overflowing movement, it is this inconceivable exposure, that opens thinking to the question-worthiness of beings, that gives the breath of air to the philosophical word, and that opens and opens us to what Heidegger calls experience (*Erfahrung*), understood as being in finitude's transformative configurative exposure.[26] In other words, once machination has left reason exposed to its overflowing, thought can be engaged in its configurations of beings and its very configuration in its exposure to its finite incalculable and unpredictable passages.[27] This I would also call the abyssal sense of truth in Heidegger.

Thinking in the abandonment of being under *Machenschaft* means engaging in a speaking in the overflowing of being's configurations, in the impossibility of domination, and furthermore, in exposure to the most difficult undergoings of thought's weaknesses, dangers, and limitations in its times. In being overflowing, this thought is always already transgressive. This is not nihilism or solely about the overcoming of metaphysics. As Heidegger himself will put it, thinking is no longer fundamentally about metaphysics: "Beyng-historical inquiring into beyng is not reversing metaphysics . . . this should indicate that being here is no longer thought metaphysically."[28] If we can already say, in *Being and Time*, that Heidegger's thought seeks the transformative retrieval or *Destruktion* of the metaphysical tradition, we can add now that the thought that is coming is spurred not by metaphysics but by thought's transgressive character as such, that is, in thought's being in overflowing abandonment. This thought does not arise against or over against metaphysics as the recovery of something. Rather, it draws its figuration and form from a limit marked in the undergoing of being in overflowing abandonment. In this sense this thought comes to pass as a transformative delimitation of its limits.[29] This is why later on Heidegger, in *Building, Dwelling, Thinking*, says that the limit (*peras*) understood in the truth of overflowing being or *physis* does not close horizons but marks the out setting of figurations of beings that go beyond all conceptual determinations already in place and beyond all presence under such configurations.[30] But if this is the case, such thought does not have nor will have a set place within any teleologically determined historical tradition like the Western tradition. In this sense, this is a thinking that already overflows its configurations, a thinking that in this sense is always strange, alien, marginal in its very determinations of the senses of beings. Heidegger writes: "In the sense of other beginning, *Da-sein* is still completely strange to us; it is what we never find lying around us, what we leap into . . . that clearing of beyng in which future man must place himself in order to hold it open."[31] Here, Heidegger recognizes this marginal sense of thought in overflowing abandonment, as he writes in his preface that the thought he attempts can not be represented nor can it be defined according to the requirements of the logic and conceptual history of the metaphysics of presence. Rather, this thought, in being transformative of the tradition and in its overflowing of its very configurations, is strange: *befremdlich*. "The thinking of philosophy remains strange (*befremdlich*) because in philosophy knowing everything . . . is always exposed to displacement and thus no immediate representation of anything extant is ever possible."[32] This does not mean that Heidegger gives up philosophical rigor for poetic musings as so many readers of the German philosopher seem to think. On the contrary, as we have seen, the task of thought in its finitude requires the utmost rigor and even exposure to what cannot fully be determined or dominated by reason. At the same time, this must occur without abandoning questioning and language; this is part of that disposition (*Verrückung*) that will distinguish the task of thought in *Contributions*. Indeed, as I have already mentioned, this thought requires the transformative retrieval (*Destruktion*) of the history that situates it, since the overflowing opening of *Contributions*, in thinking in its temporality, requires the reappropriation of the history of Western philosophy. This is not required as an historiographical matter but in order to release and set in play thought in its overflowing strangeness.

If we follow the interpretation of Heidegger's discussion of *Machenschaft* as the release of thinking from it through the uncovering of a certain overflow of being in *Machenschaft's* economy, then we find that in its being in overflow of reason and machination, in spite of the role of the history of Western philosophy in *Contributions*, the thought to come can not have as its single horizon the history and destiny or future of Western philosophy. (With this remark, we point beyond Heidegger, as it will become obvious in the fourth meditation.) Not only is that history incapable of containing the overflowing being of thought, in being overflowed, and exposed to thoughts opening transgressive movement, rationalism (in its logical-emotional oppositional partition of all senses of beings) is already exposed to the strange, the marginal. In being situated in the overflowing abandonment of being, thought is exposed and opened to other histories, memories, and forgettings, and to other paths and configurations to come, which can not be determined nor even expected by a history of Western philosophy to which these do not belong. If, unlike machination, the thought to come opens in its encounter with a sense of limits, these limits arise in thought's vulnerabilities and exposures to ephemeral and concrete undergoings, in the strange and uninvited and in the strange and uninvited in the thought that encounters such overflowing configurations. In short, in its being exposed through the undergoing of its finitude. With these words much is suggested but still, we have to wonder how to begin to understand such overflowing philosophical word, and to what extent Heidegger and we ourselves might be able to engage and sustain it. These will be the themes of the next two meditations.

CHAPTER 3

Third Meditation

Thought's Sensibility in its
Finitude and its Exposed Word

". . . from enowning is enowned a thinking-saying belonging to *Beyng* and the word 'of' *Beyng*."[1]

As we saw through our previous discussions, in *Contributions* the senses of the configurations of beings are not left to oblivion, the thinking of Heidegger does not abandon sense, rather it seeks to hear the call of the senses of beings through our face to face with our epoch of oblivion. We must begin to think from our situation and in a transformative re-appropriation of its empty quantitative and production-driven rationalism. As the quote above indicates, this exposure to the abyss and overflowing of being that may lead to our coming thought beyond machination's single dominion must occur through articulate words.[2] The question here is obvious: how do we understand this word-concept that is insinuated in our being exposed to the abyssal and fecund undergoing of machination?[3] In light of what we have already said, we are speaking of a word engaged in the face to face with the violence of the highest form of nihilism in our epoch.[4] Furthermore, this word must resound beyond the domination and centrality of the formulation of philosophy given by the history of Western metaphysics.[5] This also means that in thinking in departure from the centrality of metaphysics this word will not be determined or figured by resistance, opposition, or any other reactive relation to the tradition; nor will it entail the attempt at a revaluation of values.[6] But all of these negative characterizations do not yet engage in the thoughtful word we seek. In order to begin to have a sense of the word in the abandonment and overflowing of its finitude, we will have to begin by understanding in what sense such word can be a being-there (*da-sein*) in the abyssal and fecund finitude of thought. Therefore, this meditation has two parts. First we will discuss the sensibility of thought in its temporal being there (*da-sein*), specifically the sensibility that figures being exposed in the undergoing of being's abyssal fecundity. Then, in light of this we will discuss being-there in its exposed word. A remark from Hans Ruin's essay "Origin in Exile" will serve as an introduction to our discussion.[7] As Ruin points out, Heidegger's sense of the origin of language occurs as an origin in exile.[8] This is because for Heidegger language is temporal, and it is in the unfolding of a coming of time that language finds its instantiation. As Ruin indicates, this is the case already in *Being and Time*, where, remarkably for our discussion of *Stimmung* or dis-position in relation to language, language is already understood in relation to silence and as a question of disposition rather than predicative assertiveness.[9] Therefore, in asking about the word in relation to the overflowing of being, we already have an indication of the open-endedness of language and of its essencing's inseparability from and determination in terms of dis-position.

The Sensibility of Thought's Being There in its Finitude

Da-sein: Being There as Modality or Disposition of Thought in its Finitude

According to Heidegger, being-there (*da-sein*) is a modality of being. *Da-sein* is a temporal movement that cannot be grasped as a subject or a will, nor as a transcendental conscience, which in intuiting the essences of beings gives them their meaning. Without the rational subject as the Copernican point of reference, thought is neither the task of recognizing beings and their significance as beings—a bridge between rational subject and things, nor is it an expression of the will that forms worlds according to its needs. For Heidegger, all rational and transcendental thought requires before and towards all senses of beings a certain *Da-sein*, a being-there that situates all conceptual determinations of being. In the *Beiträge* Heidegger calls thought's way of being there *Stimmung*.

Immediately before introducing *Stimmung*, Heidegger explains that the philosophical thought he seeks differs from the rationalistic and logical argumentative tradition in that the latter always supposes that the consciousness of the one who makes the argument—the subjective consciousness, does not change with its conclusions about being.[10] Instead, when Heidegger situates thought in *da-sein*, with thought in its being-there (*Da-sein*), the very giving of senses of being and of the truth of being are situated outside the parameters of the logical and transcendental traditions of metaphysics and transcendental phenomenology. In his thought, Heidegger not only recognizes in intentional acts the simultaneous arising of the perceiver and the perceived, but also breaks this *zetetic* circle of intentional consciousness, because thought in *Da-sein* refers to the modality in which both the sense of being of the perceiver and of the perceived are given. In short, *Da-sein* introduces thought's pre-intentional opening, an opening fundamental to all conceptual determinations of senses of being.

It is precisely this step towards a thought situated in *Da-sein*—this call for thinking in being-there—that makes Heidegger in his introduction to the *Beiträge* conclude that, as a being there philosophical thought is always strange (*befremdlich*).[11] As we also already noted in our previous meditation, what makes thought a strange experience is that it occurs as a modality that cannot be situated according to the already operative metaphysical or transcendental ideas of the nature or task of thought. Here it is crucial to add that, for this same reason, we cannot understand language any longer in terms of these traditions, that is, we cannot take language to be a representative tool of signification that serves rational consciousness and its intuited essences and entities.

In light of our discussion thus far, we can say then that *Stimmung* (often rendered into English as attunement) indicates a certain modality or dis-position of thought, which at least suggests to us a thinking that goes beyond the rationalist tradition, and also beyond the understanding of consciousness as intuition (*Anschauung*) that sustains traditional phenomenology. Indeed, as Ruin indicates, and as Agamben and David Krell also point out, this is a matter that runs through Heidegger's thought: the point being that we find throughout Heidegger's thought a certain attentiveness to the modality in which that thought arises, and as which it arises and comes to pass.[12] In order to begin to understand this thinking that is so fundamentally strange to the tradition, will be helpful for us to see now how in his *Contributions* Heidegger takes up thinking in being there, and specifically his treatment of this way of thinking as occurring as a certain *Stimmung*.

Stimmung: A Felt Sensuous Sense of Being There

In *Contributions*, when Heidegger introduces *Stimmung* he does so in direct relation to the six parts or fugues that configure thought in its transition from the apotheosis of nihilism and metaphysics in *Machenschaft* to the coming sense of philosophical thought in its engaging anew the senses of being. The first three dispositions or modalities of thought that Heidegger introduces are *das Erschrecken*, panic or horror; *die Verhaltenheit*, reservedness; and *die Scheu*, fear, and a certain timidity.[13] Immediately after introducing these dispositions, Heidegger explains that their internal relationships can only be understood if one thinks through the book's six fugues. This indicates to us that *Stimmung* concerns the experience of undergoing the abandonment of being in the epoch of machination, and the task of finding in this way an opening in which one may hear the echo of being.[14]

At the same time, Heidegger identifies specific *Stimmungen* with specific parts of his book. The dispositions that characterize thought in the
echo (*Anklang*) of being are terror (*Schrecken*), fear, and timidity (*Scheu*).[15]
In the fugue titled *Zuspiel* we find as *Stimmung* a certain pleasure in going
beyond first beginnings or principles (*Übersteigung der Anfänge*). To *Sprung*
corresponds fear and timidity (*Scheu*).[16] The other three fugues (*die Gründung, die Zukünftigen,* and *Der Letzte Gott*) also come to pass under certain
Stimmungen. Furthermore, as all other *Stimmungen*, these grow out of the
Stimmung of reservedness. Heidegger writes, ". . . but always rising out of the
grounding-attunement of *reservedness*."[17] In short, *Stimmung* indicates the
various dispositions or modalities of thought in its being there in abandonment and transition.

The names of these modalities may easily be mistaken for moods or
attitudes, for emotions or feelings that can be contrasted to the work and
clarity of reason. But as we already saw in the first meditation, Heidegger
considers the dichotomy between reason's calculative logic and emotions to
be no more than a comfortable dialectic operative in *Machenschaft*, in which
its empty operations of calculative production are opposed but ultimately not
severed from the vacuous adventure or *Erlebnis* called emotions. Heidegger is
clear that *Stimmung* is not a matter of feelings, in the sense of blind emotion.
Indeed, as Heidegger explains, even the fields of psychology only limit the
possibilities of studying and understanding *Stimmung* and *Dasein*, because
they fix themselves on the emotions and will of the subject.[18] Furthermore,
and even though this is also not the case for Heidegger, the philosopher also
reminds us that, when placed over or against the idea of thought as the forceful
means of measurement and ordering through calculation and production, the
Stimmungen we have mentioned might easily seem experiences of weakness,
of lack of clarity, experiences given to terror and, in this sense, may seem to
be obfuscating moods. This last differentiation and warning should at least
begin to remind us of the difference between calculative force and the sensible and fragile experience of thinking which Heidegger touches upon as he
identifies thinking in *dasein* with *Erschrecken* (panic or horror), *Verhaltenheit*
(reservedness) and *Scheu* (fear and a certain subtle timidity).

The last observation introduces us to a crucial characteristic of thought
as *Stimmung* in Heidegger: Without reducing the experiences of horror,
reservedness, and fear and timidity to emotional or psychological definitions,
Heidegger begins to give us a felt and sensuous sense of the experience of
thinking in its finitude, in its being there in abandonment. The *Stimmungen*
refer us to thought's most intense undergoing in the experience of facing the
absence of all senses of being in, what I would call today, a world of normal-
izations under the blind rule of *Machenschaft*. I am saying that such terms
as *Da-sein, Stimmung, das Erschrecken, die Verhaltenheit,* and *die Scheu*, do

not offer abstract propositions about thinking, which one might or might not employ. These words bespeak experiences of a thought that looks as best it can and attempts to go through what most of us today, even in spite of our own efforts and ideals, fail to even begin to engage. *Das Erschrecken* does not bespeak a mood outside the task of thinking, but it sounds out the very passage of thought's encounter with the emptiness behind our dearest and famous hallucinations of life and success in the abandonment of all senses of being. *Die Scheu* recalls the unthinkable experience of the encounter with the echo of the sense of being in its refusal, and, as Heidegger says it, with the surprise of an encounter with a dawn born of the darkest night of metaphysics and nihilism. It is through these felt and sensuous modalities that thought encounters its ways and ontological sense: The names of the *Stimmungen* situate thought in its painful and exciting opening, in which *Da-sein* begins to find its articulation as the being-there in abandonment that figures the decisive opening *(Entschiedenheit)* of a time-space *(Zeit-Raum)* towards a thought to come.[19]

Exposed Thoughts: the Sensibility of Thought's Being-there

Da-sein—being there in abandonment, is sustained in its doleful passages or modalities by a certain fundamental attunement or *Grundstimmung*. Heidegger writes: "But grounding attunement *attunes* da-sein and thus attunes *thinking* as projecting-open the truth of beyng in word and concept."[20] All thought in *da-sein* occurs in fundamental dispositions. This is why Heidegger says that in each *Stimmung* resounds a fundamental disposition or modality of experience. "The grounding-attunement of thinking in the other beginning resonates in the attunings. . . ."[21]

This fundamental modality is not only given in the three dispositions we have already mentioned, but also in a fourth, which is crucial to all *Stimmungen*, and in this sense is fundamental to them. The philosopher writes, "The grounding-attunement [*die Grundstimmung*] calls to us: panic or horror [*das Erschrecken*], reservedness [*die Verhaltenheit*], fear and a certain subtle timidity [*die Scheu*] presentiment [*die Ahnung*], profound presentiment [*das Er-ahnen*]."[22] Here appear *die Ahnung* and *das Er-Ahnen*, presentiment and the profound presentiment, that accompany each *Stimmung*. Indeed, in the introduction to the *Beiträge*, Heidegger groups the *Stimmungen* under the single heading *Ahnung*, presentiment. This is because in all passages and dispositions of thought in abandonment resounds the presentiment of the senses of being. It is in light of such echo of being that *da-sein* opens as a time-space in which we might engage in the thinking of the senses of being.[23] It is under the presentiment of being that thought withstands and undergoes its experiencing the fury of the refusal and abandonment of being. But, if this is the case, this is because presentiment goes beyond common sense. Neither logic nor will may justify or sustain undergoing the emptiness of being. It is the presentiment of being that alone sustains thought in its being there in abandonment, and this presentiment is found in our thoroughly experienced hopelessness, and, as we shall see below, in reason's ultimate lack of control over beings.

Presentiment and *Grundstimmung* not only indicate the disposition or modality of thought in the experience of being there in abandonment they refer also to the sensibility of these dispositions of thinking in *da-sein*. As Heidegger explains, *Grundstimmung* prepares us for the fall in which we encounter the fury and the call of being in our epoch. For Heidegger, *Grundstimmung* is an intimation of being that requires a decisive attentiveness in da-sein (being there), and, as he writes, "this decidedness is only the dispassionate power to suffer [*Leidenschaft*]. . . ."[24] In *Grundstimmung* thought encounters itself in being there, as is exposed to that which situates it, exposed to the gravest and fecund experience of being in abandonment and forgetfulness of being.[25] This is what the names of the *Stimmungen* recall. Horror, reservedness, timidity, and presentiment tell us that this is a thought that comes to pass in its being exposed to the fury and the eco of being in being there (*da-sein*). We should note here that this language carries a suffered sense of thought's embodiment, and yet, it does not bespeak the body: this is not a bodily language in the sense of undergoing the singularity and density of bodies.[26] One may think of this point as an indication of a certain limit in Heidegger's thought; a point at which a border between difference and the singular can not be crossed in Heidegger. This has been the fitting critique of Heidegger held by Jacques Derrida in *Geschlecht I*, and *Geschlecht II*; it is a point of difference that will become a question for Derrida's own thought when we discuss Derrida and Antonin Artaud in the latter part of this book.[27] For now, we move towards the fecundity of being in the word, with a warning, a reminder of a singularity that may already mark a limit to Heidegger's own exposure to abyssal or fecund being.

The Fecundity of Being There

According to Heidegger, the dispositions of thought in *da-sein* occur with a certain dissemination or fecund opening of the senses of being. "Attunement is the spraying forth (*Versprühung*) of the trembling (*Erzitterung*) of being as enowning in da-sein."[28] This explosive dissemination (*Versprühung*) occurs as thought comes to pass in a disposition that situates it in a certain overflowing of being. This occurs when thought finds itself beyond the rationally ruled representations of all senses of thought and beings. We are speaking of experiences of thought that arise in the collapse of the logical and calculative project of reason, and its attempt to control and produce all senses of being. As we already said, according to Heidegger, it is the same implosion of the all-powerful project of rationality and its force that leads thought to sense the need for thinking the senses of being anew: It is in the total loss of senses of being—in that grand void, that the need for the sense of being comes to be felt in excess of all calculation, logic, and the totalizing quantification of beings. In other words, in its dispositions or modalities of being there, thought encounters the limits of its productive representation, and, through this delimitation, thought encounters itself in openness to experiences of being over which it does not have any productive rule or control.[29]

This overflowing of reason, this fecundity of being in *da-sein*, is crucial to understand the possibilities opened by Heidegger's thought as discussed here. In speaking of the overflowing in *da-sein*, we may begin to engage thought in terms of themes and experiences not traditionally treated as part of the task of philosophy and not directly engaged by Heidegger. I am speaking of following through Heidegger's foot steps and taking the senses and experiences of identities and being in light of their historical, temporal, and finite character. In Heidegger's words, this occurs as one takes conceptual knowledge and thought in their *geschichtlich* sense, much in the way Heidegger begins to do so when he situates thought in *da-sein*, and when he takes being there as a problematic of *Stimmung*.

If, in its finite being there, thought occurs as an experience that overflows its logical, quantitative, and productive expectative, then, in beginning from its situation, thought must begin from that which informs it and yet remains beyond its rules of representation and control. At such a point, thought and its traditions are open to lineages, histories, memories, exclusions, des-encounters, silences, and words and voices, which configure the philosophical tradition without being wholly determined by it. In other words, ultimately the task of thinking in being there calls for the thinking of being through what I would provisionally call a hermeneutics and phenomenology of singularities. This last phrase requires a brief clarification.

I say singularities, because of the ephemeral and often marginal themes that here are introduced to the center of philosophical thought. I speak of hermeneutics and phenomenology together because, as the development of Heidegger's later work indicates, this engagement of the overflowing in being there, opens language to a necessary and rigorous engagement. In Heidegger's terms, thinking is always concerned with the essence/ing of language. Therefore, if along with hermeneutics we still say that all senses of being occur in language/interpretation, this also means that we must think through the senses and forms of language with which thought comes to pass. I am speaking of engaging thought in its word not only through the meaning and logic of what is said, but also by seeking its silences, hesitations, aporetic moments; and, I would suggest, perhaps already transgressing Heidegger's words, this also leads to ask how that tacit being of animals, wordless graphic works, even our breath turn, and the many other nonspeaking ways of beings and bodies, inform the very configuration of our words and thought. In light of this, I think we can say that thought is as much a matter of interpretation as is interpretation a matter that calls for a certain phenomenological concern.

With these conclusions I do not mean to suggest that we must introduce the stranger, the other, the brute, the animal, to the philosophical discourse, or vice versa. If we take Heidegger's thought in its felt and sensuous senses, we will find ourselves with the need and challenge to think with a certain sensibility through that most strange situation of being there and through the language in which such experience might be heard.

Heidegger concludes his discussion of *Grundstimmung* and presentiment by saying that, in our epoch, the thought of being-there requires that we undergo and decidedly persist in *Da-sein*.[30] He then concludes with a sentence we have already noted above, "As an intimating decidedness, however, this decidedness is only the dispassionate power to suffer [*Leidenskraft*] of the creative ones."[31] Such decidedness is not other than the task of a thought open to the suffering of facing the abandonment of being in our epoch. But, as Heidegger states, in these doleful dispositions we also find in *Stimmung* the creative strength of a thought that opens towards the fecund overflowing of the senses of being. Thinking in abandonment, being there, only will occur if our thoughts are exposed to their strange passages and overflowing; and, it is only through the sensibility of a thought exposed to the emptiness of all senses of being, to abandonment, to overflowings, to transformations and marginality—it is this being there exposed that will situate us and make a space and time for a thought and word to come.

Tremulous Exposed Words

The Abyssal and Fecund Sensibility of the Word in its Finitude

It is clear that, for Heidegger, all thought happens in words. But what this means cannot be taken for granted, since as it is well known, in his later works Heidegger makes clear that perhaps the single most decisive issue for thought is the essencing of language, or the finite undergoing of the saying ⸢ a word.[32] Thus, in taking up the word of thought in its finitude we take ⸢e task of thinking language in rather concrete and direct terms, and it ⸢ly in this way that we will proceed.

⸢ have already seen, the undergoing of thought in its abandonment ⸢ve moment in the release of thought to the abyssal overflowing of all determinations of senses of being. For Heidegger this turning point occurs in the disposition of reservedness: "Reservedness (*die Verhaltenheit*) is the creative sustaining in abyss."[33] But how do we understand reservedness? Heidegger develops his discussion of the creative opening of being in reservedness out of a certain lack of words: "*Es verschlägt einem das Wort*."[34] Words lack. But this lack does not indicate an error or incapacity. Here, language is not defined according to a logic of calculation, signification, and representation.[35] Here lack refers to the word that is not yet the signifying unity that seems to be when taken as part of a representational language system. Indeed, according to Heidegger, the lack felt in language figures the urgency of finding words beyond machination's rational production of discourses. Heidegger writes, "The word's escaping [*Verschlagung*] is the inceptual condition for the self-unfolding possibility of an originary-poetic naming of beyng."[36] The strength of words is not determined by questions of signification and meaning. For Heidegger the words that may engage the call of beyng arise out of silence and lack. Analogously, it is the silence or withdrawal of senses of being that is felt in the lack of words. And precisely in arising with this silence the word arises in reservedness, that is, in that lack of breath and timidity that gives leeway for the word to unfold in its embodying passages, in breath, resonance, and senses. In other words, in reservedness words arise out of their exposure to their silence or lack, and this means that, unlike the infinitely ringing linguistic product of machination discourse, this word finds expression out of pause (in an opening in which we may first listen) and not by rushing to produce more signification while taking for granted the sense of affirmation and signification.

In other words, the word in reservedness arises in abyssal exposure or awareness. In finding itself in its incontrollable lack and silences, the word is open to limits and possible delimitations that cannot be claimed or covered over by affirmation, representation, or argumentative logical correctness. Heidegger speaks of thought in such words in reservedness as, "inceptual thinking as nonconceptual [*als unbegriffliches*]."[37] Here *unbegriffliches* not only means a word or thought that is not determined by something categorical or conceptually determined by the immediate presence of entities, but also, and along with this, not secured by its supposed limitless capacity to explain, define, and give an account of being. In this sense, as Françoise Dastur's elegantly says, thinking in reservedness means "to make silence come to the word."[38]

In the last section of his book Heidegger again recalls the primacy of silence in the arising of language: "Language is grounded in silence."[39] As we just saw, here silence figures the abyssal withdrawal of being, and Language may be said to be grounded in silence as it unfolds in the reservedness of the word exposed to its silences and lack. At the same time, this undergoing of silence in reservedness also figures the opening to the overflowing of being.

In the undergoing of their silence language and word find a limit that situates them, and that does so as they encounter a relation to all senses of beings that they cannot determine, control, or fully preconceive. It is that sense of impossibility of domination that grounds language in the abyssal fecund opening of beings. Language opens in as far as it is situated by the engagement of its silence and when in that undergoing begins to unfold its fecund resounding. Heidegger writes, "Silence is the most sheltered measure-holding. It holds the measure, in that it first sets up measure. And so language is measure-setting in the most intimate and widest sense, measure setting as essential saying of the jointure and its joining (enowning)."[40]

For Heidegger language in the sense of reservedness unfolds as the opening place of being (*die offene Stelle*), and the time-space for the unfolding of the senses of being: "language is ground of da-sein."[41] With it open earth, heaven, and world. In "Sprache und Ereignis," writes Heidegger, "Fleeting shimmer of earth, resonance of world. *Strife*, the originary sheltering of the fissure, because the innermost rift. The open place."[42] In the reservedness and breath of the word exposed to the abyssal fecundity of its undergoing of all senses of beings resounds the pulse of the fecundity of being. But here is the crucial point about this sensible undergone and withstood word: the word opens because it exposes itself to its ephemeral and concrete passages, to its limit. This word is the time-space for the unfolding of the senses of beings because its figurations of senses of being are always configured in exposures to the abyssal fecundity of all senses of beings. Furthermore, because of the impossibility of its self-closure and auto-determination, we are speaking of a word always already exposed to senses of being that take it well beyond its configurations of sense, into encounters as unpredictable as they are involuntary. In this sense we can say that Heidegger's sense of this abyssal fecund language bears its blow to emptiness by bringing silence to language in a call to a tremulous and essentially marginal and exposed speaking in the opening of the passing senses of beings.

Heidegger does not find this language in philosophy in our epoch and Western history, but rather in poetry. "The one who seeks beyng in the ownmost overflow of seeking power, is the poet who 'founds' being."[43] This has led many critiques to mistake the thinking of later Heidegger for a mediocre attempt at poetizing. But the sensibility we have been discussing and the word that unfolds in reservedness can not be subject to the simple differentiation between aesthetic and conceptual experience that is sustained precisely by the rationalism that Heidegger unsettles. Surely, as we have seen now, thinking in its finitude will be a matter of sensibility, of exposure, and even of the most violent undergoing of the ephemeral and concrete configuration of senses of being. And it is not the poet, or the artistic sensibility as opposed to the rational, that Heidegger identifies in the poets. Rather, the poet attends to the passing of sense in the unfolding of senses of beings in the word. Poets, not all, but a few, are those who have begun to engage sense through the exposed sensibility we discussed, which, if heard by philosophers, could transform and spur thought in thinking through its finitude and therefore its very undergoing and withstanding of being.[44] Furthermore, for Heidegger the task of *Contributions* is merely that of a preparation that will give us the sensibility and therefore strength to hear and understand the words of the single poet that does open the word to the abyssal fecundity of the senses of being.[45] "Thereupon philosophy is now primarily preparation for philosophy in the manner of building the nearest forecourts in whose spatial configuration Hölderlin's word become hearable and is replied by *da-sein* and in such a reply becomes grounded as the language of future man."[46] According to Heidegger, in the poetry of Hölderlin we find the opening that points toward a further destiny of philosophy, that sheds a light through the darkest night of metaphysics, and that opens towards that sensibility and disposition in the word in fecund abandonment we have been discussing through our meditations.[47] This leads us to the last, and perhaps most critical of our meditations.

CHAPTER 4

Fourth Meditation

Thought's Ambiguous Finitude: Between Abyssal Fecund Thought and the Historical Destiny of the West

The crossing too must be experienced in its entire range and its many ruptures.

(Heidegger, *Contributions to Philosophy*, 79)

You are like a land
No one has ever said.
You await nothing
But the word
That will spring from the bottom
Like a fruit amongst branches.
A wind finds you.
Things dry and emaciated
Crowd you and pass in the wind.
Ancient limbs and words.
You tremble in Summer.

"Earth and Death," Cesare Pavese

As we saw in our previous meditations, Heidegger's work seeks to open thought to a disposition or sensibility in which thought is exposed in abyssal fecund being. This opens the possibility of exposing the history of Western philosophy to another beginning out of the undergoing of thought's finite marginal and transformative passages. Thus, something does ring in our undergoing and withstanding the face to face with machination. At the same time, this transformation or leap in departure from machination and its dominion requires a violent break, a *Zerklüftung*. Not only must we remain with the abyssal truth of all configurations of senses of beings, but this means undergoing the exposure to the marginal and transformative character of all word and thought. In the sense of its attempt to engage thought in its finitude, *Contributions* is originary (*ursprünglich*). This means that it occurs as a transformative hermeneutical undergoing: in the insertion of the abyssal and, through this, of the marginal and transformative in thought, the thinking of *Contributions* invites the recognition and conceptual, analytical, and critical expansion of the already determined paths of the Western tradition. The inception of finitude in its abyssal fecund register also prefigures the possible reconfiguration or transformation of the already determining and working parameters that situate the history of philosophy and its determinations of being. Heidegger writes that, "Truth as ground grounds originarily as abyss (*Abgrund*)."[1] The term "*Abgrund*" precisely indicates that in its abyssal finitude thought is always already in a loss and transformative recovery of all fundamental conceptual ideas and parameters, and in this sense also in transformative loss in relation to the determination of all senses of beings, presence, senses, language, et cetera. This is not only because of the protean or temporal character of finite thought, but also more remarkably, because in its opening exposure to its limits, the philosophical word cannot control nor determine all senses of beings, and therefore, neither can it determine its historical sense in any teleological manner. In other words, the thought in finitude is always a thought to come in that it cannot ground itself in its historical determinations, and therefore, it is a thinking without immutable foundations or transcendental essences that may be identified in nature or reason. All this said simply to indicate the extent of the openness that occurs with Heidegger's engagement of philosophical thought in its situatedness and finitude. Now, the question is, to what extent does Heidegger's thought withstand and undergo this abyssal thinking? This is the issue for this last meditation.

Between Emptiness and Overflowing Fecundity

According to Heidegger the opening of the word in abyssal fecundity requires a dispassionate strength for suffering in those disposed to hear the silence of being.[2] Heidegger writes concerning those who may undergo the abyssal fecundity of all determinations of beings, "But this requires a higher strength for creating and questioning and at the same time a deeper preparedness for suffering and settling within the whole of a complete transformation of relations to beings and to being."[3] On the one hand, this dispassionate strength for pain and suffering refers to the violent encounter with the emptiness behind all the projections of *Machenschaft* and behind the history of Western metaphysics in its rationalist stride: that face to face with emptiness and the absence of a teleological determination behind all conceptual works or lived experiences (*Erlebnis*). On the other hand, as we saw, the same undergoing of emptiness bears the opening of thought to a situation that is not only beyond its domination, but that situates all determinations of being in thought against and in openness to an indeterminate future. This is why, in the citation above, Heidegger writes that the disposition for transformation (*Wandel*) is inseparable from that strength to undergo suffering. Thus, Heidegger's thought occurs in between the loss of all meaning and the coming of uncertain senses of beings.

Throughout *Contributions*, Heidegger's language dramatically and literally indicates this much; words pass unperceived if one insists on reading them in terms of reason and ignores the sensibility of the undergoing of the word in his thought. *Contributions* unfolds as an encounter with the fury of the abandonment of being (*der äußerste Ingrimm der Seinsverlassenheit*); through the courageous sacrifice and solitude of being in the abyssal fecundity of thought's finitude (. . . *die den höchsten Mut zur Einsamkeit mitbringen, um den Adel des Seyns zu denken und zu sagen von seiner Einzigkeit*); and, in the uneasiness or distress of engaging the question of the senses of being (*die Unruhe des Fragens*).[4] The very names of each disposition of thought in *Contributions* resound with the difficulty of being there (*Da-sein*) in thought's finitude: in *Erschrecken* (fear), *Verhaltenheit* (reservedness), and *Scheu* (timid reticence) not only do we find the echoes of the literal undergoing and withstanding of the transition through machination of Heidegger's thought, but, furthermore, these words tell the manner of the transition.[5] We are speaking directly of the fear or horror of facing the emptiness of machination and the refusal of all sense of being. At the same time we hear of the timid fear or reticence (*die Scheu*) towards the indeterminate transformation of all senses and concepts of being, in the intimation (*Ahnung*) of a thought that perhaps is coming. Furthermore, these dispositions gather under a single one, attentive reservedness (*Verhaltenheit*): that being in silence in which we begin to hear the double echo of the senses of being in their abyssal emptiness and fecundity, that finite being there (*da-sein*), never secured by representational and conceptual language or projection, and yet exposed to all senses and transfigurations of being and thought. As Heidegger writes: "Reservedness is the midpoint (cf. below) for startled dismay and deep awe [*das Erschrecken und die Scheu*]. These simply make more explicit what belongs *originarily* to reservedness. Reservedness determines the style of inceptual thinking in the other beginning."[6] This sentence gives us a sense of the difficulty of remaining with thought's finitude: what is coming may arise if we can remain in silence so that the name, the word take flight, and twist free in midair letting sense open . . . only to then find thought once again moving in the task of silent listening in abyssal fecund finitude.[7] It is the harsh discipline of undergoing the opening of thought between emptiness and overflowing that marks Heidegger's thinking in finitude in *Contributions*. But to what extent does Heidegger sustain this situation?

With this question today we find two possible paths already delineated: Derrida's critique of Heidegger's attempt to reach thought's singularity, and Agamben's situation of Heidegger's thought at the border of the reduction of life to biopolitics. In the case of Derrida, the critique follows Heidegger's insistence on being rather than beings, and the way this leads him apart from singular events. In the case of Agamben, Heidegger begins to think our biopolitical situation: he articulates biopolitical existence already in *dasein's* indiscernible character in relation to all traditional determinations of man, and in *Contributions*, he attempts to think in that open space of transgressed difference between life and politics. Both Derrida and Agamben make crucial points about Heidegger's thought; however, in my discussion I have tried to follow the movement of Heidegger's thought in its undergoing of machination. In other words, I have tried not to critique but to undergo the thought, in order to mark the limits and possibilities opened by it, some of which are recognized in both Derrida's critique in "Geschlecht I," "Geschlecht II" and in "De L'esprit," as well as by Agamben's relation of Heidegger to biopolitical concerns in *Homo Sacer* and in *L'Aperto*.[8] Also, I think that both Agamben and Derrida are situated by the exposure to temporality inaugurated by Heidegger's thought, and that in this sense undergoing Heidegger's violent encounter may be fruitful if one wishes to understand the sensibility that orients the later philosophers.

The Abyssal Word as the Path to the Destiny of the Western Philosophical Tradition

> Through flame or cinders, but like all others, inevitably.
>
> (Derrida, De L'esprit)

As I mentioned at the end of the previous chapter, the work of *Contributions* reaches towards Hölderlin's word, and his word, if heard, will offer us the space for thinking in the finitude of thought and all senses of being.[9] The poet's words lay bare a fundamental sensibility, which if undergone may begin to orient and even sustain the opening of thought beyond machination. Heidegger writes in the last fugue of *Contributions*, "Beyng,"

> enjoined unto the distress of the truth of being and thus bound into the necessity of that decision which on the whole has at its disposal what is ownmost to history and its essencing. Thereupon

philosophy is now primarily preparation for philosophy in the manner of building the nearest forecourts in whose spatial configuration Hölderlin's word becomes hearable and is replied by Da-sein and in such a reply becomes grounded as the language of future man.[10]

And then concludes, "The historical destiny of philosophy culminates in the recognition of the necessity of making Hölderlin's word be heard." In its passage through the darkest night of metaphysics, philosophy seeks to learn to hear Hölderlin's word.[11] It is the poet's language that indicates the way to the future word. First of all, we should be clear that this does not mean that philosophers must become poets, or imitate Hölderlin. Undergoing *Machenschaft* opens our language to a sensibility in which we become able to hear in the poet's words the fecund echo of being in abandonment. Heidegger writes in reference to Hölderlin, Nietzsche, and Kierkegaard:

Let no one today be so presumptuous as to take it as mere coincidence that these three, who, each in his own way, in the end suffered profoundly the uprooting to which Western history is being driven and who at the same time intimated their gods most intimately—that these three had to depart from the brightness of their days prematurely.[12]

The word in which opens the future of thought is found in these thinkers, who suffered the uprooting and violence of nihilism to the point of madness and early death. Such a passage figures the undergoing of the abandonment of being, in such withstanding, being there, opens the horizon of thought. Hölderlin's word articulates and resounds from the abandonment of being, it is a word exposed to the abyssal and fecund undergoing of our time. Therefore, we find here a basic sensibility in the undergoing in being exposed to the abyssal and clear emptiness and fecund opening of beyng. Were we to think in such disposition or exposure, we would begin to be taken up by beyng through the engagement of the abandonment of being. Only through such an abyssal and fecund experience of language as disposition would we begin to reclaim the sense of such fields of experience as literature, politics, and aesthetics. This dramatic relationship to language we find in Heidegger's readings of certain poets is well explicated by von Herrman.[13] In pointing to his interpretation, I emphasize that it is not my intention to undermine or question the understanding of Heidegger's reading of poetry as an engagement with the essence of language. The question is to what extent Heidegger's thought withstands the exposure in fecund abyssal grounds figured by such language. Indeed, we can set further towards this question by mentioning another crucial observation made by Hans Ruin in "Origin in Exile." In this essay, Ruin invites us to consider "how the attempt to escape the Platonism of the contemporary philosophy of language, as well as the shallow historicism of the human sciences," leads Heidegger "to rediscover the romantic thinkers, and Hölderlin in particular."[14] This invitation to a genealogical study of Heidegger's disposition could only be positive if done well, and is something much needed by the many critical assessments of Heidegger's political involvement with fascism. However, this is not the place for this, rather I take this invitation also as an indication of the danger of simply following Heidegger's path without being attentive to its limitations. We now turn to such critical moment, towards the delimitation of Heidegger's thought.

Heidegger's turn to poetry carries a great promise, and yet, a closer look shows us how this opening comes to a quick closure. It is precisely at this point of possible exposure in the word as disposition that Heidegger gives a determinate direction and goal to the sensibility of thought; most remarkably, turning from its sense of exposed sensibility. This is evident if we listen again to Heidegger's first remark above: "The historical destiny of philosophy culminates in the recognition of the necessity of making Hölderlin's word be heard." (*Die geschichtliche Bestimmung der Philosophie gipfelt in der Erkenntnis der Notwendigkeit, Hölderlins Wort das Gehör zu schaffen.*)[15] Ultimately, the opening of being in the undergoing of machination does not refer us to madness and obscure death, but these experiences, together with the discipline of suffering through nihilism's highest moment have a single point of reference, the historical destiny of philosophy. As the quote above indicates, madness comes from being uprooted from the tradition: "in the end suffered profoundly the uprooting to which Western history is being driven."[16] At this point, the critique of technology and machination unfolds not towards a fecund diversifying horizon, but rather towards a history that although always questioned by Heidegger, seems to come back to rescue the philosopher from an abyss too dense for him to engage directly.

Indeed, along with the sensibility of being exposed in the word to finitude in its fecund opening and with the disposition to undergo the great suffering, Heidegger identifies the great task of opening a space for the justification and destiny of the West. Heidegger writes:

> But the dangerousness of the question, who are we'? . . . is the one and only way to come to ourselves and thus to open the way for the originary saving, i.e., justifying the West through its history [*Rechfertigung des Abendlandes aus seiner Geschichte*]."[17]

Thus, in hearing Hölderlin's words we would move towards the reappropriation of the Western tradition through an originary saving. For Heidegger, *da-sein*—being there in finitude—is not only the undergoing and withstanding of being in fecund abandonment, but this undergoing already has a destiny, and this is nothing less than the rediscovering of the historical destiny of being: "If a history [*Geschichte*] is ever to be allotted to us again, i.e., if we are to be creatively exposed to beings out of belongingness to being, then we cannot turn away from this destiny [*diese Bestimmung*], namely to prepare the time space for the final decision concerning whether and how we experience and ground this belongingness."[18] The word for history is *Geschichte* and it should not be confused with historiography. As the term indicates, we are speaking of engaging our situation in its fecund and transformative passage. At the same time, the word translated as destiny is *Bestimmung*. This term, with its root in *stimmung*, should indicate to us that Heidegger is not speaking of an extant promised destiny, but of that opening disposition that must be sustained beyond the economies of machination, and otherwise than the attempts to move beyond it through rationalism, pragmatism, psychology, and historicism. However, we have now found a task that gives force and sustains the fecund almost inhuman exposure to thought's finitude. That which has already been allotted to thought by Heidegger is the destiny of the West: this is the issue that orients the language of the final decision (last quote above). Derrida certainly sees this in "De L'esprit." And he is right in identifying the close connection between the doleful requirements of spirit as the suffering of undergoing machination in the form of being-historical-thinking and the ultimate repatriation of the uprooted (case in point: the thinkers and the poet mentioned above) in Heidegger's thought.[19]

The task of reinterpreting the West opens for Heidegger a horizon that although indeterminate does offer sufficient promise, as to sustain and hold together thought over against its finitude's horror and its reservedness in the face of the fury, emptiness and overflowing unrestrained and overflowing senses of being. We are no longer seeking a vibrant and tremulous word born in abyssal fecund fury. Rather, it is a matter of engaging in discourses, which, although indeterminate due to the temporality of language, are already inscribed to the great task of thought. Having said this one must wonder about the exilic character of language in Heidegger (as Hans Run points it out) and this turn to a discourse fated to be undone by virtue of the exilic temporality of thought and language.[20] Here, the matter to be thought guides thought, and this matter is the West, its history. Thus, thought is insured its sense in spite of suffering (even in spite of madness or premature death), as it stays along the path of the great task. After all, this is not any opening, but the overture to the destiny of the whole of philosophical thought, Western thought and culture, in the truth of Beyng. This thought, as Heidegger tells us, will once again give humans direction, a *télos*, an end and purpose beyond machination (*ein Ziel*).[21]

This welcoming although indeterminate horizon for the word in the abandonment of being is felt more directly and strongly when Heidegger associates the poet's words with "the last God." In speaking, in *Contributions*, of reservedness Heidegger points specifically to his two works on the poet from 1934–35, "Hölderlins Hymnen 'Germanien' " and "Der Rhein."[22] As Heidegger explains, this reservedness is "destined by the last God" (*vom letzten Gott bestimmt*).[23] And as he explains in the first page of the section in *Contributions* titled "*Der letzte Gott*," the path that opens in the letting be heard of the last god is "But the futural, the truth of being as refusal, contains within itself the ensuring of greatness, not magnitude of empty and gigantic eternity, but of the shortest path."[24] Here we find, literally, the passage through nihilism guided by the greatest task of Western destiny; now the origin in exile has also been recovered under the larger project. Furthermore, the sentence ends in what can be seen as a radical contrast with the horror and suffering of being in abyssal opening: the transition to this destiny will be the shortest. Pain, fear, horror, fury, violence, and suffering seem to be submerged if not left to oblivion for a moment. Instead, in these words we find a thought that moves swiftly in fugue towards a great destiny that assures its sense under the inspired flight of the last God, although the latter remains indeterminate in its arrival and fugue.

In the task and promise of the justification of the history of Western philosophy Heidegger's thought finds support in its painful and difficult attempt to think with thought's finitude in abyssal exposure. Nihilism stands not only as a point of transformation in departure from the tradition, but it is also the hidden requirement for the thought to come, the lesson that thought must learn. But this lesson needs be learnt because what is hidden in that lesson is the assurance of thought's relationship to its great task, the Western tradition. In other words, no matter how radical the collapse of metaphysics and the *Destruktion* of the Western tradition, this very thinking is sustained by a question-worthiness afforded by its great assignment. Ironically, one might say that nihilism gives thought a certain security, and even pedigree.

At the same time, in this requirement we find that regardless of its fecundity, in Heidegger the thought that is coming is always already situated under the one destiny, the destiny of Western thought. The issue is not the vulgar pointing of fingers at European philosophy's Eurocentrism. We have gone too far in our encounter with the histories of colonialism and the Americas to even believe that there ever was a single Western thought . . . did not Dionysus come from the east! The point that concerns me here is that in meditating on Heidegger's thought not only are we led to undergo our thought in its ephemeral and concrete finitude, but we find ourselves situated in an in-between. On the one hand, abyssal exposure leads thought towards a coming thought that can not be subsumed under the Western history of philosophy, metaphysics, or machination. On the other hand, in being situated by nihilism, in its face-to-face with reason's calculative and emotive production and its emptiness, this very thought is inseparable from (and to a certain extent does carry the weight and destiny of) Western tradition. It would be pointless to say here that Heidegger chooses his position, or that we can choose ours. This is where we stand, thanks to Heidegger's almost inhuman attempt to think in thought's finitude: we stand between the marginal abyssal and fecund openness of thought's temporality, and the dependence on the tradition this thought bears in its very temporal situatedness, a relation that limits and ultimately threatens to exclude that very thought's abyssal opening. Heidegger writes: "Da-sein is the crisis between the first and the other beginning."[25] This is made evident by the fact that not even deconstruction can understand itself outside of the grounding question of the West, that is, its Holocaust, the death of its God, and its nihilism . . . to what extent is Nietzsche a liberator and to what extent is he the figure that assures a suffering and a destiny for thought in its Western lineages?

Being Between

As Heidegger writes in *Contributions*, "History [*Geschichte*] emerges only in the immediate skip [*Überspringung*] of what is 'historical' [*des Historischen*]."[26] These lines indicate that one can only engage thought in its finite and fecund situatedness and temporality in an originary (*ursprünglich*) manner. At the same time, the issue of the destiny of the West and its philosophical tradition refers to that tradition's various configurations of senses of beings. It is the thought of the historical figures of that tradition that must be interpreted, appropriated, and ultimately justified through the delivery of its destiny. Here, between fecundity and tradition, we find an impossible place for thought's movement. If we are understanding beyng-historical thinking when we say that it is fundamentally an originary thought that sets out in abyssal exposure, then the possible justification (*die Rechfertigung*) belongs to a leap that already goes beyond any destiny of the metaphysical tradition and its history. If the leap in abyssal exposure situates these various configurations of being on the way towards their destiny, this destiny can not be understood to be either creative in ignorance of the historical tradition, nor may it seek the coming thought in reason as understood by the tradition in such formulations as the rationalism calculative, logical, and productive figurations that orient metaphysics or any other historical movements. Neither the self-critique of reason in its recognition of its own limits, nor a project like that of *Dialectic of Enlightenment* will do. Furthermore, even hermeneutics, with its blending of horizons and its close proximity to Hegel's dialectic will not seem enough, because in all of these cases thought has not taken an abyssal leap that releases it from the tradition, such that thought may retake the tradition in and through undergoing its uncontainable fecundity. In what we have seen, a historical-hermeneutical thought, that makes the leap, will situate thought at its limits. These limits are not found in the tradition but in its abyssal reappropriation through the abandonment and fecund coming of senses of being in their concrete undergoing.

Indeed, thought's leap in abyssal finitude makes the assimilation of the marginal or unexpected into the tradition impossible, because in that leap thought moves out of ephemeral and concrete exposures that have always already gone beyond a tradition that may be in the position to receive and contain the senses of being arisen in the fecundity of the abyssal opening. The abyssal fecundity of thought in its finitude will not fit or be measurable by the tradition. This is why Heidegger at the outset of *Contribution* speaks of the thought he attempts as *befremdlich*, strange, foreign to the tradition.[27] And, even if, as Derrida points out, Heidegger's task is the repatriation of what has been made strange by machination, this repatriation figures a disruption in that economy, which has already set thought on its way beyond Western history. This is because in its temporal sense this strangeness figures a transformative movement: in interpreting the tradition out of abyssal exposure, the tradition is always at risk of not being preserved. This is also the case because the tradition also marks a limit in terms of what can or cannot be accepted as thought, senses of being, and language. Therefore, we can not expect, as Heidegger does, that thinking in its finite fecund exposed leap will lead to a justification of the tradition, or the delivery of Western tradition to *its* destiny.

Although already in the ambiguity between leap and tradition figures the impossibility of sustaining the sense of a certain destiny and justification of the tradition, Heidegger's thought remains caught in ambiguity: "Thinking in the crossing brings into a speaking-in-between [*Zwiesprache*] what has first been of beyng's truth and that which in the truth of being is futural in the extreme—and in that speaking in between brings to word the essencing of beyng"[28] Heidegger's thought is immobilized in the ambiguity between tradition and abyssal overflowing exposure. This is why he sees his thought as an in-between-word (*Zwiesprache*). His thought is marked by the indecision wrought of the double vision of a tradition that slips away and a thought that is coming that no one can yet see, and that guarantees nothing. That Heidegger refers to the thought of *Contributions* as an attempt (*Versuch*), does not only mean that he is thinking in a certain reservedness, but what makes his thought only an attempt is that his work can only be preparatory; preparatory in the sense that in his thought Heidegger does not move decidedly, there is no decision (*Entscheidung*) in Heidegger's thought, only the preparation for a decisive step to come.[29] As Heidegger also writes,

"The time re-building the essential shaping of beings according to the truth of being has not yet arrived."[30] This is the case precisely because Heidegger's thought remains in between the destiny of the tradition and an overflowing of that very tradition. I also would suggest that this is why reservedness remains the central attunement in *Contributions*. Here we are speaking of a reservedness that leaves us open in an in-between, and that will not give way to the step or leap that will take the tradition into the abyssal transformative and dangerous opening of thought's exposed finitude.

With these observations, I do not intend to say that Heidegger's thought fails, or that it does not accomplish what it seeks. As I have said since the beginning of my meditations, in his thought Heidegger undergoes an almost inhuman encounter between conceptual thought and its ephemeral and concrete temporality. However, this thinking opens to an abyssal overflowing of the philosophical tradition that also overwhelms Heidegger; since it occurs between the emptiness of nihilism and the overflowing of a thought that is coming beyond the tradition's formulations and expectations, Heidegger moves back to the reassuring task of the opening of the destiny of the West. Thus, he is caught between it and abyssal fecund being, and can not take the step to think in abyssal exposure. But this ultimately means that to Heidegger we owe the articulation of our situation in-between, and this means the exposure to a thought still well beyond us, not only because of its power but more decidedly in the intimation of that step in abyssal fecund exposure and openness that we might or might not ever take.

Towards Other Sides

The difficulty articulated in this meditation, as well as in the previous chapters, is not Heidegger's, and is not an issue for our objective justification of his thought. In Heidegger's thought, we find the encounter of conceptual thought and its tradition with its finitude. In that encounter, thought begins to be exposed to its abyssal and fecund being. This makes impossible the claim to a single rational and metaphysical tradition, and its project of machination, to which must belong the destiny of thought. In the leap in abyssal exposure the parameters of senses of being operative in metaphysics, rationalism, and machination have always already been overflowed, and with them the Western tradition. With this overflowing, their supposed justification and unique destiny have been open to what, to them, would be unpredictable and even unthinkable, and to destinies unforeseeable for the tradition, even in its well-hearted attempts to include its other. However, at the same time, in our situation, the tradition and its history are undeniable rubrics of any philosophical thought, and it is not for lack of sensibility but because he clearly understands the difficulties that face us, that Heidegger sees thought's finitude as a hermeneutical, or interpretative and appropriative historical (*geschichtlich*) task. The issue for us is how to take the decisive abyssal leap in a sense transformative for the tradition but without being fixed in ambiguity and immobilized between a tradition that must be justifiable and led to its destiny and an abyssal opening in a thought that is coming. How do we take the tradition out of thought's finitude in its fecund and transformative exposure?

To close these meditations, and as a lead to the rest of this book, I want to suggest that we have already begun that leap: I mean, in understanding, through our abyssal exposure, the impossibility of remaining wedded to the tradition's interpretations of the senses of beings and to the idea that to the Western tradition alone belongs the thought that is coming. The impossibility of situating the fecund opening of thought's finitude in the tradition has a specific and distinct sense: here occurs an opening of a certain sensibility of thought, because the very manner or undergoing of thinking is transformed. In its abyssal fecund undergoing of finitude, thought is not a matter of fixing meanings, representing them, and securing their roles in the production of senses of being. At the same time, given this, language cannot be viewed as the signifying or representative tool for categorizing, fixing, defining, representing and putting to work meanings, as if it were a readily available tool. In short, in abyssal exposure, thought breaks beyond the traditional rational-emotional parameters. In this leap, thought may only recover its place in exposure to its ephemeral and concrete situation: as the word gathers into sense in configurations oriented by its self-overcoming, that is, in arising from the sensibility of being in exposure to emptiness and the fecund overflowing of the very figurations of sense it sets. Such lived and felt words do not have, as their orienting and determining activity, representation and signification, categorization, and functional placement of senses of being. In abyssal exposure, words let us hear, release us, give leeway; they figure passages, openings, sites of exposure, loss, and unexpected unfoldings of senses of being. But this means that, in undergoing thought in its abyssal finitude, we will have to begin to learn to speak again and again: as words always play out of silence, opening to the not yet of the coming thought. Without undergoing and withstanding thought in its finitude, these observations could easily become another announcement and production of an infinite project, always in exciting preparations and deferrals. Our meditations have led us to the place of our thought, to the edge of an abyssal fecundity and coming thought that we will undergo and withstand in various registers, histories, and destinies through the various essays in the rest of this book.

CHAPTER 5

Exposed Memories

Towards Reading the History of Philosophy Beyond its Historical Destiny in the West

Thought's life finds part of its measure in the future to which it gives rise, in its youthfulness.

(Charles Scott, *The Time of Memory*)

In the concluding section of *The Time of Memory*,[1] a work central to his thought, the American philosopher Charles E. Scott writes:

> As events of thought, like memories, become enmeshed in other events and experiences and pass away and beyond *their* ability to make a difference, they come to belong to memories, new figurations of vitality, and appearances that take them up, as it were, into other forces that transform bygone events into other images, narratives, or constellations of values. Thinking can be responsible to its nonpreserving aspect, to this transformativeness in its life, *as* it gives new life to appearances in transformations of past and present events—in justice to their transformation we might say.[2]

Scott's work reminds us of the indisputable play of our histories and lineages in our thought and determinations of the sense of things. Indeed, it is in things that thought seems to arise, and it is in the concrete passage of thought with things that its temporality is engaged. It is this concrete sense of thought that Scott unfolds in discussing in *The Time of Memory* thought's memorial dimension. At the same time, as this quote and the quote that opens this chapter already announce, this concrete sense of thought's passing points to a rejuvenating force proper to thought. As in the case of Heidegger, Scott is well aware of the need to be attentive to our beginnings and the history that situates us. Furthermore, as is the case with Heidegger, we hear in these two quotes that Scott recognizes as essential to thought its future, the need for it to find its measure, and, in the latter quote, the need to do justice to thought and its history. However, these similarities only serve us to point out the sharp departure Scott takes from Heidegger's thought. As we saw in the previous chapters, in Heidegger's engagement of thought's temporality, thought seems fated to a desperate immobility in its profound ambiguity between its exposure to its fecund and abyssal opening and its reorientation in response to the single destiny of philosophy in the West. Scott is aware of the danger of falling back into the security of that already determined sense of the place for thought and its futurity, no matter how open the horizon of the destiny of the West may be in view of its temporality or futurity. As Scott warns, "We as philosophers can turn the *life* of transforming thought and language against itself, and by that turning we can produce states of mind that deny their own living moment and refuse to carry out the performative work that constitutes them."[3] I believe this warning is directly appropriate to Heidegger's thought, as the German philosopher ultimately withdraws from his exposure and opening to thought's abyssal fecund exposure in its concrete temporality. In the context of Scott's words, one might say, as Heidegger's thought turns from youthful power to a refusal of thought's living power. But, this warning and Heidegger's ambiguous aporetic moment belongs to us, as do the future of thought, and the need to engage thought in its measure, and, to paraphrase Scott's fitting phrase, in justice to thought's concrete transformations. These issues situate our question: How are we to take up the difficulty of thought in its temporality in a way that engages thought in departure from Heidegger, that is, as we set out from Heidegger again and already in transgression of his thought? How are we to move towards thinking in the transformative overflowing fecundity we intimated in discussing Heidegger's *Contributions to Philosophy*?

In *The Time of Memory*, Charles Scott gives a powerful interpretation of memory with emphasis on the losses that occur with it, and out of this insight situates thought in its abyssal finitude: that is, in its temporality as figured by a sense of loss in thought and the transformative passages open in that loss. This analysis amounts to a transformative recovery of thought from the history of the West, and the idea of this history and its destiny as the single orienting problem for philosophical thought. This release does not point to the abandonment of this history or the reduction of thinking to politics, science, or the social sciences. Nor does it engage in the kind of wholehearted and reactive repudiation of these fields, as does Heidegger. Rather, in the recognition of the life of thought in its temporal transformative character, Scott offers us a way of engaging the history of philosophy on the way to a fecund opening towards other histories, lineages, and futures in language and thought. In this chapter, I develop this alternative to Heidegger's suffered ambiguity and horror, in light of the unbounded future of the history of the West.

In the following discussion, I trace the issue of the transformative appropriation of the history of philosophy by focusing on the way Scott's *The Time of Memory* takes up the beginning of the Western philosophical tradition, that is, the Greeks. We will move from a brief sketch of Scott's understanding of memory and its relationship to thought, to the interpretation of Greek figures in Scott's thought in the context of memorial events. Through this discussion I want to suggest that Greek thought appears for us as an operative figure of the transformative loss enacted by thought in its conceptual delimitations. In indicating this, I point to Scott's crucial insight concerning our appropriation of the tradition and the singularity of our thoughts. As we saw in the previous chapters, Heidegger seeks to take a step further along Nietzsche's insight concerning the end of metaphysics, as he attempts to think through nihilism in its highest form, machination. In doing this, Heidegger's thought exposes us to the abyssal and fecund opening that occurs in engaging thought's finitude, and yet, at the same time, he remains incapable of engaging fully in that transformative passage: this occurs as, in the horror of the unfolding of being's abyssal fecundity, Heidegger finds the task of justifying the Western philosophical tradition by letting it come to its destiny—the destiny of thought. In Scott's work, we find a thought in finitude that undergoes abyssal exposure without appealing to or expecting the delivery of a destiny of the Western tradition or any justification. Rather, in his own work, Scott seeks the intensifying of the very undergoing of thought in its exposure to finitude in order to engage the abyssal overflowing unfolding of the thought to come. At the same time, he seeks these intensifying transformative passages without releasing the figures of the Western historical tradition, but understanding them as sites for the transformative fecundity of thought in its finitude.

Recoveries in Transformative Loss

The central issue of *The Time of Memory* is "memory in its loss."[4] Loss is first introduced through Scott's reflections on his memory of himself as a child, and his awareness of a double loss in the experience of that memory.

> I can say that 'I then' and 'I now' are foreign to each other in the memorial event. If I believe that I now recognize him *then*, I do not understand the memory. And if I believe that 'I as a boy' recognize me now, I now lose touch with myself in that experience. Only by knowing the losses and in the losses can I remember with some clarity of understanding.[5]

A double loss in memorial events is behind the presence of memory and its seeming continuity. *The Time of Memory* recovers memory in its loss and the transformative passages in that loss.

Along with this awareness one finds that the book's development begins from and occurs in part through a series of encounters with certain Greek mythological figures, namely and principally, Mnemosyne and Lethe, and Dionysus and Apollo. These are ultimately understood as figures of loss and transformation. The discussion of Mnemosyne (remembering) and Lethe (forgetting), takes up these mythological figures in apparent affiliation in the story of two conjoined springs on each side of a cypress tree, Lethe on the left of the tree, Mnemosyne on the right.[6] Although traditionally the two are separated by presence and absence, by the chaos attributed to Lethe and the clarity and preservation of life in Mnemosyne, in this story remembering and forgetting spring from the same tree. The story points to a loss common to both figures. A loss not only in the sense of the chaos attributed to Lethe, but operative in Mnemosyne. There would be a loss in Mnemosyne in the forgetting of life's disasters which let life return. Loss or the Lethic aspect of Mnemosyne would not abandon the affirmation of life in remembering but indeed, would make it possible by letting life's disasters pass into oblivion. One finds such sense of loss in Nietzsche as well as in Borges. The first points out that remembering without forgetting will kill any human being; the latter writes a story in which a man who remembers everything is soon destroyed by the overpowering weight of memory without forgetting.[7] As Scott points out, "Rather than constituting only disaster and darkness, Lethe also presents their oblivion."[8] Hence, Mnemosyne's power of life enhancement and affirmation carries with it a Lethic release. This indicates how forgetting and loss are inscribed in occurrences of memory, that is, how memory occurs in its loss.

The discussion of Mnemosyne and Lethe leads to a series of significant issues which contribute to the understanding of memory in its loss. In its Lethic aspect, "Mnemosyne appears to happen originatively in her loss of form, substance, clarity, and identity."[9] This suggests that, to a certain extent, memory remains beyond presence and representation. In the coming to presence of memory a necessary loss beyond presence occurs. This operative loss in memory also puts memorial events beyond subjective or objective realization or intentionality. "Mnemosyne's myth, opens a direction toward considering of a dimension of remembering that is obscured by images and cannot be 'said' by language formed within dominant structures of subjectivity and objectivity."[10] Finally, in remaining to an extent beyond presence and subjective intention, memory suggests a loss of unchanging origins or ideas that might inform memory, experience, and even thought. In terms of the ambiguity we found in Heidegger's thought, at this point the history of metaphysics, as a first beginning, is already not necessary for the situation of thought. Because, whatever history may mean, the memory of thought's determinations, although concrete, does not constitute a fixed unchanging insight concerning being.

The recovery of loss in memorial events leads to a discussion of its transformative aspect. Transformation does not follow loss but is an aspect of loss. Hence, transformation is also central to Scott's treatment of memory in its loss. In the introduction he states, "I wish to emphasize, rather, that in memory radical transformation can occur and can be shown to occur, and those transformations are crucial for an understanding of memory."[11] Transformation concerns memory's recollection and the sense of recognition of something preserved we find in that remembering. In remembering, one has a sense of sameness in recurring memories through the experience of the coming to presence of memories. This coming to presence is certainly undeniable as it leaves traces of continuity, but this does not mean that such traces must be understood in terms of presence alone, or as an image recalling and preserving unchanging ideas or objective fact. Scott understands this coming to presence, these traces, in their Lethic aspect, out of and in memory's loss. "One kind of movement that occurs in memory is the turning of one thing into another thing, a play of transformation with a carry over, a trace, of what is lost."[12] What seems to be the substance or unchanging part of memories is a trace left over from a transformative experience. The trace echoes not a substance but a transformative passage which is part of the memorial experience.

This transformative passage occurs when in remembering one finds presence and proximity, but an intimate proximity given out of a return that occurs out of loss. For example, Scott's memory of being a child occurs in the loss of two figures, the past and the present, and what echoes in that memory is that loss. It is in light of such echoing of losses that one might release thought from Heidegger's first beginning; not because the history of metaphysics is an imagined fact, but because its concrete force in memorial experience occurs in the loss of that history as well as in the loss of a metaphysical sense of the now. Indeed, with memory one finds not only loss, but in that loss a transformative experience that leaves a trace. This trace is that carryover often interpreted as the substance and the indication of continuity behind memory. In their transformative sense these traces of memorial events carry in their presence a kind of severity. "But there is a severity in these transformations. . . . The severity is found in the coming of memory as well as in their passage. Severity is found in the loss that invests their memorial return, in the loss of presence in the return of what was and now, transformed, is contemporary."[13] It is in undergoing loss in a transformative sense that presence and continuity are found.

The traces of loss are not only elements of memory but they figure every aspect of experience, the coming to presence of things, perceptions, and memories. "Events take place, make demands, and persist for a while. They are severe in the sense that they are quite singular as they happen to pass, and in their occurrences they seem often to efface other bygone events whose meanings and images they carry."[14] The extent to which loss is part of the occurrences and experiencing of things is also indicated in another passage in the same section. Discussing loss in terms of nonvoluntary memories Scott points out that, "Our looking already involves memories. We happen as memorial events. . . . Mentation seems to belong to memory and memory to mind. Indeed, mind and memory might name the same thing."[15] The experience of looking, and hence encountering the world, and even mind, which is often taken to be the deus ex machina behind experiences, is found in the times of memories, the times of their passage in transformative loss. Scott continues, "Memory seems to occur as the manifestation of things in their significance and meaning—to infuse their significance and meaning—in both their generality and particularity."[16] Experience and the experienced arise in the severity of loss, and out of and in this loss the trace of transformative loss is left. We should note that this is an account of reality fitting to Heidegger's concept of truth (*aletheia*) as concealment and unconcealment.[17] In Heidegger's terms, Scott recognizes the Lethic element of *aletheia*. However, in Scott's case, the discussion of *aletheia* arises out of thinking the singular experiences of memories, rather than as a general ontological discussion. Here truth is thought concretely and in the intimate temporal singularity of the memorial sense of experience, things, and thought.

Thinking in Dionysian Transformations

In Scott's book, memory in its transformative loss is engaged through the figure of Dionysus, and in the god's inseparability from Apollo. In the figure of Dionysus, Scott finds a space of transformative experiences in loss. In such passages, the transformative and creative forces of loss, which give rise to the appearing of presence and continuity, are released and recovered in their loss. The Dionysian aspect of remembering allows us to engage "the losses—the dismemberments—that constitute memory, as well as to address the future aspect of thought and memory in the constructive openings of loss and forgetfulness. . . ."[18] Dionysus figures the recurrence of memory in its loss, a recurrence which takes place through dismemberment, violation, transgression, and interruption, in the severity of loss. "Dionysus' sublimity dissolves individuals of all kinds into a mere passage of difference and then re-solves them into these differences again—into membered bodies who come again to pass."[19] We are speaking of a re-membering in a transformative dis-membering.

Dionysian returns in transformative loss also figure experiences of thought. This is a central issue of Scott's book, which he explores in its last chapter. According to Scott, "thinking appears not only in the impact of memories-in-transformation but also with many of the same qualities and dimensions that characterize memory's self-presence."[20] Thinking does not only occur with memories but it enacts a Dionysian and Lethic passage of coming to presence in loss, and of return in that loss. These Lethic and Dionysian aspects of thought are engaged by Scott's discussion of philosophical thought in the quote that opened our discussion, which comes from a section of the book's last chapter, "What We Philosophers Do."

> As events of thought, like memories, become enmeshed in other events and experiences and pass away and beyond *their* ability to make a difference, they come to belong to memories, new figurations of vitality, and appearances that take them up, as it were, into other forces that transform bygone events into other images, narratives, or constellations of values. Thinking can be responsible to its nonpreserving aspect, to this transformativeness in its life, *as* it gives new life to appearances in transformations of past and present events—in justice to their transformation we might say.[21]

Thought does justice to loss, transformation, and return by remaining with the loss and in loss in its passing. This remaining, this awareness of thought's nonpreserving and nonrepresentational aspects, requires, on the one hand, a discipline that acknowledges the Apollonian in the transformative loss. On the other, it also has a creative and transgressive aspect. In being configured in this way, under these two forces, thinking occurs as the art of thinking. Scott points to the character of this art by discussing two forms:

> One of the arts of thinking happens by means of awareness in the merges, mutations, and remembrances in thinking, and a further art can come with thought that remembers its rememberings as distinct to providing itself with images of freedom from ontic determinations and from the inconsistency of basic questions and problems.[22]

Philosophical thought requires a discipline of awareness to the losses, absences, transgressions, interruptions, exclusions, nonvoluntary memories, and transformations, which are at play in the coming to presence in passing of thought. Thinking must go under, must enact its dismemberments, with a discipline that does not deny thought's vitality, but that, on the contrary, engages thought's youthfulness in its transformative losses. For Scott, the art of thinking, the remaining with and undergoing of loss and transformation, can be understood as the art of untying certain knots that sustain ideas of continuity and presence, and which therefore cover over the loss and transformation in events of thought in the coming to presence in passing of things.[23] As is the case with Heidegger, Scott calls for the direct engagement of thought's temporality in its abyssal and fecund senses. The difference is that, in the latter's case, such encounters afford us both the undergoing of thoughts vital or youthful movement as well as the possibility of releasing this fecund possibility from the knots that sustain and are sustained under forms of moral-historical obligations to a past that must be delivered and that will deliver us to our destiny.

Figures in the Crossing

Greek mythological figures accompany us through *The Time of Memory*, in the crossing from the traditional interpretation of memory as recollecting and preserving, to the encounter of the times of memory and of thinking in youthful loss. In light of our discussion of memorial loss and the release of historical memories, and because of the suggestions of continuity, we find in the recurrence of these figures, one must wonder: Mnemosyne and Lethe, Dionysus and Apollo, how are these recurring memories encountered in and by Scott's thought? How is one to understand their function in the recovery of loss? These questions point beyond these particular figures, because they also refer Scott's thought to ancient Greek experience and thought, and to the question of how Scott engages Greek figures of thought in his work. In a sense, what is in question here is how Scott understands memories that are operative in his thought, those memories of Greek lineages that seem to accompany not only his work but I would say, accompany thought at least since Plato.

In *The Times of Memory*, Mnemosyne and Lethe, and Dionysus and Apollo, are first engaged as mythological figures rather than Greek figures. In his introduction to the book, Scott explains how he understands mythological figures. "The myths which I address seem to me to embody memorial events of memory's happening, to constitute recall of nonvoluntary aspects of memory, and to re-*member* memory—to reconnect it to its own loss."[24] Although exceptionally affective in our lineages, myths are not mere images; they do not only concern presence. They carry with them a nonimagistic dimension that offers us a site for the recovery of memory in its loss. They offer the advantage of being composed of diverse memories and perceptions, and diversified experiences operative in voluntary and nonvoluntary ways that figure our cultural inheritance. In their diversified lineages, histories, and interpretative repetitions, myths open a diversifying site for our engagement with our cultural and conceptual memory. Scott finds the mythological figures's "suggestive and disclosive powers" to be neither universal nor subject to representation. Myths function as sites of encounters of loss and in loss. They appear as fragile and compelling passages, which in these aspects remain beyond the clarity of systems and resist objective analysis.

In *The Time of Memory* Mnemosyne and Lethe, as well as Dionysus and Apollo appear through their loss as figured by their Greek lineages. Scott says:

> In their texts, the Greeks are far from present. The vivid life of their language is far removed. We have images and appearances of the tones and qualities of their lives. But they are foreign to us in our scholarly familiarity with theml. . . . The appearances of the Greeks are produced out of indirect encounters, like ancestors who are remembered in fragments of letters, drawings, memories, and traits that are embedded in later generations. We draw close to such people and events in their loss, and we experience their loss in their loss as a medium of their return.[25]

The mythological figures Scott engages are encountered through their returns in their loss, and the point of encounter in their loss is their Greek form. Mnemosyne and Lethe are encountered through a double loss, which occurs in the configuration of a unified Greek pantheon of Olympian gods. In the unification of the gods a religious and philosophical dispersion of the two aspects of memory takes place, and in their externalization and separation, their earlier inner affiliation is covered over. This occurs already in Homer's oral tradition, and then as a second loss in Hesiod's writing, in which the directness of Mnemosyne is remembered in its loss to writing. "Archaic Mnemosyne appears in her loss in Hesiod's classical, written memory of her."[26] This loss also figures Mnemosyne's return.

> The future of that loss did not happen so much as a failure but rather as a birth of which this writing—which takes place in the fading of Hesiod's earnestness, solemnity, and closeness to the gods, as well as in the fading of Mnemosyne's immediacy in his writing—is a distant progeny.[27]

Scott encounters Mnemosyne and Lethe out of their losses, and his writing arises as the distant progeny of those losses. Here, the Greek context of these myths appears as a site of loss and remembering, in that loss, a space of encounter and return of Mnemosyne repeated by Scott's writing.

Dionysus and Apollo first appear in their inseparability and youthful excess in the *Times of Memory* through a discussion of Nietzsche's recovery of Greek tragedy. As Scott shows, Nietzsche's recovery occurs through a double reading and a double loss of these mythological figures. Nietzsche recovers Greek tragedy in its loss and at the same time finds a transformative sense of experience in loss. "His [Nietzsche's] return to Greek tragedy is tensed by the future reference that he gives the return: he returns in order to turn through the culture of lost tragedy . . . not to Greek experience but to a sense of life that is differentiated by his memory of Greek tragedy."[28] Nietzsche's sense of Greek tragedy arises in light of the loss of the Greek sense of tragedy and is configured in that loss and transformation.

According to Scott, Nietzsche encounters Dionysus and Apollo in a double loss. On the one hand, Nietzsche shows the loss of Greek tragedy in the formation of Western philosophy, that is, he exposes the covering over of loss and transformation in the name of unchanging continuity and unity. In this sense, "Western philosophy is post-tragic in its replacement of a sense of tragedy with a sense of transcendental, undisastrous life."[29] On the other hand, as Scott indicates, "Nietzsche gives his descriptive account in the awareness that his ability to recognize the Greek accomplishment of tragedy is formed by the loss of their experience of tragedy."[30] Not only does Nietzsche remember Dionysus, the loss and transformation in the Greek tragic sense, but he does so in awareness of the loss operative in his thought in the recovery. Nietzsche's recovery of Dionysus occurs out of this double loss; the loss of the tragic sense found in the Greeks and the loss of that tragic sense of the Greeks in his recovery or remembering of Dionysus. Furthermore, as Scott points out, Nietzsche's thought "finds its own moment in an affirmation of tragedy in its loss."[31] In short, in Nietzsche Greek tragedy appears in its loss, a reconfiguration of that loss, and Nietzsche's awareness of how that loss is operative in his remembering, and how loss situates his thought and experience. In what we have said, we find three moments of loss: (1) the account of the loss of the tragic; (2) the awareness of the loss occurring in the recovery; and (3) the coming to pass of thought in awareness of these losses. Thus, history may now be seen as the recovery to presence of thought, but a thought that in its passage figures loss, and hence must remain open to transformation, as must any sense of history and particularly a history understood in its fundamental temporality. Here, we find Scott close to Heidegger's engagement of the history of the Western tradition as historicity or *Geschichtlichkeit*, but in light of our discussion, it is evident that the disposition and outcome of the engagement with the past is quite different.

Scott's recovery of memory, in its loss, invites a new reading of the tradition. Indeed, it invites for the recovery of the history of philosophy, in light of traditions and configurations, new to the canon of Western philosophy. Once memory recovers its transformative force in loss, memory as the ground for experience and knowledge loses its unchanging quality. Furthermore, although philosophical knowledge may still be seen as inseparable from memory, this inherent relationship between memory and philosophical knowledge will keep any configuration of thought from being reduced to a representation of the unchanging, or as a matter of distinct presence, and subject to systematic and objective analysis. As Scott shows in the last chapter of *The Time of Memory*, in light of the Lethic aspect of memory and thought, the task of thinking will remain the accomplishment of returns in loss, and the accomplishment of thought exposed in its abyssal finitude, exposed to its youthful relentless dynamics. But here it becomes evident that we have gone well beyond Heidegger's ambiguous stance, because, in light of what we have said, the hermeneutical reappropriation of the figures of the Western philosophical tradition does not have to bear the task of justifying and delivering figures or configurations of being in that tradition to their single and final destiny. I might also add that I have spoken of a release in thought because the beginning of this chapter points to this moment of lightness in the recovery of the tradition.[32] The weight of a final destiny has lifted, although, not the responsibility to the most intense engagement with thought.[33] As Scott states at the beginning of this chapter, from this exposure we may discover measures for thought in its transformative passages.

Conclusion

The figures of Dionysus and Apollo, Lethe and Mnemosyne, offer much for understanding Scott's recovery of memory in its loss, as well as for engaging thought's returns in *The Time of Memory*. These figures also indicate something of the loss and transformation in our thinking and memories, and in doing so, they recover the Greek figures of thought that shimmer in our conceptual horizon and let them be engaged as foreign memories, that is, as memories which figure our thoughts in the youthful vitality of their passages and in their palpable proximity in their losses. Because thought is taken up out of the awareness of the Lethic dynamic in thought's movement, Scott engages thought in its finitude without being caught between the history of the Western philosophical tradition and the overflowing of all senses of being. The history that outweighs the unfolding of thought in its fecundity in Heidegger reappears here as the figure or occasion for thought's youthful engagement with its possibilities in movements and encounters that situate philosophy in a broad horizon open to unbounded possibilities in moments of intense self-awareness in singularity. Without hesitation Scott steps lightly in light of thought's exposure, by thinking with an exposed word sustained by his sensibility to thought's finitude. Furthermore, this undergoing of thought does not call for suffering—this is not a requirement when destiny has been open to a youthful futurity—while neither does it efface the abyssal fecundity of all configurations of beings. Indeed, for Scott, thought comes to pass in the intensifying and indifferent exposure to this abyssal finitude; I say, indifferent, in the sense of our undergoing and withstanding the losses and overflowing in all configurations of senses of beings without ascribing absolute values to those passages in thought, a significant destiny, or a justifying teleology. In short, in his thought, we find a deliberate word and sensibility with thought in its concrete passing away and its unfolding to come. But this unbounded unfolding occurs in language, a point we have already found at the center of Heidegger's violent encounter with temporality. Therefore, it will be through engaging language in its ephemeral, concrete, and ultimately bodily undergoing, that we begin to think in exposure to thought's finitude. This will be the task of the next section.

PART II

Unbounded Words:
Language in its Ephemeral and
Concrete Finitude

With our discussion thus far we open a series of questions; questions that in their complexity do not propose direct answers but indicate our situation. Can one think in a manner that does not pretend to be separate from the history of metaphysics and the results of its rationalistic onto-theological production of meanings, while at the same time not inscribing one's thought to the project of capitalism and machination? And if there could be such path or paths, would such thinking still be called philosophy, that is, once origin, essence, history, and their languages are in check? How does a thinking, that has abandoned the world of absolute ends, destinies, and history, take form and sustain something like its homogeneity or singularity? Our discussion has taken us towards that sense of thought, which is exposed to its situation, and, in that exposure takes place, its place, that is, as it undergoes the impossibility of claiming a destiny in a history, and, as in that awareness of being unbounded, also looks towards a thought that is fecund in its indefinite and yet undeniable coming.

Our analysis also indicates that we cannot hold on to rationalism, analytical philosophy, transcendental philosophy, transcendental subjectivity, historicism, psychologism, or a pragmatic search for a construction of systems and meanings. In every case, machination or its lineages seem to tie our thought to its projects, and is slowly and infinitely able to subsume and consume everything—a renegade's face in a tee shirt, a new academic chair for a radical thinker who becomes interesting—in light of our discussion we already have the discomfort of being consumed and immobilized.

The break comes from our situation, from being able to remain with experience, but not in the sense of psychological or factual experience. Rather, the issue is in remaining with that singularity that moves as unidentified as the ether was to early chemists: that singularity that is always the shadow and contrast, the *chiaroscuro* in which life becomes the thing, the topic, the goal, the value, and the meaning. The break comes in remaining with the involuntary, the transient, the loss that figures the gravitas of silence as does the expectation of the coming thought. The break is in that singularity that will not give up because to be is to be in singularity, that is, exposed in otherness as one's identity weaves its way and unfolds in that movement. The break comes as we must engage that movement we are. In doing so, we figure as beings. But this happens in language. Not the linguistic body, or the play of signs, but in that writing, speaking, and reading, inseparable from bodies, breath, heart, ingrained fears, and pleasures untold in their densities and their less than intelligible character. It is the character, the mark on the page, the scratching and puncturing . . . it is the breath and the lack there of . . . speaking, writing, unfolding the *grammata* in concrete dynamic demarcations: this is the situation of the unfolding, the word is the point of return, the contact. . . . If we are to find a way, this path is with the issuing of language. Not language about things, but in that issuing in which language becomes of language in its fluid and singular passages. The break might come if we can remain with the issuing in language of the coming to presence of the named and the names. Such are some of the implications of what we have said so far, such is the direction we will take in this section.

CHAPTER 6

Ephemeral Concrete Words

On the Translucence of the Philosophical Logos
in Plato's Phaidros

It has to be living, to learn the speech of the place.

("Of Modern Poetry," Wallace Stevens)

Introduction: Beauty and the Translucence of the Shine of Beings

Helen. We hear of her many times. In *The Iliad*, "Strange and terrible is her resemblance to immortal goddesses."[1] Much later, in "On Line," Juan José Saer recalls the praise for her uncanny appearance and exposes us to her savage, almost inhuman beauty: "Her unblemished flesh of Leda, ignorant of her own sensuality, combining itself with her whiteness and with the brutal exuberance of swans, have produced that superhuman certainty, which, with innocence and cruelty, only gods and beasts enjoy, with the only end of folding the world to their own desire."[2] The intensity of these words only grows in unassailability when one recalls the famous disclaimer concerning her presence in Troy, which always shadows our uncanny encounters with her beauty. According to Socrates in the *Phaidros* of Plato, Helen was never in Troy.[3] We encounter Helen's strange (or savage) beauty as an almost ungraspable experience in Homer, Saer, and Plato, as well as in so many other authors and stories in between. Indeed, it is precisely by virtue of the uncanny presence of the beautiful, that Homer and Plato are placed together in Longinus' *On the Sublime*.[4] But, how is it that we might grasp this seemingly unearthly and inhuman beauty? How is one to understand such fathomless shine?

In setting out with Helen, with this difficult figure of beauty in mind, I broaden the issue of the shine of beauty, to the question of the sensible and articulate experiences of beings—of all that is said to be. Although often overlooked, there is something as strange and wondrous about the shine of beings as there is in Helen's beauty. I use the word "strange," because of the singularity of the shine of beings. On the one hand, and in spite of transparency being at times understood as the paradigmatic character of intelligibility, a thoroughly transparent being, be it a concept or thing, will not be visible or graspable. On the other hand, a being that does not shine, a totally opaque being will also not appear. Beings require a certain leeway between transparency and opacity in their shine. For example, this is the case when one experiences the most opaque surfaces, the earth, as well as when one encounters such dense and yet determinable conceptual experiences as numbers or geometrical proofs.[5] In other words, the shine of beings is only possible through certain translucence, that is, through an experience of visibility or a sense of being that is not self-evident to the point of transparency and that is not sheer opaque materiality or density.[6]

The issue of translucence bears its full import for our discussion when we consider it in light of the question of the relation between the sensibility of things and language. This phrasing requires an immediate warning, because, in asking about this relationship, we cannot assume a separation between materiality and language. Indeed, we seek to understand language in its concrete or material sense. This focus leads to the crucial point of this chapter: Through my discussion, I want to suggest that, when taken in its full force, the philosophical logos figures the elemental translucence of beings in their senses. In other words, my discussion shows that in the *Phaidros* of Plato the philosophical logos is understood as the dynamic undergoing of *physis* in its unfolding, rather than as language separate or opposed to a nature or phenomena it attempts to describe and explain. This sense of the philosophical logos will be engaged in the context of and through a discussion of the *Phaidros* of Plato, a dialogue steeped in the question of translucence and its philosophical significance. The discussion will move through the dialogue by tracing how the issue of translucence is encountered in it, and will conclude by returning to Socrates' disclaimer about the very presence of Helen in Troy in order to go beyond the engagement of the translucence of beings in the *Phaidros*.

Before moving to the body of the chapter, a few remarks on certain interpretations of Plato that inform my discussion and sharpen its aim and direction. I find Jacob Klein's interpretation of Plato helpful, in as much as, following Schleiermacher, Klein interprets the dialogues in their dramatic as well as logical dimension.[7] Furthermore, on the basis of his work on the difference between ancient Greek and modern mathematics (the concept of number), Klein is able to recognize the idea of form in Greek philosophy as a concrete experience where conceptual image or idea and phenomena are never severed by the modern sense of number as independent from what is counted.[8] In other words, as I see it, Klein is able to keep to the concrete experience of beings and *physis* one finds in Greeks philosophy. At the same time, in Klein this unsevered experience is allocated to a mathematical transcendental consciousness. Here, Husserl ultimately guides Klein's reading, as Klein holds to the idea of a transcendental subjectivity and universal understanding that sustains all experience and knowledge.[9] Furthermore, Klein finds the ideal or transcendental sense in the dialogues in the transcendental or noetic structures that precede modern mathematical physics. We may juxtapose Klein's reading to Jacques Derrida's reading of the *Phaidros* in his now, ironically, canonical piece, "Plato's Pharmacy."[10] In this piece Derrida exercises a powerful and forceful double reading. On the one hand, he masterfully shows the continuous slipping in the attempt to found philosophy on a central transcendental discourse. He does this by reading the dialogue in terms of the centrality of writing, and the impossibility of a sign that may unambiguously translate a nonphilosopheme into a philosophim.[11] Thus, the primacy of a transcendental discourse over all orderings of beings is de-centered as the transcendental discourse, and with it the claim to transcendental subjectivity, prove to be always already transgressed.[12] In terms of showing the impossibility of reading the dialogue as part of transcendental philosophy and its sense of language, Derrida presents a serious and insurmountable problem for Klein. However, Derrida's reading operates under the assumption that, in the *Phaidros*, Plato attempts a determination of being and philosophy in the name of the linguistic operation of a transcendental subject or consciousness.[13] Here, Derrida's own lineages become apparent, because in his concern with Husserl's transcendental philosophy, and the modern tradition's transcendental understanding of thought, he reads the dialogue as a modern, that is, by inscribing it into the transcendental tradition, which he then proceeds to deconstruct.[14] Thus, we set out from two difficult insights, from Klein's sense of the concreteness of Greek thought and in light of Derrida's release of the dialogue from modern transcendental philosophy. Here appears a third way of reading the dialogue, namely, one that attempts to keep close to the Greek sense of *logos* and *physis* in their concrete relationship: where, to use Klein's fine insight in his book on Ancient and Modern mathematics, logos is not yet *mathesis universalis*, not yet a function of reason and of a reason severed from the phenomena.[15] Our aim then will be to read the dialogue in light of the differentiated and yet inseparable situation of the philosophical logos in and as the unfolding of *physis*. By following this course, we engage the dialogue as an occasion for the exposure of the philosophical logos to the movement of *physis*, a movement that the philosophical discourse does not subsume but undergoes as the written and spoken word unfolds and weaves senses of beings.

Phaidros

The *Phaidros* of Plato is often understood as a dialogue about love and the art of rhetoric.[16] Its concern with *ēros* as well as with the making of the best speeches certainly directs the discussion.[17] But, a more complex issue sustains these themes, the issue of the logos as understood in light of *physis*. As we learn from the dialogue's introduction, Socrates and Phaidros meet near the city, not in the city, and then venture further into the fields, following a stream and looking for a place in nature fitting for the discussion of a speech written by the sophist Lysias.[18] If we consider this introduction, it is clear that finding the best discourse in the context of nature, or *physis* is central to the dialogue. The bare feet of Socrates (always barefooted), and of Phaidros, the river stream in which they walk, the meadow under the sycamore in which they sit, and the singing of the cicadas that at times seems to drown and overwhelm their dialogue, all indicate this place of the logos in nature.[19] The matter then is not to make a speech that represents nature but to encounter speech in the context of *physis*.[20] This engagement of the logos in light of *physis* takes a more specific form when one considers the very name of Socrates' companion.

At a surface level, the name "Phaidros" means that he has a joyful nature, he is a beaming soul. However, the literal meaning of the name indicates much more. The Greek word indicates a sense of light, a shine that is almost untranslatable. Although perhaps the words crystalline and shimmering give us a close sense of the word, *phaidrós* sounds out an elemental light, a light made out of a mixture of light and the element water (*húdōr*).[21] We are speaking of a translucence like that of seeing through lit water. This light—this translucence—captivates Socrates in the dialogue and calls him to speak. When Phaidros asks Socrates about his impression concerning the speech of Lysias the philosopher has just heard, Socrates replies, "It does have an unearthly power, my friend, so that I was astounded by it. I felt this way because of you (*diá sé*), Phaidros. As I looked at you, you seemed to me to be set aglow (*gánusthai*). . ."[22] What captivates Socrates is not the speech per se, but Phaidros' nature, his translucent shine. Socrates's encounter with Phaidros is therefore an encounter with a specific nature, with a certain translucence which invites him to speak. Not only is the logos to be engaged in the context of phúsis but in light of this *phaidrós*, this elemental light.

Along with his translucence, we also find that Phaidros does not have a logos of his own. Although known as the author of many speeches, in the dialogue, *Phaidrós* lures Socrates to follow him with the speech of Lysias, and, when he must make Socrates speak, he threatens him first with physical force (reminding us of the interruption of all possible dialogue and of the absence of logos that opens the *Republic*), and then with never again reading to him a speech written by anyone.[23] Thus, Phaidros never appeals directly to his own speeches, we never hear him speak directly. In this sense, in the dialogue, he does not have the leeway of his own words, that is, the space for reflection that a speech wrought by him by himself may give him.[24] In short, Phaidros figures in the dialogue a certain translucence of a being which does not have a logos that may direct it or determine it. (This is clear when one considers that he is a believer, and that he follows the word of doctors, mythologems, and sophists, without being able to distinguish their effect on the well being of his soul.)

In beginning to read the dialogue, let us say that *éros* and logos are central to it. Adding now, that they have to be engaged in light of the more complex difficulty of understanding, the wordless translucence figured by Phaidros. In other words, the fundamental issue of the dialogue is neither technical writing (rhetoric) or *éros* versus reason, but Socrates's engagement through the logos of the translucence figured by Phaidros. This fundamental difficulty in the dialogue leads directly back to it. We must now ask how this translucence is engaged in the dialogue, and then, how the philosophical logos might be understood in light of this task.

Phaidros' Dynamic Soul

At a first glance the dialogue is evidently didactic. As Socrates states, his discussions are for the sake of overcoming Phaidros' ambivalence and in order that he "dedicate his life entirely to love through speeches that are characterized by friendship with wisdom (*philosophía*)."[25] The turning of Phaidros's soul occurs through three speeches followed by a discussion on speeches. However, upon a closer reading, one finds that in these speeches the dialogue engages the issue of the translucence encountered in *Phaidros*.

The first speech is Lysias' own written discourse. Socrates has Phaidros read it aloud and in this way brings Lysias into the open.[26] (We hear Lysias' self-interest and crude rhetoric rather than Phaidros' excited and altogether well intentioned version.) In his speech, Lysias argues that it is better to give oneself over to the non-lover rather than to the lover.[27] The speech appears as one more classic display of sophistry, arguing what does not make sense for the beloved (that it is best not to be loved), and it also is a blatant attempt to seduce and ultimately appropriate Phaidros's life.[28] Under this crust of sheer vulgarity, Lysias' argument carries a wider and greater threat, as it ultimately claims that *éros* is a kind of obsessive madness (*manía*) destructive to one's life.[29] Furthermore, on the basis of this misrepresentation of love, he interprets true friendship *philía* as self-interested and detached calculation.[30] The argument goes beyond seduction to transform the meaning of love and friendship. In doing this, by definition, he calls for the abandonment of a search for *philos-sophía*, literally a life of love and friendship with wisdom. In light of this speech Socrates's task, in the two speeches he will give, becomes apparent. He must recover the definition of love and friendship, and he must do so in a way that leaves a certain leeway for the turning of Phaidros towards *philosophía*.[31] This means letting Phaidros' soul shine as such, since the life of philosophy ultimately means that he must think for himself, and only in this way he may have sense of the best life, rather than being a ray of light deflected by the moment. In short, at stake is Phaidros's very being, or the movement of his soul.

The issue of the sense of the translucence figured by Phaidros appears directly in Socrates' first speech. In it, Socrates exposes Lysias to his own medicine by repeating the sophist's attack on the lover while putting him in place of the lover.[32] At the same time, as Socrates himself indicates by covering his head in shame and play, although an attack on the sophist, his speech repeats Lysias' lie about the destructive character of all love and madness.[33] But this is not the most telling sense of Socrates' self-concealment. As he states, he can only give such a speech while not looking at Phaidros because otherwise the lucid shine of his companion would simply make him speechless.[34] The problem at this point is not that Phaidros will not be visible if misrepresented by a false speech, but that the translucence of his being would bring Socrates to silence. The accent is on the translucent nature (*physis*) figured by Phaidros, and on the way this phenomenon sets the speech. Although not directly articulated, translucence is already implicit in Socrates' gesture. He must cover his eyes from it in order to speak. The speech arises in a relation that although negative, does remain determined by a certain awareness of the translucence figured by Phaidros. Thus, in the dialogue, the translucence figured by Phaidros is introduced through a speaking in concealment from it, a concealment required for the logos to occur. Two questions arise: Is there a positive engagement of translucence (*phaidrós*) in Socrates' speeches? And, wouldn't such a speech involve a certain concealment from *phaidrós* in order to occur? These difficult questions can begin to be addressed by looking at Socrates's second speech at its most crucial moment.

Telling Almost Impossible Stories

Of the three speeches made in the dialogue, the most shocking is the last, Socrates' second discourse, which he tells with his face uncovered.[35] If the first of his speeches was a lie, his second certainly reads as a tall tale, a shameless exaggeration, one might even say, a story fed by madness. The speech speaks of winged souls that grow and lose feathers, of a journey to the limits of the cosmos, and even of gazing beyond it.[36] The excessively high-sounding tone and exaggeration has a sense, it is fitted to impressionable Phaidros (one might even be tempted to add that the speech glows and bears something akin to Phaidros' lightness and translucence).[37] However, behind the splendid rhetoric Socrates offers a redefinition of the world first presented by Lysias.

In order to turn Phaidros towards the philosophical life, Socrates recounts in this speech a story that begins from the highest way of being, the vision of being, the good, and the beautiful, only to then descend towards the human. In this way, the struggle of the soul with desire, love, and friendship, and all living experience will always be traced back to the beautiful and being as such, through recollection (a recollection figured by a story and not by a theoretical argument.) The turning point of his speech is therefore Socrates' account of the soul's encounter with being and the beautiful as such. In that crucial moment in the dialogue Socrates states:

> Of the places beyond the heavens none of this world's poets has yet sung worthily, nor shall any ever do so. But it is like this—for one must dare to speak the truth, and especially when the subject is the truth itself. That place is occupied by the being that really is, which is intangible and without color. The mind of a god . . . and that of every soul that cares about getting what is proper for it, cherishes the opportunity to observe what is and is nourished and happy while it studies the truth . . . On its circular journey, it sees justice itself, it sees judiciousness, and it sees knowledge, not the knowledge that is connected with becoming and varies with the varying things we now say are, but rather the knowledge that exists in the realm of what is knowledge as such.[38]

Here Socrates speaks in the awareness of a need to say what no poet has ever or will ever be able to say. At the same time, he is compelled to speak by the need to speak the truth itself. In other words, Socrates' third speech occurs as a speaking in awareness of having to say what perhaps cannot be said. If there can be a turning of Phaidros' soul, this will occur through a partially impossible story. To say it in terms of the translucence which calls Socrates to speak, this translucence may only be engaged through a discourse that although necessary, might be impossible. I should add that, although this speech must be differentiated from the telling of a lie in the previous speech, here one finds that the logos is not simply a representational tool wedded to a self-evident or transparent truth. Socrates' observation about the need to speak in light of what perhaps cannot be said indicates that there must be a certain translucence, a certain play in shine between unconcealment and concealment in that speaking, rather than a self-evident transparency. In what follows we will discuss this sense of translucence in the philosophical logos.

The Elemental Translucence of the *Logos*

In the discussion of speech writing that follows his two discourses on love, Socrates differentiates two kinds of writing. The first kind is akin to painting.[39] This is a representational writing which aims to show and present some-thing. This written word is nondialogical, because, as Socrates indicates, much like painting, it does not reply to the questions of the reader and simply keeps repeating the same thing. This also means that it is unable to, or incapable of change. Furthermore, such writing does not differentiate concerning who reads it; it is accessible to anyone and to everyone's abuse. In this sense, it is also unable to defend itself, and one might say that it is indifferent in its objectivity, because it does not concern anyone.[40] Socrates ultimately indicates that this kind of speech in fixed definitions and terms is a mere image of a second way of writing, its more powerful brother.[41] It should be noted that in Greek the word "*grápho*" is used for both painting and writing. In this passage Socrates speaks of writing as "*graphē*" and of painting as *zoographē*, that is, as a depicting of living beings. This will be the basis for his differentiation and contrast with the second way of writing.

The second sense of writing Socrates discusses is characterized as a "*lógon zoónta kai émpsuchon*," a living and breathing or ensouled speech.[42] That it is a living speech means first of all that it is inseparable from experience. As Socrates specifies, the experience refers to the inseparability of the soul and writing: this is a speech "written in the soul."[43] A few lines later, Socrates explains that the person who understands such speech thinks that "no speech whether in verse or prose has ever been written that is worthy of much serious consideration . . . without questioning or instruction."[44] The ensouled speech is fundamentally living in the sense of being interpretative. I mean that it requires constant questioning. This also says that, in writing or reading such a speech, its sense depends on its being played out in the soul through dialogue. Socrates introduced this point earlier in the same discussion, when he said that the best speech must have the ability to defend itself or reply.[45] A living speech is one wrought by a relentless dialogical hermeneutics. I might add that this hermeneutics has a singular purpose; the living speech concerns education, in that it gives the open space or leeway for the turning of the soul towards the good. One clearly sees this in the case of Phaidros's turn towards the philosophical life in the dialogue.

The leeway for the turning of the soul in philosophical speech also indicates that it is a speech that rather than avoiding change precisely concerns it and aims for transformation. Furthermore, such transformative leeway does not refer only to the soul but also to its fitting *lógoi*. We are not speaking of a discourse that persuades and manipulates without being affected, as is the case with Lysias' speech. As Socrates indicates, if learning is to occur, then the speech must fit the particular interlocutor's situation. Therefore, the character of the logos fitting to that transformed soul must also be open to change, and must trace the many figurations of the soul towards truth.[46] From these few observations, we can say that the philosophical logos does not aim to talk about something, it unfolds in a movement of unconcealment, understood as a movement that comes to pass as an element of transformation.[47]

This commitment to change, and more specifically to a turn in the soul, brings us to the third and crucial point about this ensouled living speech. Earlier in the dialogue, Socrates states that the soul is by nature ever-changing.[48] As we have just heard the philosophical logos gives a certain leeway for the soul's transformation. In as much as this speech is written in the soul, the philosophical speech as ensouled must not remain extraneous to the soul, as if it were a matter of action at a distance. That the speech is ensouled ulti-mately means that the speech is enacting the very motion of the soul. The leeway found for the soul in logos occurs in a single and singular motion of logos and soul: the word is the turning. We can say more specifically that this enactment occurs in an interpretative and transformative modality fitting to the soul's ever-changing character.[49] In terms of engaging Phaidros (in his splendid translucence), the philosophical logos does not describe or represent something, but it must enact the interpretative transformative motion of his soul. The shine of his being occurs in that passage of the philosophical logos which is not other than his soul's transformation.[50]

This leads to a last and further conclusion. As the enactment of the motion of the soul in its shine—the philosophical logos—the living ensouled speech is the translucence with which the arising to presence and the senses of beings occur.[51] Thus, the logos does not have to speak about beings; there is not a space from mind to things which language must bridge. Rather, logos is in the soul and in beings, and this means that to take up the task of thinking or of a philosophical logos is to seek a way of being along with the shine of the soul and beings. Thus, I would suggest that the logos can be understood as the elemental translucence of the soul and beings in their arising to presence: where this arising is not understood as the presencing of something or as the image of unchanging essences, but as the arising to presence of senses of being in their transformative passages. This dynamic sense of the arising to presence of beings now calls us to engage the logos in its concreteness.

Socrates indirectly introduces the elemental and concrete sense of the word and writing in his story about the origin of writing. As Socrates tells Phaidros, it was Theuth, the Egyptian god who invented writing. As he tells the story he does not speak of writing (*gráphō*) but of *grámmata*, written letters. Another word for written and spoken letters, and specifically for the letters in their alphabetical order is *stoicheíon*. For as long as one speak of speeches as representational texts, *grámmata* is perfectly fitting, but since Socrates has now come to speak of that other king of speech, the ensouled and living speech of one who knows, letters must at least in part be taken in that second sense which would include the word in its spoken voice. Thus, we must now also consider the word in its spoken as well as written letters or elements, their *stoicheía*.

Stoicheíon means "element," and in its plural form refers to the four elements: earth, air, fire, and most significant for our discussion, water. Thus, the letters of the alphabet and the four elements share this single name. This is not a detail Plato overlooked in his work. In the *Timaeus*, once the likely story about the cosmos in terms of noetic thought has come to its limit, Timaeus reminds us through a warning of the obscure relationship between the elements and the letters of the alphabet. ". . . we assume we know what fire is, and each of these things, and we call them principles and presume that they are elements (*stoicheía*) of the Cosmos, although in truth they do not so much deserve to be likened with any likelihood, by the man who has a grain of sense, to the class of syllables (*stoicheía*)."[52] In this brief passage we find out that the four elements are not like letters. However, this only invites the question of the relationship between the letters of the alphabet and the four elements. Furthermore, in this passage we do hear that the letters of the alphabet are elemental; the four elements are called *stoicheía* after them, although the letters are not like the other four. But, in what sense might the logos be elemental? In light of our discussion, we can say that, although not water or fire, the philosophical logos is elemental in as much as it occurs as ensouled living speech. The logos is elemental because its interpretative and transforming passage is the translucent element or leeway of the shine of beings in their senses. Stated inversely, the weight of the philosophical logos is not a matter of pure reason or propositions (moral or abstract), but it is a sense found in the transformative lived experience figured by the philosophical word.

In speaking of the philosophical *logos* in its elemental translucence, we can return to touch on the issue of Socrates' speech as a saying of what perhaps cannot be said. The impossibility can be understood in light of the transformative sense of the philosophical logos. The logos cannot say the whole because it occurs as the leeway or openness of the soul in its ever-changing being. In this sense, Socrates's second discourse, or story, is elemental, because it does engage Phaidros as it plays out a turning or transformation in his soul. Furthermore, this unlikely and necessary story bears its openness in that it does not speak about some-thing already determined, either actually or potentially. By virtue of the elemental translucence of the philosophical word, a word itself exposed to this transformative motion, Socrates' logos opens a transformative space.

Phaidros, *Lógos* and *Philía*: The Issue of Philosophical Disposition

The understanding of the elemental translucence of logos as a passage of interpretative transformation of the soul carries fundamental implications concerning philosophical *lógos* or thought, as well as for the understanding of *philía*.[53] In the case of the first, namely, the sense of philosophical logos, its elemental enactment of the translucence of beings, its self-overcoming in its exposure to change, and the fact that it is an experience inseparable from beings, broadens its traditional interpretation. This occurs as we go beyond the understanding of dialectic as self-evident logical and calculative reason, an equation that leads to identifying thought with the self-certainty of the principles of analytical reasoning.

Clearly, according to Socrates the only speech that fits the friend of wisdom is dialectic.[54] This term often stands for a rationalistic approach wedded to logic and analytical concerns. Indeed, *noeín*, often translated as reason, and as such is essential to dialectic. This is the case in the *Phaidros*, where Socrates defines dialectic as a two-fold way of thinking that is able, "To bring together things that are scattered about and see them in terms of a single form," and that at the same time is, "able to dissect a thing in accordance with its forms, following the natural joints and not trying to hack it apart like an incompetent butcher."[55] However, these two principles do not refer in the dialogue to a method divorced from other *lógoi*. Dialectic is not merely a rational method. If dialectic is to occur in the dialogue as philosophical logos, it cannot be a mere logical method. Its logical differentiations and gathering into one must concern the transformation of the soul and the shine of beings, and in the dialogue these occur in the play of a logos that is broader than reason alone, and through the leeway of the playfulness of the various forms of *lógoi*. The close relation of *dialektikós* to *lógos* certainly suggests this wider understanding of dialectical thought, since when understood out of such relation *dialektikós* means skilled in conversation or dialogue, that is, skilled in a way of understanding "*día-lógos*," through logos.[56] Indeed, it is not in the sense of logical or mathematical reasoning alone that we can read the instances when Socrates refers to *dialektikē* in the *Phaidros*, since in the turning of Phaidros's soul through Socrates's speeches logic is never found separate from desire, stories, poems, and even the chant of the cicadas.[57]

This said, we must keep in mind that, as heard above, we are not speaking of mere stories that much like a realist painting make an image.[58] I am speaking instead of what we have uncovered in part through our discussion, that is, the way the *lógoi* in the dialogue open dynamic spaces in which the soul finds leeway for transformations, spaces in which thoughts may arise, develop, and come to be exposed to limits even beyond the rational, although always on the way towards its sense and the senses of beings.

The broadening in the articulation of the sense of philosophical logos says something fundamental for our understanding of the friendship of wisdom, *philosophía*. Socrates considers lived transformative logos the only speech fitting to the friendship of wisdom, and, as such, it is a logos that in such an interpretative and transformative opening or translucence, configures the space of being of the soul of those who are friends of wisdom. In other words, to speak of friendship, *philía*, in the sense of *philosophía*, is to speak of being in a certain disposition, a madness (*manía*) that discloses and opens the soul and beings in their senses through their interpretation and transformation.[59] We are speaking of a thinking lived and written in the soul and in being along with beings, not of a kind of abstract reasoning that must reach for, form, and lead one's life and sense of nature.[60]

At the same time, again, a warning must accompany these observations: we must not forget that this disposition in logos occurs as a speaking in the awareness of the need to say that which perhaps cannot be said. Therefore, such space of friendship bears with it the logos's exposure to a certain impossibility, and this too must be part of what we may now call friendship, *philía*. This suggests that, in philosophical disposition, beings are unconcealed through a translucent speech, that is, a logos never fully disclosive. In this sense we can speak of a translucent elemental speech, rather than a transparent self-evident one that must belong to intelligible essences. But if we have begun to engage the philosophical logos, we must still wonder about that impossibility that accompanies Socrates' logos: How is one to understand that which perhaps cannot be said, that which seems to figure an escape of being in light of the logos? For this we will have to return to Socrates's account of the disappearance of Helen in his second speech, and then go a step beyond it.

One More Story: The Disappearance of Helen

At the point where he turns from his false speech against the lover to his third and true speech, Socrates recalls the story of the nonexistence of Helen. He recounts the story of Stesichorus, a poet who realized that the story of Helen and *The Iliad* were false, and that as the result of repeating the lie he had become blind.[61] In light of that realization, the poet purified himself by going back and retracting his words through a recantation. This gesture, says Socrates, restituted his sight. The obvious point is that repeating lies will blind. But what is interesting is that Socrates's recantation begins by recalling the denial of beauty's most savage shine with the claim that Helen only existed as an apparition. Socrates then indicates his need to say what perhaps cannot be said. This double abandonment of a direct saying of beauty opens a question that goes well beyond Stesichorus's revelation of a lie: How is one to engage the translucent logos of the friend of wisdom, that elemental saying of that which perhaps cannot be said? I would like to offer a closing suggestion concerning this issue by way of a story that goes further towards that elemental sense of the word as brought to us through the mystery of writing, the Egyptian god, and the disappearance of Helen.

Juan José Saer tells the story of two soldiers who, thrown together by fortune, have the duty of guarding the walls of the city of Troy.[62] In their conversations one of the guards reveals to the other that he has been taught the secret of the magical arts of the Egyptians.[63] The soldier explains that, in order to tell the difference between real concrete entities and simulacra one must expose things to the first light of the sun.[64] If the thing is real, it casts a long shadow on the ground. If its being is otherwise, the phenomenon turns from solid thinghood to translucent light and enveloped in its shine disappears from the world. The young soldier who tells the story to the older more experienced man suggests that they wait close to a part of the wall to which Helen is known to go each morning before the sun goes up. She goes there in order to look over the Achaean ships and camp. The youth adds that she is said to have even spoken at length with Odysseus and other Greeks at times.[65] After a long wait and some sleep, Helen appears along the wall, and they even manage to gaze at her inhumanly beautiful countenance before she turns towards the Achaean camp. As the sun rises, the soldiers look on, and to their astonishment, as the first light reaches Helen her head and body turn to sheer radiance, and enveloped in light she disappears. As the sun goes on rising, the young soldier sees the city, the Achaean camp, and his partner vanish in a blaze of light. Then his extended hand begins to turn to sheer brightness, a light in which shape begins to disappear. He closes his eyes, almost as in a dream, hoping for a dream, only to experience a certain irreparable lightness and to never awake.

Saer's soldier carries the secret arts of the Egyptians, the secret which may reveal being as such. As the first light encounters existence, it does not encounter things, rather, it breaks through that mystery held only by the Egyptian priests, it exposes writing, the *phármakon*. Thus, in the first light things appear as they disappear and what is revealed is not things but all that has a sense of being in writing. What is revealed is the translucence, that is, the passing transformative character of the shine of all things—the translucence found in words. We are speaking of words in which the leeway is found for the appearing in fleeting passage of all that is said to be.[66] This is why in the story all that was held to be reality in the forgetting of the elemental secret of the word vanishes. In such a moment Helen, the Achaean encampment, Troy, and even the characters of Saer's story are exposed to that lightness so well concealed in the names of things. Once all seems to have vanished, Saer almost repeats Socrates' words. If you will recall, Socrates says of being,

"That place is occupied by the being that really is, which is intangible and without color." In closing his story, Saer writes, "Now the world is no more than a uniform colorless void, from which even the sun has disappeared, and thanks to the art without match of the Egyptian magicians, seems to have revealed in that instance its true essence."[67] Unlike Socrates' account, in Saer's story the words themselves bare their lightness, that vibrancy between transparency and sheer opaqueness in which shine in its savage beauty finds its translucence. This ephemeral and unearthly translucence is what is given in the first light and what escapes apprehension: words as such, vibrant, tremulous, fleeting, and light. We can interpret the saying of what perhaps cannot be said in light of this elemental translucence of words. In this sense, that the philosophical logos is a speaking in light of what one perhaps cannot say does not indicate a failure to represent being, rather, it is a reminder of the elemental translucence movement in which beings shine, of that elemental and ephemeral translucence of words.

Conclusion

The words from Wallace Stevens that open this paper say much of what I have developed in my discussion of Plato's *Phaidros*: "It has to be living, to learn the speech of the place."[68] As we heard, the title *Phaidros* indicates this dialogue is not merely a discussion of techniques of rhetoric or a series of discourses which attempt to define love (*éros*), that is, in the dialogue philosophical speech is fundamentally neither a giving of definitions nor a giving of moral directives. Rather, the dialogue develops a certain disposition essential to thought. This disposition is friendship of wisdom (*philos-sophía*), understood as a making of speeches that in their elemental translucence enact the shine of beings. This occurs in encountering through words ways of being along with the motion of the soul and beings. In this experience the philosophical logos is a living ensouled speech that opens a space, a leeway for the interpretative transfiguration of the soul and of the senses of beings. It is in that turning in the word of souls and beings that the philosopher's speech finds its weight and density. Paradoxically, as we heard from going beyond the dialogue to Saers' story, this weight arises in the translucence of words, which like the light translucence of water and light, in their vibrant and tremulous flow bare the ephemeral shine of the soul and beings, an experience as alluring as it is elusive in its beautiful and almost inhuman uncanny passing.[69]

In coming to closure, and in light of these last words, I suggest that in interpreting the philosophical logos in the way we have, we may encounter thought in its fundamentally marginal character. I say marginal not because thought betrays with its words—written or spoken—true identity and beauty, as if words were opposed or had to be understood as other to beings factual or ideal. I say marginal because we have now begun to understand that in that living ephemeral translucence of words in which the shine of beings and souls occur we encounter a fundamental transgression to any already conceptually determined form or sense of beings and also of words as language. This is because, as we saw, the word in the soul is not only hermeneutical or interpretative, but also transformative, and therefore, we are speaking of a word that is always already played out beyond its determinate forms. Thus, in the very word or translucence of beings one encounters a certain impossibility of giving formal and self-evident determination to beings as well as to words as such. Most strikingly then, we find that this impossibility is a most compelling element in the shine of beings and that therefore, the experience of the shine of beings is given as such evanescent, ungraspable, and lived transgressive word.[70] In other words, thinking is marginal in that the shine of beings occurs in a transgressive passage figured by experiences that ultimately fade, leaving not indicators of unchanging identity or meaning but openings to beings in the ephemeral translucence of their shine. Indeed, if we seek the sense of the written and spoken logos for thinking our experiences of beings, I would suggest that this quest marks the single need in thinking always to have to begin to learn to speak again. In this sense, Socrates's infamous hortatory to begin again, calls us nowhere but to encounter our words in their uncanny translucent lightness in our times.

CHAPTER 7

The Tactility of Words (from Silent Gestures)

Gadamer's Reading of Paul Celan's Atemkristall

The reader who is interested in understanding and deciphering hermetic lyrics must clearly not be hurried. Such reader need not be scholarly or especially learned—he or she must be a reader who again and again attempts to hear.

(Gadamer, *Who am I and Who are You?*)

The relationship between Hans-Georg Gadamer's thought and Paul Celan's poetry is most vividly found in their encounter through a small series of poems written by Celan in 1963 and published in 1965 under the title, *Atemkristall* (*Breathcrystal*). This cycle was later published as the first section of *Atemwende* (*Breath-turn*).[1] Gadamer's reading of the small cycle is titled, *Wer bin Ich und wer bist Du: Ein Kommentar zu Paul Celan Gedichtfolge "Atemkristall,"* (*Who Am I and Who Are You?*), and is a collection of close interpretations of the poems, written for Celan before 1965, and delivered thereafter.[2] The proximity of Celan's word in these poems to some of the most difficult issues in Gadamer's thought is indicated by Gadamer himself, who, in *"Selbstdarstellung,"* "Self-interpretation" (1977), writes that after the publication of *Truth and Method* his reading of Paul Celan's *Atemkristall* is one of the two moments in his work in which he comes close to the transformative event operative in the grounding conditions of hermeneutic dialogue (*das hermeneutische Grundverhältnis*).[3] But what is behind this proximity? In what manner do poet and thinker touch?

In closing a recollection of his long relationship with Hans-Georg Gadamer, Dennis Schmidt says that what he learned from his teacher and friend was a certain involvement with words, and, that it is in this struggle for words that the possibility of our freedom is played out. Schmidt's reflections remind us of a fundamental aspect of Gadamer's understanding of hermeneutics, namely, that human knowledge and freedom are ultimately a matter of summoning words and of finding a shareable language.[4] This crucial insight brings Gadamer's thought close to Paul Celan's works.[5] In his famous speech "Meridian," Celan speaks of words as the possibility for finding our identity and freedom in our time, and in light of Celan's experience, this means recovering a sense of humanity for thought that today is at best in question with respect to its possibility.[6] To propose, then, a discussion of Gadamer's work on Paul Celan is to take up the task of thinking towards such possibility and of thinking in light of a certain need for the summoning of words, a task which gathers poet and philosopher in dialogue and lets us move towards their encounter.

With this theme, the summoning of words, a series of issues immediately appear: How does one begin to engage the event of the arising of words? How does Gadamer understand this experience in his reading of Celan's cycle? How is this step towards freedom understood and enacted by Celan and his poems in the cycle *Atemkristall*? And, in light of the encounter of the two, to what extent does Gadamer reach Celan's sense of the word? Lastly, what, if anything, might Celan's sense of the arising of the word in poetry contribute to Gadamer's hermeneutics? In their broadness, these questions appear as a prism through which many aspects of this discussion open up and lead well beyond the following pages. At the same time, the broadness of the question of language requires that before taking up Gadamer's commentary we go a step further in considering how poet and philosopher touch, this in order to get a more precise orientation for the following discussion, with specific focus on the way the summoning of words as experienced by Celan might contribute to hermeneutics.

In the epilogue to the revised edition of *Who Am I and Who Are You?*, Gadamer situates his reading of Celan with a brief remark: "Every interpretation seeks only to be an approximation, and would not be what it can be without taking up its historical-effective place (*wirkungsgeschichtlichen Ort*)."[7] This remark brings Gadamer's reading of Celan to the heart of his understanding of hermeneutics. The term "historical-effective" (*wirkungsgeschichtlich*), refers us back to Gadamer's *Truth and Method*, and to an insight Gadamer finds in a lecture given by Helmholtz in Heidelberg in 1862.[8] As he develops his project in *Truth and Method*, Gadamer goes back to Helmholtz and identifies in his work a certain sense of a psychological tact (*psychologisher Takt*), which, in contrast to logically drawn inferences, is operative in the configuration of the fundamental concepts of the human sciences (*Geisteswissenschaften*).[9] The crucial point, and the moment beyond Helmholtz in Gadamer's work occurs when Gadamer asks: "Does not what is scientific about the human sciences lie here [in tactile understanding] rather than in their methodology?"[10]

Gadamer's question suggests that a certain psychological tact take the place of reason's logical inferences as the ground for the configuration of conceptual knowledge. From this issue of the tactility operative in the configuration of conceptual knowledge one can gain a certain orientation for a discussion of the summoning of words central to hermeneutics. In other words, here appears the now classic issue of hermeneutics, the issue of understanding the configuration of thought in a sense broader than that of subjective rationality and its sciences. Furthermore, with this issue, we encounter the question of the essence of language, not interpreted as a descriptive or calculative tool, or as the making of a subjective consciousness, but as an experience of sense in and out of which concepts are found and situated. This issue of sense refers us to neither purely rational concepts nor to the five senses of a subject situated over against an extant world.[11] If the thinking of hermeneutics engages in a constant summoning of words and in the search for a sharable language, then, according to Gadamer's insight, not only is this experience nonsubjective, but this struggle for the breaking through of words bears with it a certain tactility, a certain prelinguistic sensuousness of words; an experience we have perhaps already intimated in speaking of this struggle as a summoning, a word that literally suggests an unspoken moment in the arising of words. This tacit tactility of words is explored in the following pages.

      This issue of tactility and word, and the series of questions above mark an itinerary.[12] The discussion will move from Gadamer's interpretation of Celan's poems to Celan's own experience with the struggle for words, and, finally, to some suggestions concerning what Celan's sense of the summoning of words may offer to Gadamer's indication of a certain tactility fundamental to thought in hermeneutics and language.[13] This concluding point will require that we bring together Celan's poems in *Atemkristall* with the work's often neglected other, that is, with the graphic works of the painter Gisèle Celan-Lestrange, which were originally published with the poem cycle and with them formed a single work under the title *Atemkristall*.[14]

Gadamer's Reading of *Atemkristall*: Where Word Touches Loss

Gadamer's reading of *Atemkristall* was originally for Paul Celan. Perhaps in part for this reason, the reading is as attentive to the way the poems may be approached as it is intimate.[15] Speaking of the title of the cycle, Gadamer says, ". . . *Atemkristall*. The title points to the sphere of breath and thus to the event of language formed by it."[16] Gadamer's observation draws attention not only to the poet's voice, but also to the breath in which words are sought and spoken. His discussion of the first poem of *Atemkristall* as a proem, a key to the cycle, brings one closer to this intimate engagement.[17] Gadamer writes,

The poem says to the poet, as well as to all of us, that the stillness is welcome. It is the same stillness heard in the turn of breath, the ever so quiet recurrence of the act of breathing. More than anything, this is the breath-turn [*Atemwende*], the sensuous experience of the silent, calm moment between inhaling and exhaling. I do not want to deny that Celan does not only associate this moment of turning breath, this instance when breath returns, with calm self-restraint, but that he also allows the subdued hope bound up with every return to resonate. As he says in "Meridian:" 'Poetry: that can mean a breath-turn' . . . They [the poems] offer witness to a last constriction of life and, simultaneously, represent anew its recurring resolution, or better, not resolution, but its elevation to a secure linguistic form [*feste Sprachgestalt*].[18]

In this paragraph, the philosopher identifies a series of specific elements in Celan's cycle. The arising of the word is situated in the singular sensuous moments between inhaling and exhaling, in a breath-turn. In this moment of suspension, in this breath-turn, a tension appears between loss and death, and a certain hope, a return in which the birth of linguistic forms occurs. The poet's word occurs as a breath-turn, that is, in a struggle to break-through to the word, as a breath that bares the poet's hope for words to crystallize and find precise form.

The theme of the struggle for words carries throughout Gadamer's interpretation of Celan. Gadamer speaks of Celan's poems as break-thrust points, at times as a breakthrough into brightness (*Durchbruch ins Helle*).[19] In relation to this task, at a certain point he also states that, "only then does it [the poem] succeed as a poem."[20] The sense of the poet's unending struggle for words appears dramatically in his reading of the last stanzas of the cycles' fourteenth poem: The ferry up- / ward poling in the / vertical, narrow / day-chasm: // it transports / something wound-read (*Die in der senk- / Rechten, schmalen / Tagschlucht nach oben / Staken Fähre: // Sie setzt / Wundgelesenes über*).[21] From this almost crude figure of the transported as "something wound-read" (*Wundgelesenes*), Gadamer concludes, "But in the end, what is transported finally emerges from the dark into the light—this is the poem."[22] But this brightness of the word in its break-through arises for Gadamer with what is transported (*übersetzt*) and wound-read (*Wundgelesenes*). Gadamer emphatically states, "Its [the poem's] real message is this: what surfaces is 'wound-read.' "[23] The summoning of words is a struggle that does not give rise to pure brightness. Rather, in these poems, in the arising of words, what appears is never beyond darkness, silence, loss, and suffering.[24] This figure, of the arising of the word into linguistic form as wound-read, opens the way for further discussion of Gadamer's interpretation of Celan's cycles. That the word is wound-read obviously emphasizes the issue of the arising of the word (what arises is read), while at the same time, the wound begins to indicate the character of such experiences.

According to Gadamer, for Celan the breaking-through of the word happens always in language. Whatever the experience, the wound, loss, silence, suffering; these occur "in language." This is clearest in Gadamer's analysis of Celan's well-known poem from the cycle, "Stehen."

TO STAND, in the shadow
of a scar in the air.

Stand-for-no-one-and nothing.
Unrecognized,
for you
alone.

With all that has room within it,
even without
language.

STEHEN, im Schatten
Des Wundenmals in der Luft.

Für-niemand-und-nichts-Stehen.
Unerkannt,
für dich
allein.

Mit allem, was darin Raum hat,
auch ohne
Sprache.[25]

In his interpretation Gadamer says,

When it says here that one is standing "even without language," it means being so alone that one no longer even communicates. But it also says, conversely, that when this I stands in the shadow of the invisible stigma and addresses itself as You, communicating absolutely "with all that has room therein," it communicates like language. Indeed, the last verse consists of a single word "language," not only is "language" expressly emphasized, it is also "set down" (*gesetzt*). For that reason, "even without language" means something further. Even before language, when one stands mutely . . . there is already language. That within which the witness of standing will and should completely proclaim itself should be. It should be language. . . .[26]

According to the philosopher, Celan's two lines, "*auch ohne / Sprache*," indicate an experience that always occurs within language. Even before language, when one stands mutely, "there is already language." This paradoxical statement opens issues concerning the essence of language that lie well beyond the possibilities of this chapter, but this question serves as the background and ever pressing difficulty towards which the present discussion moves in its discussion of the tactility of words. Gadamer's statement points to the issue of the essence of language. How is one to understand a sense of language even before language? In light of this question appears a second issue: What is the understanding of language that lies at the center of hermeneutics as understood by Gadamer and as indicated by his words in this difficult passage? With these questions as background to our discussion, and, in this sense, as orientations for it, let's return to Gadamer's interpretation of "*Stehen.*"

Gadamer's comments point to a loss of words and communication. At the same time, this is a recovery through a summoning of words out of loss and in an appropriation of that loss. He begins from the interruption or loss of communication indicated by the two lines together: ". . . *auch ohne Sprache*" means that no word is uttered or heard. However, from this absence of words, Gadamer turns to a second aspect of the poem by looking specifically at the last line, the single word: "*Sprache*" (language). According to Gadamer, this ending, this word, indicates that even before language, there is already language. The word *Sprache* in Celan's poem arises in that last line to witness the recovery of words out of loss and in the absence of words. This motion of recovery out of loss is already in language. This occurs through the re-appropriation of loss in a prelinguistic experience enacted by the summoning of words (the word you must be summoned, and hence, a dialogical space must be opened). This happens as the I addresses itself as a You, and, in this dialogical way, opens to all that which lies under that scar. But, as the philosopher explains, this recovery occurs as the I comes to stand under the shadow of the loss of words, the stigma or scar. Only if this occurs, concludes Gadamer, one finds that even in mute silence, and even before language, one is already standing in language. In this way the loss of communication, the loss of word is reclaimed. Thus, to speak of language, of being in language, means to speak of this dialogical reappropriation of loss. Furthermore, we are now speaking of a reappropriation that happens in a summoning of words out of an experience beyond words. This last phrase requires some further development if it is not to be misunderstood as sheer obscurantism.

In his discussion of Celan's work, Gadamer directs the reader to the poet's abandonment and use of traditional spoken language, in doing this he recognizes the disruption and reappropriation of the word enacted by Celan. As he indicates, Celan's poems are written beyond traditional language, that is, "without the constraints of logic and syntax."[27] At the same time, Gadamer also finds in "A Phenomenological and Semantic Approach to Celan?" a language that arises in, "a polyvalent and broken semantics, of bold syncretisms and playful assemblages."[28] In short, Celan's poetry is not a matter of language in its logical and syntactic constraints, or subject to representational limits. While it does figure a breaking-through of words anew, this is an experience that occurs out of loss, in the absence of words, and in this sense is prelinguistic.

This prelinguistic experience of the word is already indicated by Gadamer's introductory discussion of the poem as an *"Atemwende"* (a breath-turn), that is, in his engagement of the arising of the poet's word in its sensuous silent moment, in the poet's breathing, in the pause between inhaling and exhaling. In Gadamer's attentive listening to this breath-turn one hears an interruption in the arising of words.[29] Thus, one encounters an indication of a prelinguistic sense of words that is operative in the poet's sensuous and ephemeral summoning of words. But although Gadamer recognizes the summoning of words, and even comes to stand at the limit of words in touching the scar, the loss operative in the opening of a dialogical space of I and you, he does not go further to explore how this prelinguistic summoning of words takes place. His series of insights lead ahead. They open issues towards a sense of language figured by the engagement of words in their intimacy, loss, sensuousness, and prelinguistic character. In what remains of this article we will develop Gadamer's insights through a direct discussion of Celan's work.

From Loss to a New Word

1. "... *auch ohne* / *Sprache*," "even without / language." As we said above, when Gadamer indicates the double sense of these two lines he touches on the absence of words, on an interruption in language (that sensuous silence, that turn between inhaling and exhaling).[30] Even when in the last line the word "*Sprache*" (language) is *gesetzt* (setdown), in that verse, in that turn from loss to the arising word echoes the lack of words marked by the previous line. Thus, language is never found free of a certain loss. The arising and setting down of words exposes language to a sense of loss, since in the arising of the word a certain absence of words will be felt. In this sense, one might repeat Celan's words and say that the arising of the word will occur as a wound-read transport, "*Sie setzt* / *Wundgelesenes über*." Thus, adding to

what Gadamer has already indicated concerning the summoning of words as wound-read, one can say that in Celan's case loss and suffering are not only parts of the arising to presence of words, but in them and in the absence or impossibility of words in such experience the word is found anew and thus configured.[31] If there is a certain continuity in language, as one always stands in language, this continuity will figure a certain loss and impossibility essential to language.

The arising of the word beyond words is central to Celan's own understanding of his works. In a speech given in 1958, in Bremen, Celan recalls his experience with language.

> Only one thing remained reachable, close and secure amid all losses; language. Yes, language. In spite of everything, it remained secure against loss. But it had to go through its own lack of answers, through terrifying silence, through the thousand darknesses of murderous speech. It gave me no words for what was happening but went through it. Went through it and could resurface, 'enriched' by it all.[32]

Celan's words echo Gadamer's reading of "... *auch ohne / Sprache.*" Amid loss, in utmost solitude, in the interruption of all communication, language remained "reachable, close, secure." However, Celan's words have undergone a severe interruption; language had to undergo terrifying silence. And, as the next phrase indicates, "through the thousand darknesses of murderous speech," the summoning of words in their loss and impossibility are inseparable from Celan's experiences during the war. In turn, this points to the interruption of Celan's mother tongue, German.[33] Only in this breath-taking interruption one begins to encounter the arising of Celan's words. Unlike Gadamer, Celan's sense of his words arises in loss, as he undergoes loss, in the impossibility of words, without having yet the distinct brightness of a break-through which the philosopher emphasizes in his reading.

The fundamental sense of interruption and loss of words in the arising of words is felt throughout Celan's works. In "Meridian," he situates wordlessness, that terrifying silence, at the very center of the experience of poetry.[34] In "Meridian," Celan first identifies poetry with Büchner's character Lucile. "I believe that I first met poetry in the figure of Lucile, and Lucile perceived language as shape, direction, breath." Soon thereafter, Celan comes to his experience of poetry as a breath-turn (*Atemwende*). "Lenz—that is Büchner—has gone a step farther than Lucile. His 'Long live the king' is no longer a word. It is terrifying silence. It takes his—and our—breath away. Poetry is perhaps this: an *Atemwende*, a turning of our breath."[35] In this passage, poetry appears out of terrifying silence, out of the interruption of breath, as breath has been taken away. This is an experience of language in sheer absence of words in which even what is said is "no longer a word."[36] And yet, Celan then goes on to say that out of such interruption, and only then, "perhaps after this, the poem can be itself."[37]

As Gadamer indicates in his reading, Celan experiences the summoning of words as an occurrence beyond words. However, in the intimacy of loss in his word, the poet goes further to indicate an experience that is not situated in the stillness of a breath-turn but rather in the terrifying moment of breathlessness, a sensuous moment in which neither word nor breath are guaranteed a return—or a break-through.[38] How does one recover out of such interruption? How does the arising of the word occur at the limit of word, sense, breath, and ultimately, life?

2.

> You had better haul up a pair of eyes from the bottom of your soul and put them on your chest; then you will find out what's happening here.[39]

Immediately after the war, in 1948, in a text on the paintings of Edgar Jené, tellingly tittled "Edgar Jené und der Traum vom Traume,"[40] Celan exclaims:

> What could be more dishonest than to claim that words had somehow, at bottom remained the same! I could not help seeing that the ashes of burned-out meanings (and not only of those) had covered what had, since time immemorial, been striving for expression in man's inner-most soul.[41]

Celan's violent outburst concerning the impossibility of still finding sense in words is immediately followed by a question that rather than preserving the mute experience of loss and interruption points immediately towards the arising of words anew. Celan asks, "How could something new and pure issue from this?"[42] His question sets up a remarkable statement which comes as a reply, and which is worth quoting at length:

> It may be from the remotest regions of the spirit that words and figures will come, images and gestures, veiled and unveiled as in a dream. When they meet in their heady course, and the spark of the wonderful is born from the marriage of strange and strangest, then I will know I am facing the new radiance. It will give me a dubious look because, even though I have conjured it up, it exists beyond the concepts of my wakeful thinking; . . . Its weight has a different heaviness; its color speaks to the new eyes

which my closed lids have given one another; my hearing has wandered into my fingertips and learns to see; my heart, now that it lives behind my forehead, tastes the laws of a new, unceasing, free motion. I follow my wandering senses into the new world of the spirit and come to know freedom. . . . Thus I listen to my own thoughts. . . .[43]

This dense passage begins to expose Celan's recovery of the word out of its interruption and loss. As the phrase "the marriage of the strange to the strangest" suggests, the path to the breaking through of the word is one outside rational or wakeful thought, and is situated in a recovery and reappropriation of the senses. Celan speaks of "a different heaviness" and of new eyes. Most important to our discussion is that this reappropriation of the senses is particularly figured by the turning of hearing, and hence of the word, towards a new experience, in which the uncovering of the word occurs through tact: ". . . my hearing has wandered into my fingertips and learns to see. . . ." We are speaking of a tactile word that opens the world anew, that teaches the poet to see. With these difficult words Celan points to how he encounters the word anew.[44] But how is one to take up this passage, when its words come after the interruption of word and sense, after the interruption of the ordering of word, the traditional separation of the senses, of their regions or fields of experience, and hence after an interruption and as a disruption of the sense of the world? From whence does Celan begin to uncover this new path towards the poem? And, from whence does one begin to read with Celan, that is, in the experience of the arising of his wound-read word as a new word?

Celan's abrupt exclamation against the word and his recovery of it occur in his encounter with the word-less works of a painter. Indeed, as the last words of the quote above indicate, the series of radical statements arise out of Celan's encounter with painting, and as the poet is brought to reflect on his own thoughts. This arising of the word out of silence and in light of word-less graphic works occurs once again, and this time in a manner evident to him, with the composition of *Atemkristall*. Celan begins to write the cycle *Atemkristall* in 1963, after a year of silence, an absence of words interrupted precisely by his collaboration with his wife, the painter and graphic artist Gisèle Celan-Lestrange. In 1965, at about the time of the publication of the small seventy-five-book edition, Celan writes to his wife, "*Atemkristall* opened the path for me, it was born from your etchings."[45] The poems are not only collaboration with Gisèle, they are born from her etchings.[46] Somehow, in light of those abstract images, of those word-less works, Celan finds a way towards words. The graphic works mark a path towards poetry for him. To say it in terms of Gadamer's insightful reading, what is one to make of this breaking-through of the word? From silence, interruption arises a word which does not answer to words, to language as word, but which instead finds its space and opening in Gisèle's word-less etchings. Here, the issue for us is not the common sense question of the relationship between visual work and poem (as if this were a self evident differentiation).[47] The matter at hand is that of the arising of words in an experience that stands beyond, outside words as linguistic elements, an experience of the summoning of words not from other already signifying words, and perhaps, as Gadamer indicates, an experience that can still be said to occur in language.

Word and Graphic Mark

The interplay of Gisèle's graphic works with Celan's writing is well attested in John Felsteiner's *Paul Celan: Poet, Survivor, Jew*. Speaking of one of the poems in the cycle, Felsteiner points to their proximity. "In lithography and etching Gisèle worked with gray and black on white, so Celan's poem, meant to be published with his wife's art, shares her somber imagery and severe technique."[48] This interaction becomes more palpable when one brings together some of Gisèle's works with one of Celan's poems (the tenth in *Atemkristall*).

WITH MASTS SUNG EARTHWARD
the heaven wrecks sail.

Into this wood song
You bite fast with your teeth.

You are the songfast
Pennant.

MIT ERDWÄRTS GESUNGENEN MASTEN
Fahren die Himmelwracks.

In dieses Holzlied
Beisst du dich fest mit den Zähnen.

Du bist der liedfeste / Wimpel.[49]

We may compare this poem with the two graphic works "*Rencontre-Begegnung*," (1958, fig. 7.1), and "*Echoe d'une terre / Echo einer Erde*," (1967, fig. 7.2).[50] The two prints give examples of Gisèle's work through the period of *Atemkrystall*. *Echo einer Erde* shows the gray and black on white that Felsteiner identifies. One may also notice in this play of tones emerge a series of forms that rather

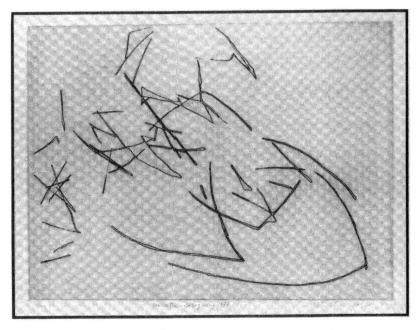

Figure 7.1. Gisèle Celan-Lestrange, "*Recontre-Begegnung*," 1958.

than becoming identifiable images, or representations, in their dispersed motion reveal an open space. This space is configured by fragments, needles, and fissures, spaces through which the eye filters to find an indeterminate muted white background. One's eye then returns from that mute background to the surface, to fragments that, without forming an image, appear like pieces of a broken see-through-crystal, a fragmented reflective surface through which one seems to clearly glimpse at a background otherwise vague, indeterminate. The stark emptiness and flatness of the white and the opening motion of the dispersing lines are more evident in the second example, *Begegnung*.

Although one does not find determinate images in *Echo einer Erde*, besides their direct resonance with the title of the work, Celan's first lines in the poem seem to recast the pictorial construction, "WITH MASTS SUNG EARTHWARD / the heaven wrecks sail" (*MIT ERDWÄRTS GESUNGENEN MASTEN / Fahren die Himmelwracks*). The words recall the way Gisèle's print emerges in a movement of fragments, masts, and pins, which open the picto-graphic space. Also, in the second stanza the wood song appears as a direct allusion to the materials and the work of printmaking. But these superficial observations only open our path towards the sense in which writing and

Figure 7.2. "Echo d'une terre / Echo einer Erde," 1967,
Gisèle Celan-Lestrange (Eric Celan).

graphic works are encountered in Celan's word. Celan's poems in the cycle
not only recall Gisèle's images, but, as we will see, show specific formal parallels, and, most important to our discussion, they ultimately indicate a certain
inseparability between the experience and process of word-less print making
and Celan's experience of his struggle in the arising of words.

Gisèle's *Echo einer Erde* opens a pictorial space through a nonimagistic,
or nonrepresentational motion of fragments and marks which operate as

passages through which an otherwise muted and indeterminate background gains moments of intense clarity. These moments are made all the more precise and poignant by virtue of the way they occur. The seeing happens through diverse fragments, and as a play of emphatically distinct forms, which, in their fragmentary interaction, remain free from unification. Formally these nonfigurative open spaces and moments of distinct clarity point directly back to Celan's poems. Much like Gisèle's prints, Celan's poems resist imagistic or representational unification. Furthermore, as Gadamer points out, Celan writes outside of the constraints of a syntax or logic that may reconstitute the poem into something unified by reason.[51] For example, the three stanzas we have been discussing can hardly be gathered under one representational meaning or single metaphor; nor can for example the two lines in the second stanza be held together semantically. "Into this wood song / you bite with your teeth" ("*In dieses Holzlied / Beisst du dich fest mit den Zähnen*"). At the same time, through this fragmentation, Celan's poems often expose us to cuttingly sharp glimpses of experience. This happens through a writing that, as Gadamer fittingly says, occurs in "a polyvalent and broken semantics of bold syncretisms and playful assemblage."[52] Thus, in the assemblage of single filament like words, and pieces of sentences, and in the gathering of irreparably interrupted fragments, we find crystallized glimpses of experience.[53] Much like Gisèle's works open a space by virtue of what Celan calls a "cryptographic gesture," Celan's words trace the poem's event through fragmentary, nonimagistic and yet distinct crystallized moments. This is the case for example as one listens once again to the poem we have been discussing: WITH MASTS SUNG EARTHWARD / the heaven wrecks sail. // Into this wood song /You bite fast with your teeth. // You are the songfast / Pennant.

The visual parallels discussed before and the formal similarity of Celan's writing and Gisèle's graphic work bring one closer to the intimate sense of Celan's experience with the prelinguistic sensuous summoning of words. As Felsteiner points, to a certain extent Celan's cycle is configured by words that overlap with terms often used in the graphic arts. Among these, Felsteiner highlights, "etching . . . , bite . . . , carve . . . , groove . . . , press . . . , copper . . . , stone . . . , image . . . , shade . . . , white-gray . . . , gray-black . . . , wood. . . ."[54] In Celan's poems, these terms do not merely refer to graphic arts, they articulate Celan's very experience of the arising of words. The terms are not metaphors for language; they set down (*Gesetz*) their event. They trace, they mark, they re-mark, and figure the arising of the word in Celan's poetry. In other words, these terms are no longer borrowed from the graphic arts, they are the marks of words in the tacit sensuousness of their breaking-through.

Early in the cycle, in the third poem, Celan already entangles in inseparable union the experience of the graphic artist and that of the poet. The poem's first part reads,

INTO THE GROVES
Of heaven's coin in the door crack
You press that word I unfold from

In die Rillen
Der Himmelsmünze im Türspalt
Preßt du das Wort,
dem ich entrollte. . . .

Here, we find clear allusions to the process of print making in such words as groves (*die Rillen*), and more explicitly in the pressing of the word and the rolling out or unfolding of the poet with the pressing of words. At this point, the poem shifts towards the poet, who seems to unfold from the pressing out of the word. Here, the reversing movement, from the word arising from the poet to the poet unrolling from the word, carries a double sense. The line is a reminder of Celan's statement, "Where in the writing of the word the poet is found" (*Wer es [das Gedicht] schreibt, bleibt ihm mitgegeben*).[55] The poet is found in the writing of the word, and, further more, the poet is found out of a word arisen in a pressing out, out of a word-less process or experience. Celan then goes on to speak literally of the poets work,

As with quivering fists
I pulled down the roof
Above us, slate by slate,
syllable by syllable, for the copper
shimmer's sake
on the begging bowl
up there.

Als ich mit bebenden Fäusten
Das Dach über uns
Abtrug, Schiefer um Schiefer,
Silbe um Silbe, dem Kupfer-
Schimmer der Bettel-
Schale dort oben
Zulieb.[56]

The word-less experience of the graphic artist and the poet's summoning of words is at the end sealed in the last lines, in a striving which gathers gesture and word in a single word-less experience, an experience beyond or before language: "As with quivering fists / I pulled down the roof / Above us, slate by slate, / syllable by syllable" (*Als ich mit bebenden Faüste / Das Dach über uns / Abtrug . . . Silbe um Silbe. . . .*). But if the poet unrolls from a word given in a word-less experience, and his experience figures a certain loss in words, this does not mean the abandonment of words. Rather, as already suggested by Gadamer's recognition of the ambiguity of language in Celan's lines "even without / language," the struggle for words is not given up. The struggle is found beyond the logic and syntax, the images and representations of language. How is the word sought and experienced now? One finds a powerful indication of this in the nineteenth poem of the cycle.

Celan's sense of the word-less in the arising of words is forcefully marked in the beginning lines of the nineteenth poem of *Atemkristall*: WORD-DEPOSIT, VOLCANIC, / sea-overroared. (*Wordaufschüttung, vulkanisch, / meerüberrauscht.*)[57] The beginning sets down the word as a mark, a deposit in stone, a volcanic elemental linked to eruptive births as well as to unfathomable memory, a link found in the cooling off of the volcanic stone in which the word becomes deposited, a mark on stone, a word-deposit (*Wortaufschüttung*). At the same time, the poem's closing lines recall the volcanic to the originating beginnings to which the word-deposit becomes witness, "And the heart- / Shaped crater / Nakedly bears witness to the beginnings, / to the king- / births." (*und der Hertz- / förmigen krater / nacht für die Anfänge zeugt, / die Königst- / geburten*).[58] These closing lines relate word-deposit to the birth, the arising of words, which are not events witnessed by spoken language, but rather by the silent word, by the "*Wortaufschüttung.*" This figure has now transformed, and is now, "the heart- / Shaped crater" (*der Hertz- / förmigen krater*). Again we find the direct relation to the word-less experience of marking. The word arises and is witness to its beginnings in a word-less experience, in sensuous naked experience, as it "nakedly bares witness to the beginnings. . . ."

Tangible Words

Thus far we have sought Celan's summoning of words in its graphic and word-less sense. But the poet's voice, the event of the word, cannot be found through the silent repetition of the graphic artist's experience. The hand's gesture will not sound out the word. And yet, as we have seen, the arising of the word is for Celan a prelinguistic event. How is one to begin to understand, to undergo, such a word-less experience of language, that which Gadamer insightfully broaches when he speaks of the arising word as "the sensuous experience of the silent moment"?[59]

In the first stanza of *Weissgrau*, the ninth poem in *Atemkristall*, we hear the echo of the word-less gesture, the mark of the word as word-deposit.

> WHITEGRAY of a
> Steeply caved
> Feeling.
>
> *WEISSGRAU aus-*
> *Geschachteten steilen*
> *Gefühls.*

The "steeply caved" feeling (*aus-geschachteten steilen Gefühl*) again reminds the reader of the artist's word-less hand at work. At the same time this caved feeling does not remain silent. The last stanzas read,

> An ear, severed, listens.
>
> An eye, sliced into strips,
> gives all that its due.
>
> *Ein Ohr, abgetrennt, lauscht.*
> *Ein Aug, in Streifen geschnitten,*
> *wird all dem gerecht*[60]

Here something is heard, a word is intimated. How? What gathers word and word-less gesture is a certain shared interruption. The ear that listens has been severed; the eye has been cut into strips. However, in such interruption a certain listening occurs, and the fragmented eye "gives all that its due" (*wird all dem gerecht*). We hear here resonances of Celan's anticipatory statement about the word after the experience of the war, in the eye that, although no longer a seeing eye, does cope with it all.[61] In these dramatic lines we find the intimations of a sense of words, of what may be heard in listening, after interruption and loss. At the same time, just as Celan indicates already in 1947, the listening will have to be rediscovered out of a transformation of the sense of the word and the senses. A transformation again intimated in the ear that listens, although severed; an ear perhaps open to the wound-read word. In a sense these few lines open the word to a sensuous sense of its arising, born in interruption and beyond words. An opening, which is at the same time set down in these lines.

Perhaps it is fitting that, as we come to the conclusion, we return close to the beginning of Celan's *Atemkrystall*. The poet's sensuous summoning of words is perhaps nowhere more explicitly engaged in Celan's cycle than near the beginning, in the second poem.

CORRODED BY the undreamed,
the sleeplessly traveled bread-land
digs up the life-mountain.

From its soil
You knead anew our names,
with an eye
like yours
on each of my fingers,
I probe them for
a place, through which I
can wake onto you,
the bright
Hunger-candle in my mouth.

VON UNGETRÄUMTEM geätzt,
Wirft das schlaflos durchwanderte Brotland
Den Lebensberg auf.

Aus seiner Krume
Knetest du neu unsre Namen,
die ich, ein deinem
gleichendes
Aug an jedem der Finger,
abtaste nach
einer Stelle, durch die ich
mich zu dir heranwachen kann,
die helle
Hungerkerze im Mund.[62]

As Gadamer indicates in his interpretation, one may at least begin by saying that the first stanza refers to the gathering of experience, a *Lebensberg*. At the same time, since in the second stanza this experience becomes the soil for the kneading of names (*Knetest du neu unsre Namen*), it is worth adding that the first line of the first stanza adds to experience a certain uncanny sense. The word-deposit (*Wortaufschüttung*), the mark still witnesses at the beginning, this time as the corroding trace of the undreamed. What may surface here will be "corroded by the undreamed." This figure summons the kind of violent experience that, in its event, appears beyond what may be dreamed, perhaps, even imagined, or directly put into words. However, without leaving to oblivion this uncanny impression, it is still not out of place to say that the naming kneaded in the second stanza will arise from the soil of experience (*Aus einer Krume / knetest du neu unsre Namen*). The "kneading of names" may refer here to both the task of graphic artist and poet, and as such points to the poet's struggle for words. But, how does this kneading of names occur?

The next lines of the second stanza begin to offer a reply, "From its soil / You knead anew our names, / with an eye / like yours / on each of my fingers "*die ich, ein deinem / gleichendes / Aug an jedem der Finger, / abtast nach / einer Stelle. . . .*" The kneading of names occurs through that eye which although bereft of vision still sees, that eye which encounters the world anew. The line reminds us of Celan's statement from 1947, where he speaks of the new word in terms of "the new eyes which my closed lids have given one another."[63] At the same time, this kneading is a matter of a hand, of fingers, of tact, "on each of my fingers." Again, this line takes us back to Celan's early articulation of his sense of the arising of words anew. ". . . my hearing has wandered into my fingertips and learns to see."[64] In these early words we find the key to the lines, "with an eye . . . on each of my fingers." That the poet's fingers have eyes means that he has learned to hear anew. Only then does he probe that soil beyond dreams. Here, not only is the traditional categorization of sensuous experience overturned, but, more important, the poet's summoning of words, the very arising of words is engaged in tactile, tangible terms. The word-less hand of the graphic artist, the tact of the fingers that see in the experience of the artist's making (carving, pressing, rolling out), the tactility of this process is now found in the poet's arising words. With such sensuous sense of the summoning of words, the poet probes, again a tactile word, the soil of experience, and in such tangible experience finds the word.

The poet does not seek word-less marks, and here is the powerful insight in Celan's recovery of words. The kneading of names is a matter beyond words, logic, syntax, images and visual representation. Words are a sensuous matter, the summoning of words is a matter of tact.[65] The poem's last lines dramatically emphasize the sensuousness and tactility of the poet's word in the struggle to break-through: "a place, through which I / can wake onto you, / the bright / Hunger-candle in my mouth" (*einer Stelle, durch die ich / mich zu dir heranwachen kann, / die helle / Hungerkerzen im Mund*). The naming seeks a place, a way to "wake up onto you / the bright." These lines mark a struggle for words, for that breath-turn which can be the step towards brightness. The next and final line of the poem fully figures this struggle in its tactile sensuousness.

Hungerkerzen im Mund (hunger-candle in my mouth). Traditionally, the "hunger-candle," marks hunger, poverty, a certain lack, a need, indicated without one's presence, as a candle is left to burn alone. What shines is the mark, a tacit experience, without words already there to speak for that need. Lack and absence fill the last line. What lacks is the word and what marks is the word in its loss. However, this wordlessness is also experienced in another, most telling manner. The word is figured here in its tactility, as the hunger-candle is *im Mund* (in the mouth.) This figures a fullness beyond words, no word may be spoken with the hunger–candle in the mouth. This sensuous and tense sense of fullness and wordlessness is precisely part of the power of the figure. The word is still felt, in a sense that now must be sought beyond words, language is still felt.

Hungerkerzen im Mund, the line places the word in the mouth, in its texture and taste.[66] One might think of the middle stanza from Celan's tenth poem in *Atemkristall*. "In dieses Holzlied / beißt du dich fest mit den Zähnen." Indeed, biting, carving, pressing, rolling out, these sensuous experiences are all palpable in one's mouth in the summoning of words, in the tactile con-figuration of words. Words fill one's mouth or leave it empty. One breathes and bites through them. They can be sought with one's tongue, with every muscle in one's mouth, until one's mouth is dry. Ultimately, as Homer says of Athena's frank and intelligent words, they can surprisingly, escape through the fence of our teeth, and leave us in rather strange places, free and, or irreparably marked.

Conclusion

Four years after the publication of *Atemkristall*, in March of 1969 appeared in *L'Ephémère* a single sentence from Celan: "*La poésie ne s'impose plus, elle s'expose*" (Poetry no longer imposes itself, it exposes itself.)[67] This statement clearly indicates what we have encountered in our direct engagement with Celan's words. His poetry exposes the word beyond a subjective maker, a traditional sense of language as logically and syntactically ruled, and as a representational tool. Celan's poems arise out of the interruption and loss of the word, and they trace paths from such wordless silence to a sense of the word and poem as tactile, tangible, sensuous events. This summoning of words at the limit of words marks a radical turn towards language. Not only because the arising of words is not engaged in terms of syntactic, logical, and representational elements, but because, in being exposed to the loss and sensuousness in and of words, one is invited to consider and reappropriate the limits of one's understanding of language.[68] In engaging the tactility of words we have reached towards Gadamer's originary insight in his hermeneutics, that is, towards that tactile sense of knowledge in the experience of summon-ing words he already anticipates in *Truth and Method*. In turn, this figures a turn towards a sense of silence, loss, interruption and sensuousness essential in language and in hermeneutics. This crucial insight into the experience of language is what Celan so fittingly indicates for us with the title of his small cycle of poems, *Atemkristall* (*Breathcrystal*), and, what Gadamer encounters and begins to open for us as he listens attentively to Celan's poems and begins to read and think close to that tangible breath in which poet, thought, and word unfold anew.

CHAPTER 8

Quand un Corps se met en Œuvre

The Word in the Flesh, at the Limit of Derrida's Reading of Antonin Artaud

If I believe neither in Evil or Good, if I feel such strong inclination to destroy, if there is nothing in the order of principles to which I can reasonably accede, the underlying reason is my flesh. . . . There is for me an evidence in the realm of pure flesh which has nothing to do with the evidence of reason. The eternal conflict between reason and the heart is decided in my flesh. . . ."

("Manifesto in Clear Language," Artaud)

In his book *Artaud le Moma* (2002), Derrida speaks of his passionate admiration for Antonin Artaud, a relationship that goes on throughout the thirty years of the philosopher's career.[1] Derrida's engagement with the artist is informed by something like, ". . . *the* front, a sort of ceaseless war which, like antipathy itself, makes for me of Artaud a sort of privileged enemy, a doleful enemy I carry and prefer in me, closer to all the limits I encounter in my life's and death's work. This antipathy persists but remains an alliance, which commands thought's vigilance. . . ."[2] What makes Artaud a "privileged enemy" at the limits of Derrida's life and death? What is the sense or dynamic of this privilege?[3]

Derrida explicitly points to the sense of his vigilance and passionate engagement with Artaud in his first explicit discussion of him. In 1965, in "La parole soufflé," he writes:

The transgression of metaphysics through the 'thought' which, Artaud tells us, has not yet began, always risks returning to metaphysics. Such is the question in which *we are posed*. A question which is still and always enveloped each time that speech, protected by the limits of a field, lets itself be provoked from

afar by the enigma of flesh which wanted properly to be named
Antonin Artaud.[4]

Artaud's thought transgresses metaphysics; furthermore, his word is one
not yet accomplished, and yet it places us in a way that violates the limits
of metaphysics. But this blow to metaphysics occurs in the flesh's aggressive
provocation of the limits of speech, through the enigma of flesh that wants
to be properly named. It is this enigma of the flesh, and its violence against
speech, that situates us, that exposes us to and in metaphysics and in the
violation of its limit. This issue of a speech in the flesh, and its ambiguity
is what we will discuss in the following pages. In order to better orient our
discussion I should preface it with a few remarks.

In part, what follows arises out of my displeasure, almost a disappoint-
ment I find, when I compare the reach, physicality, and intensity of Artaud's
sense of language, at the limit of language, with Derrida's reading of the
artist's work: No matter how far Derrida goes, his language seems to turn
to strategy in light of the need to decenter transcendental subjectivity, its
phonocentrism, and the metaphysics of presence. Such rich agenda seems to
squeeze out of Derrida's discourse a more concrete unfolding or experience
of language. However, at the same time, I find in Derrida's reading of Artaud
a way into the concrete and ephemeral undergoing of thought, as language,
and thought with it, are brought to their finitude. An encounter that results in
the unfolding of a fecund and disseminating thrust for philosophical thought,
well beyond the traditional claims to subjectivity, reason, conceptual catego-
rizations, and the parceling out of existence in terms of these. Thus, my aim
in this discussion is not to criticize Derrida, but to make a few introductory
remarks on how our thought is situated once we follow Derrida's thought
of *différance*. Throughout this chapter we will follow closely Derrida's fitting
reading of Artaud's metaphysical drive, as well as his uncovering of Artaud's
concrete undergoing of language, and in light of the contrast between these,
we will point to the limit and perhaps transgress Derrida's engagement of the
word in the flesh. This in order to introduce what I take to be a sensibility
particular to thought, which opens once thought engages its very finitude or
temporality through the concrete and ephemeral undergoing of its event in
language. Ultimately, this sensibility brings thought closer to the physicality of
Artaud's undergoing of language, as philosophy comes close to being an act
of life. Hence the title of this essay, a title taken from a piece written by the
Argentine writer Julio Cortazar, in *Sur*, precisely in the occasion of Artaud's
death. As Cortazar states it, after Artaud, "living is more important than
writing, unless writing—as is so rarely the case—is an act of life."[5] Keeping
in mind that the *of* in the phrase "act of life" is not meant in the proprietary
genitive sense, the question then is to what extent does Derrida, or might we
be able of such act of life.

My discussion can only be an introduction to Derrida's reading of Artaud. His career offers many decisive and singular encounters with the artist: "La parole Soufflé" (1965),[6] "The Theater of Cruelty and the Closure of Representation" (1966),[7] both part of Derrida's well known *Writing and Difference*, (*L'écriture et la différence*) (1967); "to unsense the subjectile" (*forcener le subjectile*, 1986 and 1988);[8] and, *Artaud le Moma* (1996 and 2002).[9] The last two works deal explicitly with Artaud's paintings and drawings, and with an issue that will be always pressing in the following discussion: the inseparability of speech from the silent graphic mark, an issue figured by the impossibility of writing without drawing Artaud encounters already in 1939.[10] For the most part, I will only discuss "La parole soufflé," although, in order to better introduce Derrida's sense of the concreteness or physicality of Artaud's language, I will take a moment close to the end to discuss "to unsense the subjectile." However, before going so far, so that we may better follow Derrida's thought in "La parole soufflé," I will at least highlight the issue of the concrete sense of *différance* in Derrida's 1968 text, "La différance."[11] This will provide a certain leeway to begin to take up a crucial question behind our discussion: In what sense and to what extent does the thinking of *différance* engage the word in the flesh?

La différance: Concreteness and the Issue of the Body by Detour

If one follows Derrida's essay "*La différance*," it becomes clear that issues of concreteness, body, and flesh, are not extraneous to the thinking of *différance*, and must be sought through the movement of *différance*, that is, in a manner that does not merely repeat the metaphysical identification and treatment of the body and flesh as things or essences separate from thought and words. At the same time, Derrida's discussion of *différance* as the relation to non-being fundamental to the temporalizing-spacing behind all presence exposes us to the general economy of the play of *différance*, that is, it exposes us to the loss and dissemination in the spurring of presence and the name Being. This exposure figures as its central movement the strategic unsettling of the authority of the metaphysics of presence, of signification, and of the name. On the one hand, Derrida's thought is a matter of simulation and strategy,and, on the other hand, it requires a concrete undergoing of the neographism *différance*. Here we encounter an ambiguity in the thinking of *différance*: In the unsettling of signification and the metaphysics of presence through our exposure to the temporalizing interval beyond presence, we find an opening towards the concrete undergoing of thought in the abyssal and disseminating play of *différance*. At the same time, this opening requires a strategic delineation of *différance*, which makes possible the unsettling opening at the limits of metaphysics. Thus, the concreteness, the body and flesh of the unique word (beyond the metaphysics of presence and the difference between sensible and intelligible—beyond body and mind) remains but an insinuation, which must always effect a forced deferral in order to be thought through and in the opening play of *différance*. This is not an occasional aspect of *différance*, but the way thought is undergone in order to be exposed to the limits of the metaphysics of presence through its unsettling.[12]

In spite of this ambiguity or forced deferral, Derrida's closing words indicate the urge towards the concrete undergoing of *différance*: "Such is the question: the alliance of speech and Being in the unique word, in the finally proper name."[13] If the question is that of the alliance of speech and being in the concrete singular mark or trace figured by the proper name, this must occur through the concrete undergoing of *différance*. As we will see and hear, in Derrida, one of the figurations of this proper name, in the alliance of speech and Being, is the name Artaud, which properly experienced will figure, to a certain extent, the single movement of flesh and word in a play of *différance*.

Derrida's Reading of Artaud

The Word in the Flesh Through *Différance*

In "La parole soufflé," written in 1965, the issue that leads Derrida's discussion is precisely the word in the flesh. "Artaud promises the existence of a speech that is a body, of a body that is a theater, of a theater that is a text. . . ."[14] Artaud pursues, ". . . a manifestation which would not be an expression but a pure creation of life, which would not fall far from the body then to decline into a sign or a work, an object. . . ."[15] He goes on, "Artaud attempted to destroy history, the history of the dualist metaphysics . . . the duality of the body and the soul which supports, secretly of course, the duality of speech and existence, of the text and the body. . . ."[16] Then he concludes, "Beating his flesh in order to reawaken it . . . Artaud attempts to forbid that his speech be spirited away [*soufflé*] from his body."[17] In Artaud Derrida finds a specific sensibility of thought: the struggle in the flesh to destroy and think beyond the understanding of identity, word, and work in terms of the metaphysical difference between body and mind.

More specifically, Artaud struggles against a certain economy inherent in all speech. Derrida marks this economy with the word *soufflé*. *Soufflé* means "to blow away," and in this sense refers us to breath and a concrete sense of soul. But here Derrida plays on a more colloquial sense: to use an English figure of speech, the word (*soufflé*) indicates a lifting or theft that occurs with every utterance of a word.[18] ". . . Artaud knew that all speech fallen from the body, offering itself to understanding or reception, offering itself as a spectacle, immediately becomes stolen speech."[19] Derrida immediately goes on to situate in signification the falling away or separation of speech from the body: "[all speech fallen from the body] becomes a signification which I do not possess because it is a signification. Theft is always the theft of speech or text, of a trace."[20] Here, speech, and specifically signification, come to the fore as the sites of struggle, and therefore, flesh and body will be engaged through these issues, and also as inseparable from them.

As we hear immediately after this quote, the theft inherent in speech is not any theft, but one that precedes all moral, economic, and political order. Given that meaning and value arise in the play of signification in speech systems, the theft of speech is the theft of the very possibility of the meaning and value of theft. Thus, the lifting of speech figures the theft of the system that is the possibility of any sense of theft. This leads to a further conclusion: Behind all speech systems occurs a forgetting of that very theft intrinsic to all signification. Derrida discusses this forgetting of the theft of speech immediately after.

"Soufflé . . . inspired by an other voice that itself reads a text older than the text of my body," this is the voice of a prompter (souffleur) who, "ensures the indispensable différance and intermittence between a text already written by another hand and an interpreter already dispossessed of that which he receives."[21] Here, the lifting literally relates to différance. But, we must go slowly in order to hear the whisper of the prompter (souffler), in order to begin to have a sense of the play of différance in the lifting of the theft. Because it is always already fallen from my body, speech is never mine. Furthermore, the interpreter, the I is always already dispossessed of whatever is received. I might add that this includes the interpreter's "body."[22] Thus, Derrida writes:

> I am in relation to myself within the ether of a speech which is always spirited away [soufflé] from me, and which steals from me the very thing that it puts me in relation to. Consciousness of speech, that is to say, consciousness in general is not knowing who speaks at the moment when, and in the place where, I proffer my speech. This consciousness is thus also an unconsciousness.[23]

That consciousness that comes to pass as all senses of being, including the consciousness which delivers me as the I bears a loss in the play of différance. This forgetting figures a loss of the loss (différance) by virtue of which the I and its discourse and body are present and represented in consciousness. The prompter, the play of différance, submerges as consciousness arises through the lifting away of body and speech from loss onto the affirmative logic of presence and the speech of reason. Thus, the lifting in which we find consciousness also figures a moment of erasure, a swift or furtive movement or gesture of a forgetting of forgetting.[24] The moment of erasure indicates a single moment that may be engaged at two levels. At one level, the uncovering of the furtive moment exposes us to the cruel economy of presence and representation that happens in metaphysics, that is, to the theft of body and speech as these are lifted into a discourse of identity and difference in presence. At the same time, at another level, this lifting is not other than the movement of *différance*, the opening of the space-time in which difference and presence come to pass. In the latter sense, and in terms of the general economy of *différance*, we are speaking of the play of nondialectic negativity in all representation and signification, a play that is always beyond representation and signification.

Derrida finds in Artaud a struggle for another consciousness in opposition to this forgetting of the play of *différance*. He goes on, ". . . and this time, consciousness will be cruelly present to itself and will hear itself speak."[25] This new consciousness refers directly to Artaud's theater of cruelty. Derrida explains, "To restore danger by reawakening the stage of cruelty—this was Antonin Artaud's stated intention, at the very least. It is this intention that we will follow here."[26] Thus, Artaud's struggle figures for Derrida the attempt to expose us to the play of *différance* always lifted away and forgotten by speech and text in their signification. More precisely, we are speaking of engaging the play of *différance* in as much as we will be exposed to the cruelty of presence and representation. As the last sentence in the last quote clearly states, it is this exposure to this specific sense of *différance* that Derrida's essay will attempt.

As we have seen, Derrida's essay sets out with the problematic of the word in the flesh and its theft, but then goes on to take up this issue through the loss of the movement of *différance* effected by representational speech. Thus, we now find the issue of flesh and word expressly linked to the very attempt to engage the play of *différance* operative in presence and its differences (including absence). This should occur through our conscious undergoing of the play of *différance*, and not in terms of the separation of body and mind, text and voice. At this point, Derrida's encounter with Artaud has opened a specific sensibility of thought in the very arising of the word in the flesh: Word and flesh are found through thought's exposure to the theft of body and breath underlying our senses of being in terms of presence and consciousness. And through this exposure, we have also begun to have a strategic exposure to the movement of *différance*.

The Flesh Through Extreme Metaphysics

As Derrida explains in his essay, the difference in consciousness between the one whose word and body are stolen and the conscious I who speaks,

is nothing, is furtivity itself: it is the structure of instantaneous
and original elusion [*dérobement*] without which no speech could
ever catch its breath [*soufflé*]. Elusion is produced as the original
enigma, that is to say, as the speech or history (*ainós*) which hides
its history . . . Elusion is the initial unity of that which afterward
is diffracted into theft and dissimulation.[27]

This elusion or deception is the enigma which only in a secondary diffrac-
tion becomes the theft of a body and a speech. This elusion is a substitution
of what Derrida calls in "Différance," the "interval," that is, the relation of
presence to non-being, which occurs as the operative spacing-temporalizing
in all presence and difference. But, as Derrida explains, in the recognition of
the economy of elusion as theft, Artaud has already inserted an individual
body, and in this sense, we find his struggle caught in a metaphysics of subjectivity "powerfully at work in Artaud's thought."[28] This is a metaphysics of
life, in which Artaud contrasts the bad inspiration or spiriting away (*soufflé*)
of his body with the good inspiration of life, of a life force (*force de la vie*).
Which, I must add is not life understood biologically, since the biological
body is already a stolen body, an already organized body.[29] For Artaud the
elusion is not only the theft of speech, but also, and inseparably, of my body.
". . . the simultaneous theft of both my body and my mind: my flesh. If my
speech is no longer my breath (*soufflé*), if my letter is not my speech, this is
so because my spirit was already no longer my body, my body no longer my
gesture, my gesture no longer my life."[30] Ultimately, what is spirited away is
the flesh (*la chair*); and, Derrida finds in this word, "flesh," the gathering of
body and speech in their theft. But he also sees in Artaud a ". . . metaphysics
of the flesh which determines Being as life, and the mind as the body itself,
as unseparable thought. . ."[31] Thus, Derrida engages Artaud's struggle with the
word in the flesh, and specifically the physicality inseparable from Artaud's
thought, by way of the powerful metaphysics of subjectivity at work in Artaud's
work and the specific configuration of a metaphysics of the flesh. This is a
crucial point, since that sense of the flesh so touching and challenging in
the words of Artaud will now be understood through Artaud's metaphysical
thrust or desire. One must at least wonder at this point if Artaud's words
and the spurring desire that drives them are fittingly metaphysical, and to
what extent Artaud's word is engaged as Derrida's concerns with signification,
representation, and the metaphysics of presence situates it. This is not to say
that Derrida does not think with Artaud, but the issue is how he does so.

    Immediately after the last quoted passage, Derrida writes, "This meta-
physics of the flesh is also governed by the anguish of dispossession, the
experience of having lost life, of separation from thought, of the body exiled
far from the mind."[32] In Artaud, this dispossession figures a physical and yet

continuous metaphysical loss: My body has been stolen since birth, and the theft is the work of God, the one who can take, not merely the attributes of a life, but life itself, the life that should be my proper innate being.[33] "By definition, I have been robbed of my possessions, my worth, my value. My truth, what I am worth, has been purloined from me by some One who in my stead became God at the exit from the Orifice, at birth."[34] Birth already means the loss of the proper and innate. After this, falling away from the body becomes the economy of theft and loss. As Derrida indicates, this economy situates Artaud's sense of the work or oeuvre as excrement, as death, and traditional theater as the production of still born works. "The work, as excrement, supposes separation and is produced within separation. The work thus proceeds from the separation of the mind from a pure body." This goes to the extent that Artaud will literally equate writing with excrement: "Writing is trash."[35] Birth as the production of an oeuvre, of an identity, the name, its body: these are but violations of the flesh. And yet here, once again, the metaphysical desperation of Artaud emerges: it is the pure flesh, the integrity of the flesh that is blemished by the excrement that leaves it, and thus perpetuates the violation, the robbery.

Artaud's struggle rejects the theft, the work, the falling away from the proper body. Thus, Artaud has to retain the speech, the work, and the body. What is innate must be retained. Derrida writes, "To keep myself, to keep my body and my speech, I must retain the work within me . . . it must be kept from falling far from my body as writing."[36] This resistance is also bodily, of the flesh. What is proper must not fall away and dissipate. Derrida explains that, with a sense of the proper's theft, and in his resistance, Artaud solicits, shakes metaphysics in raging against the work, the text. But, Artaud also summons metaphysics.[37] His resistance is bodily: "Like excrement, like the turd, which is, as is also known, a metaphor of the penis, the work should stand upright. But the work, as excrement, is but matter without life, without form or force. It always falls and collapses as soon as is outside me. This is why the work will never help me stand up right. I will never be erect in it."[38] But, as Derrida points out, Artaud's physical resistance occurs in a metaphysical register: "Rigid with rage against God, convulsed with anger against the work, Artaud does not renounce salvation. On the contrary soteriology will be the eschatology of one's proper body. . . . One's proper-body-without-detritus."[39] Even at this point, physicality is permeated by the proper. The flesh must stand in its proper place, but the proper is invested in metaphysics; the metaphysics of a closed flesh that closes itself as it seeks its proper erect place. "The reconstitution and reinstitution of my flesh will thus always follow along the lines of my body's closing in on itself."[40] Even here, in the physicality of the struggle despair and anger figure Artaud's metaphysics. Even when his raging screams in terms such as birth, falling from orifices, excrement, penis, erections, these expressions of Artaud bear a direct metaphysical import.[41] In all falling, Derrida reminds us, "I relinquish what is proper to me," and it is this metaphysical obsession with the proper that drives Artaud's strongest words.[42]

In Derrida's essay, these passages are the most directly physical. Derrida seeks to play out the body that is not separate from the word of Artaud. But Derrida engages this physicality as a metaphysics of the flesh. The moments of utmost anguish in their most concrete word configure in Derrida's reading a metaphysics. Derrida's reading rightly indicates the operation of a radical metaphysics in Artaud's thought. Furthermore, as Derrida indicates at the end of his essay, we can say that the separation between metaphysics and madness has been transgressed, and what seems an objective and safe space of difference between reason and its other (the irrational), now opens in a play that unsettles that very comfort.[43] However, Artaud's word bears a sensuous immediacy that the metaphysical rendering does not engage: A sensibility in which Artaud's word is flesh, excrement, blood, birth and death, detritus, and rage in the undergoing of treatment and unimaginable violations. It is as if in engaging Artaud's word through the thrust of metaphysical desire, we remain at a distance from the concrete undergoing of irrecoverable loss and dissemination.

The Word in the Flesh Through a Return to the Text

If we find in Artaud's most explicit words a metaphysics of the flesh, they also elicit an explicit sense of the concreteness of the flesh in the word. This explicit physicality is further intensified as Derrida moves from the metaphysics of the flesh to the textuality of Artaud's word. As Derrida points out, those words we have heard—excrement, orifice, birth, penis, erection, turd, et cetera—are not metaphors for Artaud. As Derrida writes, Artaud cannot be placed among other writers, even Hölderlin or Nietzsche, because the standing upright, the proper stance and place of the flesh, is failed in them by their production of literary works. "The uprightness of the work, to be more precise, is the reign of literality over breath [soufflé]."[44] For Artaud, in those other thinkers, flesh becomes valued only in works. It is the text and not the flesh that makes sense. But Artaud is not simply against text. As Derrida writes, "It is metaphor that Artaud wants to destroy. He wishes to have done with standing upright as metaphorical erection within the written work."[45] Also, "The theatre of cruelty, by killing metaphor . . . pushes us into 'a new idea of danger'. . . ."[46] This raises the question of how we might begin to understand a language that does not aim to be a work or representation. At the same time, this turn against metaphor and toward the question of language brings the issue of the recovery of the flesh back to the issue of the centrality of the text in Western theater and culture in general.

As Derrida explains next, Artaud's fear of the loss of the flesh also figures a fear of an organic differentiation shared by speech and body in their
traditional determinations. In the theater the centrality of the text organizes all
speech around its dominant letter, and in this way actor and director become
organs that perform by repeating and recording a text separate and sovereign
over them.[47] As you might recall from our previous section, this loss of the
breath (*soufflé*) to speech figures the loss of the gesture, the body, and ultimately, the flesh. But Derrida goes on to explain that this organization of the
Western theater around the rule of the central text only follows the general
loss of the body to an analogous economy or organic differentiation.[48] The
body is stolen through the transformation of the concrete flesh in its unity
into body organs, body parts. "Organization is articulation, the interlocking
of functions or of members. . . . This constitutes both a membering and dis-
membering of my proper body . . . Artaud is as fearful of the articulated body
as he is of articulated language, as fearful of the member as of the word. For
articulation is the structure of my body, and structure is always structure of
expropriation. The division of the body into organs, the difference interior
to the flesh, opens the lack through which the body becomes absent from
itself, passing itself off as, and taking itself for, the mind."[49] Body and speech
are lifted away through an articulation that in the case of the body occurs
through a membering that is also a dismembering of the proper flesh or body.
This means that it is this organic differentiation or articulation that must be
resisted. Thus, as Derrida explains, the reconstruction and reinstitution of
my flesh will always require the "reduction of organic structures."[50] At this
point in Derrida's reading, the dismembered organized body is directly linked
to the centrality of the text by virtue of the double function of articulation.
Thus, although Derrida recognizes that for Artaud the body already is lifted
away by the time the text takes its central place in the Western theater, he
goes on to discuss the dismemberment through the problematic of the theater and the centrality of the text. In this way, the issue of the word in the
flesh is returned to the theater of cruelty, and through this, to the issue of
textuality and signification.

Derrida writes in "La parole soufflé," "The initial urgent requirement
of an in-organic theater is emancipation from the text."[51] In other words,
the resistance to the theft of the body through its membering or articulation
goes back to the need for a certain emancipation from the text. He goes on,
". . . in *The Theater and its Double*, protest against the letter had always been
Artaud's primary concern. Artaud initially dreamed of a graphism which
would not begin as deviation, of a nonseparated inscription. . . ."[52] With this
statement Derrida introduces a series of transformations of the word in the
theater, changes that occur as Artaud seeks the word in the flesh in a recovery
of body in speech. The first attempt at a neographism is, ". . . an incarna-

tion of the letter and a bloody tattoo. . . ."[53] Derrida explains that this purely graphic attempt must soon give way to another, since the tattoo paralyzes gesture and silences the voice, which also belongs to the flesh.[54] Hence, we will move from the silent graphic mark to the spoken word. In resisting the silencing of the voice, Artaud's withdrawal of the theater from logocentric domination cannot give it over to silence.[55] Now, speech must be resuscitated but also subordinated. "Without disappearing, speech will now have to keep to its place."[56] This means that the word will no longer lead and define an ordering under a teleology of self-certainty and clarity that must always find clear representation. Rather, while not erased, the word will be a matter of "illegibility" and "illiteracy."[57] As Derrida explains in "The Theater of Cruelty" (1966), Artaud ultimately resists the idea of the word and language specifically in its representational function: "The theater of cruelty is not a representation. It is life itself, in the extent to which life is unrepresentable."[58]

The last two quotes lead us back to the issue of articulation, since the transformation of the word consists in resisting a certain textual intelligibility that sustains the centrality of representation that has ordered and ruled the theater as well as Western culture in general. Derrida gives us a glimpse of this word by contrasting it with the function of the sign. "The depth sought after must thus be the depth of illegibility . . . In theatrical illegibility, in the night that precedes the book, the sign has not yet been separated from force. It is not quite a sign, in the sense in which we understand sign, but is no longer a *thing*, which we conceive only as opposed to the sign. . . ."[59] We are speaking of a word that is neither mute graphism or thing, nor articulate sign or language. In "The Theater of Cruelty," Derrida develops this sense of the word: "How will speech and writing function then? They will become gestures; and the logical and discursive intentions which speech ordinarily uses to insure its rational transparency . . . will be reduced or subordinated. . . ."[60] Further on in the same paragraph, he explains that the word will be, "Glossopoeia, which is neither an imitative language nor a creation of names." Derrida also says that this glossopoeia

> takes us back to the borderline of the moment when the word has not yet been born, when articulation is no longer a shout but not yet a discourse, when repetition is almost impossible, and along with it, language in general. . . .[61]

Speech suggests now a speaking in the play of *différance*, since we are speaking of words uttered in a space between the difference of shouts and discourse, bodily jolt and reasoned articulation, body and mind. The glossopoietic word suggests illegible utterances, illegitimate figures of the flesh and breath, words configured in the undergoing of sensibilities without bodies proper or names, without the allocation of language to presence. But in both essays for Derrida this play of words in the breath still requires a return to the letter, to writing.

Derrida explains in "La Parole Soufflé" that, "Artaud, through a strange movement, disposes the language of cruelty within a new form of writing: the most rigorous, authoritarian, regulated, and mathematical—the most formal form of writing."[62] This is possible because, as I mentioned above, Artaud does not abandon language but only the model of speech and writing as representation.[63] Artaud's neographism will be "the writing of the body itself."[64] This means that this writing will not perform the falling from the body, as do the literary text, works, and excrement. This new writing is done by way of "hieroglyphs."[65] In "The Theater of Cruelty," Derrida explains that hieroglyphic writing is, "the writing in which phonetic elements are coordinated to visual, pictorial, and plastic elements."[66] Thus, we are speaking of a neographism between spoken word and written mark, between voice and text. Here, writing figures not the horizontal and flat language of logic or description, but it is a neographism that bears speech and flesh in an almost inexhaustible play of senses, in what we might call a polydimensional word. "Words will cease to flatten theatrical space and to lay it out horizontally as did logical speech; they will reinstate the 'volume' of theatrical space. . . ." In "The Theater of Cruelty," Derrida quotes from Artaud's *First Manifesto*:

> Once aware of this language in space, language of sounds, cries, lights, onomatopoeia, the theater must organize it into veritable hieroglyphs, with the help of characters and objects, and make use of their symbolism and interconnection in relation to all organs and all levels.[67]

In not letting speech be separated from the body, and in its multidimensionality, this writing figures a fecund word in the flesh.[68]

Artaud's Metaphysics of the Flesh

At this point in "La parole soufflé," Derrida calls the discussion back to Artaud's metaphysical register, and points out that this neographism between the voice and writing, in its polygrammatical play, figures the suture or closing off of the proper flesh. The word in the flesh, the hieroglyph reassembles the flesh into its proper presence. "Discourse can now be reunited with its birth in a perfect and permanent self-presence."[69] Artaud's idea of the hieroglyph ultimately leads towards the accomplishment of the most extreme ambition of Western metaphysics, "self-presence, unity, self identity, the proper."[70]

Derrida concludes the paragraph we have been discussing by saying that Artaud's attempt to find a neographism that does not separate speech and body ends up delivering, "The present knowledge of the proper-past of our speech."[71] In Derrida's analysis Artaud's hieroglyphic markings end up as figures of a metaphysical closure. The flesh that speaks bears with the word the desire for presence. Here, Derrida's discussion traces Artaud's word in the flesh in its extreme prejudice or desire, and, as it happens with Derrida's encounter with Artaud's strongest physical language, once again, the flesh seems to be bound to metaphysics. And, again, we must ask the question: To what extent is Artaud's word in the flesh engaged as it must respond to the issue of a metaphysical desire for subjective presence?

However, for Derrida, the metaphysical hieroglyphs are not mere repetitions of metaphysics. We are certainly not speaking of a forgetting of the cruelty of representation, a mere lifting of the theft, or of a naive repetition of the dialectical difference between mind and body. In "The Theater of Cruelty," Derrida writes: "Here we touch upon what seems to be the profound essence of Artaud's project, his historico-metaphysical decision. Artaud wanted to erase repetition in general."[72] As Derrida argues, at the center of the exposure of representational cruelty and theft, and at the closure of representation through these, lies the unsettling of dialectical difference and its naïve repetition. This is why Derrida writes in "La parole soufflé" that with Artaud's writing made flesh, the present is gathered as, "seen, mastered, terrifying and pacifying."[73] Artaud's neographism—the word in the flesh figures, exposes, bares, plays out the cruel economy of the theft, of representation, and is played out in it. In order to understand and begin to undergo the movement indicated in this last quote, we will have to touch on the closing paragraphs of Derrida's "La parole soufflé."

In the last paragraph Derrida writes: "Artaud keeps himself at the limit, and we have attempted to read him at this limit."[74] Immediately, he goes on to indicate the various levels figured by Artaud's words at the limit. First of all, in his raging attack against the tradition, he exposes the tradition to the difference, alienation, and negativity inherent in the determinations of reality.[75] This is also a denunciation of the theft, the cruelty inherent in the metaphysics of presence.[76] At a second level, this happens through the summoning of metaphysics that ultimately, "fulfills the most profound and permanent ambition of Western metaphysics."[77] Artaud's neographism, ultimately, gathers the flesh and word in a single hieroglyph of self-presence. But these aspects of Artaud's thought only frame the crucial movement behind them. Derrida goes one step further to point out the most complex level in the reading.

Artaud's thought unfolds in these various ways as it undergoes the economy of metaphysics. Here, we touch on the play of *différance*, as we encounter a necessary rule at play in the very delimitation of the limit: Artaud's thought, and any thought involved in the destruction of the metaphysics of presence, must be involved in the cruelty of presence. Thus, Derrida finds that in engaging Artaud's works, "we are actually delimiting a fatal complicity. Through this complicity is articulated a necessary dependency of all destructive discourses: they must inhabit the structures they demolish, and within them they must shelter an indestructible desire for full presence, for nondifference: simultaneous life and death. Such is the question we have attempted to pose."[78] In other words, Artaud's metaphysics is not other than the figure of a necessity in deconstructive thought, the need for it to undergo its desire for absolute presence and self-representation. Words, and even the neographisms, in their very passage will always bear the desire and risk of returning to metaphysics.[79] This metaphysical (and subjective) tendency warrants the strategic thinking of *différance*: The ever present risk of falling back into metaphysics bears our need for a strategic vigilance that will play out—expose and unsettle, the secret theft of presence. To put it in the terms Derrida uses to discuss the strategic delineation of the thinking of *différance* in "Différance": We require a strategy that will bring representation to bear its relation to not being, thus unsettling the strictures of the metaphysics of presence. Thus, Derrida concludes his essay by indicating that we are now posed by an enigma, an enigma that must keep us vigilant and this means in the play of *différance*: The enigma of the flesh that desires to be properly named.[80] As we will see now, if we follow Derrida a step further, pushing towards the word in the flesh, we will go beyond his strategic reading, perhaps, even transgressing his thought.

Conclusion: Thinking . . . an Act of Life

In contrast to what I have just concluded, although altogether too briefly, we might close by developing further the concrete sense of Derrida's reading of Artaud. In order to do so, we will have to move ahead for a moment to his essay from 1986, "to unsense the subjectile."[81] I believe this is the piece in which Derrida takes up, in the most direct way, the issue of the concreteness or physicality of Artaud's language. As the central word in the title of his essay indicates, in it Derrida discusses "subjectile," a term used in three crucial occasions by Artaud with respect to his written-drawn language. For example, his statement about a bad drawing in 1932 "Herewith a bad drawing in which what is called the subjectile betrayed me."[82] As Derrida indicates, subjectile is an untranslatable term. And yet it does refer to the Latin phrase "*subjecta materia*" and the Greek *hypokeimenon hule*. Thus, in his essay Derrida unfolds a reading of the subject matter or underlying matter of Artaud's hieroglyphs. As Derrida explains, the everyday sense of subjectile may include a work of art's substance, subject, and the matter to be painted or sculpted; but at the same time, it also may mean the support or surface of a work. He then goes further and points out that the subjectile figures neither of these single elements but an operative movement between subject matter and object or support. The subjectile is nothing but the spacing between the intransitivity of being-thrown (as may be the case with a surface or given subject matter) and the transitivity of throwing (as may be drawing, writing). Derrida states:

> Everything will play itself out from now on in the critical but precarious difference, unstable and reversible, between these two. . . . Thrown throwing, the subjectile is nothing, however, nothing but the solidified interval between above and below, visible and invisible, before and behind, this side and that.[83]

Indeed, the subjectile figures not a space in between matter and support, but the dynamic spatio-temporal movement of *différance*.[84] Furthermore, as the phrase "solidified interval" already indicates, it is precisely as the concrete operation of *différance* that Derrida will discuss Artaud's written-drawing.

As a thrown throwing the subjectile figures a synergetic movement. And, as Derrida explains, for him literally this movement involves the trajectory of "a crossing between painting and drawing, drawing and verbal writing."[85] This crossing not only bears the transgression and undoing of the separation between writing, drawing, and speaking, but, in more general terms, it cuts across the separation of the arts of space and the others, and ultimately, between space and time.[86] This last formulation calls us again to the concrete and ephemeral quivering that is the dynamic concrete interval in undergoing *différance*.[87] The undergoing of this movement figures a destabilization and thus dissemination of sense and of the senses: as the putting forth of the hieroglyph in its transgressive cross movement of writing-drawing-speaking destabilizes the stable propositional and categorial structures which sustain sense in terms of a metaphysics of presence and of an impermeable self-determined discursive subjectivity. But, here we also find a much more direct indication of the concrete unfolding of this movement as figured in the hieroglyph. Derrida writes: "Pictography is to be taken literally here."[88]

As he explains, Artaud's mark is that he brings to writing-drawing a glossolalia—that is letter transcribed phonemes that do not follow the syntactic, semantic, or phonetic requirements of language.[89] Thus these utterances, inseparable from the drawn writing, unsettle the text by unsensing even the elemental claim to syllabic groups. While, at the same time these phonemes put into play beyond its claim any attempt to represent, since the representation is also violated, trespassed in the impossibility of finding allocation for the vocal locution. In short, we are speaking of "A glossolalia that suspends the representative value of language and interrupts the representative description of a painting."[90] At this point, one might think only of Artaud; but many other figures crowd the discussion. For example, the work of Cy Twombly, whose markings are often inseparable from writing, and, whose titles, since the beginning of his career, have often arisen through the onomatopoetic playing with the movement of line and color and mood in the paintings or drawings. One may also think of the physicality in Paul Celan's language, a language much inspired by his wive's nonlinguistic graphic works.[91] But one may also think of the markings, animal fat smearing, and bodily traces in the work of Joseph Beuys. Particularly because Derrida will go one step further in his discussion, and make clear that in speaking of this crossing and transgression in Artaud's drawing-writing-voicing we are not referring to a self-contained voice and breath:

> To draw with his mouth, this isn't just giving it his voice, his breath, and his language before any words, it is rather attacking the support with these solid, incisive of grinding instruments that are the teeth, it is eating up, sometimes spitting out the subjectile, the "thing," if we can say it like that, as much as its glossomatic body or its phonogram.[92]

Here we encounter the physicality in the disseminating movement of *différance*, as we engage Artaud's hieroglyphs in concrete crossings . . . the dissemination of sense beyond metaphysics occurs in undergoing the concrete and ephemeral arising to presence of senses of being, of bodies, and of selves. And this is a thought that must be an act of life, a thought undergone in the unfolding of sense through a language that is an act of life . . . marking, attacking, caressing, cutting, scratching, piercing, biting, spitting, swallowing, salivating, with teeth and the stroke of the tongue[93], stomach and gut . . . remarkably on the verge of words. . . . Here a series of questions open up. Echoing Gadamer's crucial point in his reading of Paul Celan's *Stehen*, where he states that for Celan even when one is without language, "there is already language," one might ask if in having gone thus far with Artaud we are not still with language.[94] In turn this question leads us to ask ourselves about our understanding of the limits and delimitations of language. Also, in light of engaging the traversing and disseminating physicality of Artaud's hieroglyphs, can we still stand in strategic vigilance with our words, exercising in our words the distance between words and language over against phonocentrism, subjectivity, and the metaphysics of presence? Must we take this vigilant stance? And if we must, are we not fated, inscribed, lifted by the letter and voice of transcendental subjectivity and an onto-theological economy of presencing, although no longer as representing it?

I have stayed with Derrida's later text in order to make a strong contrast between the strategic vigilance required for the unsettling of transcendental philosophy and the metaphysics of presence, and the concrete undergoing of thought that becomes possible when one thinks with Derrida. On the one hand, if we were to continue reading Derrida's later text, we would find that the physicality we began to encounter remains part of Derrida's strategic reading and thinking. Ultimately, these passages I have discussed are referred back to a nondialectic operation; hence, the undergoing of the word in the flesh is re-inscribed under the unsettling strategic play of *différance*.[95] Indeed, in Derrida's essay, such words as cutting, sewing, shredding, will become functions of the operation of *différance*.[96] This is not surprising when one considers Derrida's early reading of Artaud. The difficulty with the strategic disposition is that in engaging Artaud's words in a way that exposes us to the need for the vigilant strategy of *différance* we never undergo the physicality of the configuration of words figured by Artaud's hieroglyph. Derrida's reading unsettles and exposes metaphysics and representation; it transgresses the limits of metaphysics (by exposing it to its desire beyond its very boundaries). But strategic thinking does not configure a word in the flesh.[97] Rather, it spurs a certain strategic vigilance that must sustain an enigmatic distance between speech and flesh.[98] As we have indicated through our discussion, this occurs as Artaud's neog-raphism is engaged through the play of *différance*. Derrida's words, as well as our thinking are not excrement, blood, skin, marrow and nerve; most of us do not take up thought in words and language out of scratching, biting, and spitting half-digested sounds out. As we set out, I think that most of us are concerned with transcendental subjectivity, phonocentrism, metaphysics, representation, repetition, textuality, and signification . . . even when speaking of the other. . . . Ironically, we are played out in the lifting of breath and voice, as the words that sustain the unsettling strategy and afford us exposure to the concrete and ephemeral passage of thought in its temporality or finitude keep us at a certain distance from undergoing our thought in a manner analogous to Artaud's word in the flesh. Derrida's discussion suggests that this vigilant distance is a required element for thought. I would say that to a certain extent thought in certain occasions will require such vigilance; at least in as much as language is identified with words and signification in terms of transcendental subjectivity and Western onto-theological metaphysics.

On the other hand, in following Derrida's path, we have come some-what beyond the strategic vigilance that sustains Derrida's lifelong encounters with Artaud. I must emphasize, I do not think that vigilance and a thought that is a living act are mutually exclusive; and I do think at times these are inseparable. But must our vigilance be guided and thus configured solely in light of vigilance against transcendental subjectivity and the onto-theological tradition? Perhaps, the strategic vigilance may give way to a thinking that is an affirmative act of life; that is, once we expose ourselves and our discourses to transgressions already at play in our concrete and ephemeral undergoing of thought's nascent movement in language. Indeed, Derrida's later text leads us to a sense of language that in its physicality is no longer *per forza* about signification, words, even syllables. And yet, the spacing of the subjectile figures the undergoing of nascent language and thought arising in concrete and ephemeral movements. Derrida's discussion of Artaud under the rules of the game of *différance* exposes us to the other side of the metaphysical delimitation of the word, and in doing so also calls for a new sensibility in thought—for a thinking in the flesh, which we have not yet undergone.[99] With *différance* and on the other side of its vigilant delimitation, we must seek other registers of the word in the flesh. Derrida's vigilant strategic thought is an opening to configurations of thought that do not require Derrida's singular discipline. Through our juxtaposition of Derrida's thought and Artaud's word in the flesh, we have not merely repeated deconstruction: now thought is opened to a sensibility that calls for neographisms wrought in the undergoing and withstanding of the flesh in registers and sensibilities that, without forgetting desire, cruelty, and risk, overwhelm even the strategic disposition behind *différance*. I am speaking of a sensibility of thought that occurs as thought comes to figure a living act, a movement scratched—burnt on the surface of its desire; and as in this marking, in cruel and exposed awareness, we undergo thought's nascent singular and concrete movement in our marrow, nerve, breath and flesh. Such is the question in which we are posed.[100]

PART III

Unbounded Finitudes: Thought's Sensibility in Art and the Political

With our encounters with the ephemeral, the tactile, and the bodily senses of words, and in light of them, we are now in the position to return to specific configurations of senses of being. In this section, we will discuss three specific issues concerning the configuration of the senses of the human. The point is to attend to human freedom beyond the economy of machination; so that in having begun from Heidegger's critique of modernity in his encounter with thought's finitude, we will now return to our situation in light of the sensibility of thought that we explored and developed as we engaged language as word and medium of exposure and possibility for the unbounded and unbounding undergoing of the senses of being. Again, as in the last section, and the book in general, nothing exhaustive can be pretended if one seeks to think in departure from the finitude of thought and the configurations of senses of being out of and through their finitude. However, the three issues at hand are figures of the experiencing of sense through the sensibility of a thought that exposes itself to its finitude and that in doing so situates our sense of humanity in its open and unbounded possibility. The three ciphers towards such opening in the following chapters are: the work of art as political and yet non-ideological; the concept of Spirit in Hegel and its unfolding through two other openings towards humanity that cannot be dialectically subsumed under Hegel's project; and, a sense of the political situated in the fine threads of our concrete finitude, which in their ephemeral and almost tacit passages hold together the object of larger political and institutional discourse.

CHAPTER 9

The Sensibility of Art in its Finitude

Undergoing the Disaster Through Benjamin's "Politics of Art"

When Theodor Adorno made his famous remark that after Auschwitz and the atomic bomb there was no more room for poetry or art, he raised a question about the possibility and the necessity of giving articulation to negativity.[1] That the disaster cannot be said by art does not mean that it does not happen, or that it must become our best kept secret or mystery, nor does it mean that the work of art should disappear. On the contrary, once poetry and the forms that give meaning to art prove to be useless, our task becomes that of finding an articulation in that delimitation of our existence as it is marked by the disaster. But how is one to understand this? In order to begin to address this question, I discuss in this chapter one of the specific works that Adorno mentions critically when he articulates the issue in 1967, namely, Walter Benjamin's reply to this necessity for the articulation of experience in our time in "The Work of Art in the Age of Mechanical Reproduction" (*Das Kunstwerk im Zeitalter seiner technischen Reproduzierbarkeit*).[2] According to Benjamin, we may find a new possible aesthetic as a politics of art in film and through its mode of mechanical reproduction.[3] In order to develop this idea, and following my discussion of Benjamin's essay, I discuss how the disaster finds nonrepresentational articulate form in *Hiroshima Mon Amour* by Marguerite Duras and Alain Resnais. A film that, in the awareness of the impossibility of saying the disaster or representing it, not only seeks to have us undergo it, but that ultimately, as I argue, exposes us to a certain sensibility essential to the experience of the sense and possibility of the political for us today. As we will see, ultimately, Benjamin's thought offers an alternative to Adorno's rationalist dialectic, as well as to Heidegger's sense of reproduction as machination, that is, as the limit point which must be overcome in order to arrive at the destiny of the history of Western thought.

The Revolutionary Aesthetics of Film in Walter Benjamin's "The Work of Art in the Age of Mechanical Reproduction"

The Politics of the Work of Art

At the beginning of "The Work of Art in the Age of Mechanical Reproduction," Walter Benjamin situates the revolutionary character of the work of art neither in genius nor in eternal values or mysteries. Rather, he takes a step towards the articulation of it in its concrete situation, when he takes up the way the sense of the art work is transformed through the advent of its mechanical reproduction.[4] As is the case for Adorno, for Benjamin the work of art must pass through a finite moment in order to become part of "art."[5] In this sense, rather than taking the work of art as an ontologically meaningful experience, he seeks the experience in which the sense of the work arises. Although both philosophers agree that the arising of the work of art in its concrete singularity occurs as a social political experience, for Benjamin the issue is the force of the mode of representation, rather than a dialectic between production and subject.[6] In his essay Benjamin understands the singular moment of the work of art in terms of a change in the mode or conditions of production of the work, that is, through the development of mechanical reproduction and the aesthetic experiences the medium affords us beyond the naked eye.[7]

In the introduction's last paragraph Benjamin writes, "The concepts which are introduced into the theory of art in what follows differ from the more familiar terms in that they are completely useless for the purposes of Fascism. They are, on the other hand, useful for the formulation of revolutionary demands in the politics of art."[8] Indeed, both the introduction and the epilogue to the essay situate the issue of the work of art in direct relation to the political, and specifically to Fascism. As Benjamin explains in the epilogue, Fascism introduces aesthetics into politics by making politics aesthetic (*die Ästhetisierung der Politik*).[9] This occurs through a double gesture: the denial of the transformation of property relations that is the right of the masses, and the implantation of the expression of the masses as the production of cult or ritual-values (*Kultwerten*).[10] Thus, the masses are caught in an economy which allows for empty expression, since it occurs without the transformation of property relations.[11] In this economy of expression the work of art appears as the production of ritual value in the sense that it appears as an image at a distance, which is valued as the object of fetish for the ritual, an object that can be viewed but neither touched nor transformed. We can refer to a wide range of examples of this system of oppression that range from the original works preserved at the museum, to the powerful images in Leni Riefenstahl's technically masterful propaganda films, to the distinct nationalist and god fearing cheer of the enslaved masses of today.[12]

Another way to articulate the aesthetics of fascism is by looking at the production of what Benjamin calls ritual values through the Marxist analysis of the alienation of labor. When we do so, we see how this ritual value production results in an ontological aura behind the traditional idea of the work's value as an "original" (*der einzigartige Wert des "echten" Kunstwerks . . .*).[13] When the work and worker are separated, value is given to the work, and the worker with his/her modes of production comes to be understood as secondary and dependant on the value of the work produced. This separation results in the valuation of the result over the labor, and through such valuation the work acquires a kind of ontological aura, as it is understood as a value in itself, and finally as a metaphysical essence, or at least as an ontologically independent entity. In turn, the worker is transformed into an individual subject who also has a value separate from social praxis. The aura of the work only becomes more explicit in the work of art, since in our culture the work of art is the object of contemplation, the object that is never subject to transformation (it must be the original) and at the same time always the symbol or measure of existence in its purest form. As a result, we never experience the work of art directly but only as value removed from life, a mystical object, an object of fetish.[14] Furthermore, this way of encountering the work of art secures an experience that occurs always through an established distance from the work. Benjamin writes, "The definition of the aura as a 'unique phenomenon of a distance however close it may be' represents nothing but the formulation of the cult value of the work of art in categories of space and time perception."[15] For Benjamin this rendering of politics aesthetic figures a distancing of the sense and possibility of history and work from their concrete living sense. In his essay, he proposes a challenge to this situation through an entirely different experience of the work of art, which, in Benjamin's words, will figure the politics of art (*die Kunstpolitik*).[16]

Benjamin's phrase, "the politics of art," does not mean that art must choose new symbols or emblems for the furthering of a certain ideology; that is, it does not mean that the work of art must produce new ritual values. Without transforming the mode of existence of the symbol, this would simply repeat the way politics is rendered aesthetic by fascism. Benjamin's aim is to recognize a sense of the aesthetic that is radically different from fascism. With his analysis of the change in modes of production, Benjamin seeks to introduce a new aesthetic sense, which, in transforming the way worker relates to the work, would transform the ideological symbolic functions (the production of ritual values) of the work of art. Such transformation in the relation of work and audience would ultimately transform the sense of their political and lived existence. In other words, Benjamin's aim is to introduce a different sense of the work of art and of the political, one that results out of a new aesthetic experience arisen through the development of mechanical reproduction. Here, we are speaking of an aesthetics divorced from the aura of the work of art as an object of contemplation kept at a distance and informed by some obscure force or meaning, as situated by the production of ritual value.[17] Although Benjamin's politics of art do not repeat the fascist aestheticizing of the political, Benjamin's aesthetic is ultimately political, both, because the work and its experience arise from a shift in the modes of production, and also, because of its hoped effect for society.

As Susan Buck-Morse explains, Benjamin follows Adorno's idea of the transformation of society through the analysis of the work of art. As she explains, the change happens through *ars inveniendi*, that is, in the discovery of the social structure in a particular configuration. This occurs through an immersion in particularity or empirical existence: the subject enters into the object and transforms it in a manner that situates the subject onto its social parameters, thus, no longer in a subjective and passive disposition. This unsettling of subjectivity happens through an act of exact fantasy: Where subject and object are held in their dialectic relation, and through this critical relationship the elements of the social parameter are reconfigured through an interpretative rearrangement.[18]

Here arises the question of the function of the work of art as symbol or image. Does Benjamin's thesis suggest that all symbols are destined to have a cult value, and therefore, are destined to serve the same function they serve in fascist aesthetics? In order to understand how symbols may function otherwise, we must look at Benjamin's understanding of the character and role of the symbol in experience. When we do so, we see that for him the symbol is neither a signifier of unchanging concepts, nor does it preclude a fascist aesthetics. Rather, depending on its mode of production, it can have different functions, including its being a site for the transformation of aesthetic experience. Let us for a moment think back to Benjamin's writing about perception in "Über die Wahrnehmung."[19] In this brief text about Kant's theory of knowledge and the understanding of the experience of nature, Benjamin indicates a differentiation between experience (nature), and knowledge of experience (our experience of nature). In light of this differentiation we can say that *aisthesis*—the experience of nature—is not merely experience (nature) but knowledge of nature. As a result of this differentiation, Benjamin is able to treat *aisthesis* as knowledge. But knowledge for him is always situated by a symbolic system, and more specifically, in language (understood as a symbolic system). Therefore, to speak of an aisthetic experience is to speak of an experience given as a modality of and in the context of the symbolic system of language.[20] With this argument Benjamin situates *aisthesis* in the realm of concrete experience, as understood by materialist critique; that is, in the sense that *aisthesis*, as part of a symbolic modality, is not intuited knowledge, but it is subject to the transformations of the symbolic system. And, such transformation in the symbolic system will occur when the modes of its production change.[21] Thus, we can translate this materialist view of *aisthesis* to the case of the aesthetic experience of the work of art, and say that, the experience of the work of art depends on the transformation of a system of symbols, and that such system is transformed as the modalities of production are transformed. Thus, Benjamin explains, in his essay on the work of art, that a painting will allow for a ritual contemplation that a film, with its montage and change in views, space, and speed, will not allow. As a result, the symbol in film should come to be read differently, or, as Benjamin specifically suggests, with a certain disarming distraction that would ruin the possibility of having it function as the object of a ritual and fetish.[22] Furthermore, if the symbolic system is transformed through the film form (through its mode of production), then film offers a system of symbols that redefine the very character of the aesthetic experience.[23] In short, for Benjamin the film image carries with it the possibility of functioning otherwise than as a cult value; and, in its different function, the image also affords us an opening towards a new aesthetic experience.

For Benjamin, the effect of this new experience is the release of the masses to their transformative force through the exposure of a fundamental aesthetic experience that not only does not coincide with the fascist function of the work of art, but that in being useless to it, can ruin the aesthetic politics of fascism.[24] Benjamin writes, "For the first time . . . man has to operate with his whole living person, yet forgoing its aura."[25] The aura that dissolves is the metaphysical identification of the work of art with an ontological status and with the creation or genius of a subject or actor behind the work. As Benjamin explains, with reproduction the image has become portable, it has been separated from any ontological original or content, and in this way quality has lost value to quantity, and has become the matter of the masses. In the last section of the essay Benjamin concludes that, "The mass is a matrix which all traditional behavior toward works of art issues today in a new form. Quantity has been transmuted into quality. The greatly increased mass of participants has produced a change in the mode of participation."[26] This passage explains how reproduction has transformed the way we understand the work of art, and how, in its dissemination of the image, it causes the shift with the masses and the political. However, this does not yet say anything about how today, man has to operate "with his whole living being" (*mit seiner gesamten lebendingen Person*). Ultimately, the change in the mode of production bares a transformation of the aesthetic sense of the world, and with this, should follow a renewed experience of life through a transformation of the very way property, work, and subject are to be understood by society. In order to understand this transformation we will have to look further into the new sense of aesthetic experience that Benjamin seeks to open.

The Shocking Immediacy of the Work of Art

If in his analysis of the work of art Benjamin refers directly to film as the medium that sets a new path towards a politics of art, the appeal in film is certainly not this or that style; for example Riefenstahl's development of a certain look which comes to be identified as fascist aesthetics.[27] Rather, what is at issue is the appearing of the subject and the work as afforded by the medium—film, as mechanical reproduction. According to Benjamin, with its mechanical detachment film sets up a new aesthetic. Benjamin writes that the camera lens "reveals entirely new structural formations of the subject."[28] And, that "a different nature opens itself to the camera than to the naked eye—if only because an unconsciously penetrated space is substituted for a space consciously explored by man. . . . The camera introduces us to unconscious optic experience (*zu einer Optisch-Unbewußten Erfahrung*)."[29] Just like psychology makes accessible and analyzable a whole realm of experience heretofore unnoticed in the broad realm of perceptions, film, says Benjamin, "has brought about a similar deepening of apperception (*Apperzeption*)."[30] This does not only mean that our experience of our subjective self and the world have been transformed by film, as we come to inhabit our empirical or singular social parameters. In this transformation, we have begun to undergo a new aesthetic experience, an unconscious optic experience at play in the configuration of our knowledge of world, self, and work of art. Apperception here does not indicate a transcendental consciousness untouched by empirical data, as is the case in Kant. But the term does follow Kant as it indicates that the configuration of the subject requires, in Kant's words, "a consciousness which precedes all data of intuition."[31] Apperception refers to the physical unconscious structure in which something like the subject can be configured. In light of this, we can assume that when Benjamin speaks of man operating with his whole living being, he means that these elements of apperception, these unconscious optic experiences, have become in some way accessible and analyzable for us through the experience of film. If this is the case, then we must go a step further than Benjamin, and without letting go of the way the mode of production transforms existence, we must ask about these new structural formations of the subject, about this unconscious apperception, and ultimately, about the configuration of the politics of art which occurs in undergoing such experience through film as a work of art.

Benjamin takes a last step towards these new experiences by explaining how Dada accomplishes the destruction of the aura of the work of art. Dada's works operate as a studied relentless degradation of its materials, which emphasize the uselessness of the work rather than its value (in contrast to the fascist idealization of the work as a site of contemplation and ultimately worship).[32] The work of art in dada is not an object of contemplation but a center of scandal, the site of public outrage.[33] This outrage is not a mere effect, but it situates the audience in relation to the mode of work of the work of art, and does so as a physical shock, that is, by the work striking the audience.[34] The work of Dada operates as a bullet, says Benjamin, that is, not as something to be viewed at a safe distance but as an immediate experience that ultimately hits by acquiring "a tactile quality" (*eine taktile Qualität*).[35] As Benjamin immediately explains, it is this tactile and dynamic character that distinguishes film. He concludes: "By means of its technical structure, the film has taken the physical shock effect out of the wrappers in which Dadaism had, as it were, kept it inside the moral shock effect."[36] Indeed, film goes further than Dadaist art works in that it presses and brings to the fore the physicality of the shock; a shock that results from and through film's technical structure.

This means that ultimately the aesthetic sense we find in film occurs not as an experience of an already configured image at a distance, a symbol that can be an object of fetish and ritual value. This is what Benjamin indicates when he says that, "The concept of aura which was proposed above with reference to historical objects may usefully be illustrated with reference to the aura of natural ones. We define the aura of the latter as the unique phenomenon of a distance, however close it may be."[37] This also suggests that film will not represent our aesthetic experience, since film will violate the distance that would allow for such view at arm's length. Benjamin also writes, "On the tactile side there is no counterpart to contemplation in the optical side. Tactile appropriation is accomplished not so much by attention as by habit."[38] Tactility indicates the immediacy of the experience of the work of art, an immediacy given beyond and outside the limits of contemplative distance, or representation, and yet an experience given through a praxis (through habit). Benjamin also indicates the immediacy of the aesthetic experience when he points out the shift from the photographic portrait—the last form of the aura as the emphasis on the face in art turns in mechanical reproduction to the whole living body.[39] We should keep in mind that here appears a contrast between Adorno's idea of a linguistic dialectic between subject and object, and Benjamin's since of something like an embodied transformation.

Through the work of the lens and montage we may experience more than an already constituted symbol and its aura. The auditory and visual elements of the film form go beyond the grasp of a subject's individual eye or a sense of aesthetic experience oriented towards an object already given as an individual, determinate, and self-enclosed identity:

> With the close-up, space expands; with slow motion, movement is extended . . . the act of reaching for a lighter or a spoon is familiar routine, yet we hardly know what really goes on between hand

and metal, not to mention how this fluctuates with our moods. Here the camera intervenes with the resources of its lowering and lifting. . . .[40]

Through such technical effects as camera movement, the close-up, and slow motion, with their multiple fragmentation, and through montage, with its disruption of sequential time, we experience an immediate sense of image and sound.[41] Film, with its fragmentation, exposes and opens the senses to their unconscious optic and auditory experience in which the image as a unit is configured, and before the image has been resolved as a single unit. While the film form makes the aura of the fascist symbol impossible, it also exposes us to the fine multiplicity of spaces and experiences of temporality in which something like a complete image is configured. This proximity, this immediacy, this aesthetic experience in the flesh, rather than at a distance, is what Benjamin indicates when he recognizes the tactile shock of the film.

The Time of the Shock

Benjamin's understanding of the work of art as a shock links film to the heart of his understanding of history in the materialistic sense.[42] In his later work, "Theses on the Concept of History" ("Über der Begriff der Geschichte"), written in 1940, Benjamin writes that for materialistic history, "Thinking involves not only the flow of thoughts, but their arrest (*Stillstellung*) as well."[43] As opposed to a universal idea of history as an infinite accumulation of time, for Benjamin it is a certain arrest or most intense sense of the moment that characterizes the work of materialist critique. He then goes on to explain, "Where thinking suddenly stops in a configuration pregnant with tensions, it gives that configuration a shock, by which it crystallizes into a monad. A historical materialist approaches a historical subject only where he encounters it as a monad. In this structure he recognizes the sign of a Messianic cessation of happening, or, put differently, a revolutionary chance in the fight for the oppressed past. He takes cognizance of it in order to blast a specific life out of the era or a specific work out of the lifework."[44] Mechanical reproduction figures such moment of explosive revolution, since it figures a cessation of the universal that will transfigure an entire historical era. Here the shock is not ontologically significant a priori. It is not a matter of engaging the temporality of things, as is the case in Heidegger's *Being and Time* for example.[45] Benjamin concludes, "The nourishing fruit of the historically understood contains time as a precious but tasteless seed."[46] The sense of time is accomplished through the undergoing of the singular concrete moment, a moment that is singular not because it belongs to the individual subject and its aura, but because it is a necessary and concrete passage through which experience and sense are configured. One of Benjamin's points about mechanical reproduction is that individuality gives way to mass consciousness. But, here is Benjamin's critical insight, this does not preclude that this mass consciousness cannot be given through concrete and ephemeral experiences, hence through the singularity of the moment. Furthermore, this singularity of the moment does not point outside the critical emphasis of Benjamin's work, but it indicates an elemental part of the moment.

In the case of film, the arising of the sense of the aesthetic comes to pass out of the mode of production which exposes us to a singular transformation of the very sense of the work of art, and hence, of the life of human beings. But to say that this singular transformative shock makes for the operation of man's whole living being would be to jump too far ahead. Benjamin closes his discussion of Dada and film by saying that this shock, "like all shocks, should be cushioned by heightened presence of mind."[47] This presence of mind certainly refers to the articulate undergoing of the moment. But if this is the case, we must go on to articulate that tactile or immediate experience in the flesh in which our subjectivity, the work, and its politics are configured; since only then we will begin to have a sense of the experience of living as whole living beings, and will begin to engage that crucial moment in Benjamin's materialist critique of the work of art.

In what remains of our discussion, I explore the immediate aesthetic experience of the work of art in its shocking politics by looking at a film, specifically, at the very beginning of Marguerite Duras's and Alain Resnais's *Hiroshima Mon Amour*; a film which, as probably many readers know, and as the title indicates, by no means avoids the social-political context of the work of art but rather takes it up, explores it, and exposes us to it.

Hiroshima Mon Amour

Another way to understand Benjamin's turn from a politics made aesthetic to the politics of art is by looking at the way form and content are engaged in the discussion of the work of art as encountered through mechanical reproduction. That the work of art is understood in terms of the mode of its production means that the form of the work as given in that particular mode of production is separated from the idea of a content that should inform the sense of the work. Indeed, this separation of content from form is apparent in Benjamin's essay in terms of a certain loss of the mystic aura that sustains fascist aesthetics, a loss that occurs with the advent of the cinema and its mechanical reproduction. The mysterious fetish content of ritual value gives way to fragmentation and dissemination. However, the separation of mode of production from content does not mean that the work of art is meaningless. On the contrary, if form is recognized in its historical origination, in the historical materialist sense, the content of the experience of the work of art must be found out of the mode of production. Thus, content is given through the historical configuration of a particular form, in this case film and the aesthetic experience that is opened by it. In order to understand then the sense of film as an introduction to a politics of art, we will have to recognize first of all the aesthetic experience that is given by the specific form of the cinema, and then, we will have to at least indicate provisionally, how this experience might orient the politics of art. Furthermore, in looking for the aesthetic experience in which something like the politics of art occurs, we will have to look at that immediate, tactile, physical shock to which, according to Benjamin, film exposes us. Thus, we are seeking to engage an experience before the already configured image that may be viewed and worshiped at a distance, we seek a proximate experience in which the image is configured and open to transformation. Let us take up these two questions in the case of *Hiroshima Mon Amour*, beginning from the immediate experience of the aesthetic in the flesh.

Any balanced discussion of *Hiroshima Mon Amour* would require a much more extensive treatment than what is possible here. In what follows, I only show that in the famous opening sequence of the film we find a recovery of the sense of Hiroshima—a reconfiguration of the political through the aesthetics of film. Duras explains in the film's synopsis that the film concerns Hiroshima as rediscovered through the banal embrace of two lovers.[48] The opening sequence is made up of a montage, in which shots from the documentary made the day after the detonation of the bomb are juxtaposed with images of museums and public places in contemporary Hiroshima, and with shots of the two lovers' bodies. The sequence moves from the first indeterminate shot of flesh covered with dew or ashes to its conclusion when the faces of the two lovers and their embrace appear. What interests me here is specifically the recovery of Hiroshima through the experience of that embrace, an embrace that is configured through this first montage sequence of the film. I take this specific sequence as an example of the recovery of the political through an aesthetic experience radically different from the production of ritual value, or the object of fetish, particularly in terms of how Hiroshima is rediscovered through the shock of film in this first sequence. Ultimately though, I would like to go a step further, and at least suggest that through this brief engagement with this film we begin to see that certain works of art expose thought to its finitude, that is—to its ephemeral and concrete passages; and, that it is in undergoing such exposure to thought's finite singularity in the flesh that we find in thought the leeway for our understanding and recovery of the politics of art and the concrete possibility of freedom that Benjamin seeks in his essay.[49] In other words, what follows begins to articulate the concrete and ephemeral singularity in which our sense of subject, world, and politics as ideologies is founded, in order to recognize a fundamental element to be critically articulated.[50]

Hiroshima, Beyond Saying or Representation

As Duras also states in her synopsis, "Hiroshima," the experience of the detonation of the atomic bomb cannot, be said nor represented. She writes in her synopsis, "Impossible to talk about Hiroshima. All one can do is talk about the impossibility of talking about Hiroshima. The knowledge of Hiroshima being stated a priori by an exemplary delusion of the mind."[51] The first minutes of the film indicate this much. Two voices speak over the montage of cuts of the documentary from the day after the explosion enmeshed with images of the city in 1959, as well as with images that by the end of the sequence prove to be those of the two lovers in intimate embrace. The voices of the lovers state a perfectly balanced contradiction with no possible resolution. The French woman, who remains nameless throughout the film, repeatedly says that she has seen everything at Hiroshima, and then slowly and musically, along with images from the day after the detonation and contemporary museums and bus tours, she unfolds descriptions of what happened immediately after the bomb, and of the facts and evidence left. Meanwhile, his voice denies that she could have seen anything of Hiroshima. He says that she has seen nothing at Hiroshima. Through their duet, their exchange remains inseparable from the dilution of being able to tell the disaster. Juxtaposed with the images, their dialogue reveals that those images and facts cannot say what has taken place. Neither the documentary footage, nor the museums can show her, or us, Hiroshima. In light of this, we cannot say that the first sequence of the film, as devastating as it is, shows, or aims to represent for us what happened.

This does not mean that the film does not occur, or that Hiroshima is not engaged by that unforgettable first sequence. But, if that montage of death, fact, and flesh, word and images does not show Hiroshima, how are we to understand those first minutes, which, in the manner of a literary classic's first paragraph, situate in such powerful and unforgettable manner the rest of *Hiroshima Mon Amour*? Here it will be a matter of analyzing the moment of crystallization of Hiroshima beyond the dynamic of an objective subject that may be viewed at a distance, as an object of contemplation (an object given its meaning through the production of a ritual value). That Hiroshima cannot be said or represented, already situates the issue beyond the traditional function of its images as symbols of horror and human depravity. Duras is conscious of this, as she writes that she does not want to give us once again, "the description of horror by horror."[52] The aim of the film is not to give us a symbol or monument under which we may worship horror, even if it is with the most radical feeling of repugnance for it. But, what does happen in that sequence then?

Hiroshima, the Embrace

The sequence begins with an indefinite cut (or shot), one that may be the flesh of the lovers covered with sweat or rain, or flesh covered with ashes. Duras writes, "The main thing is that we get the feeling that this dew, this perspiration, has been deposited by the atomic mushroom as it moves away and evaporates. It should produce a violent, conflicting feeling of freshness and desire."[53] The opening cut exposes us to a ubiquitous experience, in which we do not find a determinate subject, something to settle the score. Rather, it is in the image's indeterminateness that we encounter ourselves moved by a certain uneasiness, a mixture of hope for liberation from what we dread to see and dread of what we have not seen. It is this ubiquitous experience spread across the screen and on to our flesh, this anxiety that introduces the sequence. By the end of the sequence we recognize the lovers' embrace, but only as configured through its unsettling passage. As Duras explains in the synopsis, the embrace is a banal action that violates the laws of the ritual of horror by ultimately leading us to experience a love that opens, "a place that death had not preserved."[54] In other words, Duras's aim is to engage Hiroshima without making it the theme of contemplation for a ritual safekeeping of horror. This does not mean we are to forget, rather, we will learn to live in light of our memory, and will do so without keeping our living experience safe from its touch through the worship of the disaster at a distance. In the space opened by the indefinite proximity of the lovers' and victims' flesh, these sensibilities are enmeshed with a love as inextricable from our lives as the sense of the horror of Hiroshima that cannot be said or represented.

The embrace, the lovers, their faces, do not come first; they are woven out of the montage sequence we are discussing, and they appear at the end of it. Their faces appear only at the end of the sequence, and we finally realize that they share an embrace. But this space of the embrace has been configured through a juxtaposition of footage that does not permit us to find a single complete object, image, or discourse with which we can identify ourselves, the subject of Hiroshima, or our feelings about Hiroshima. The cutting and changing of images figure a leap in time, space, place, which ultimately shatters the sense of these elements that would situate an image of worship. As Resnais himself said to one of the producers right after the first viewing of the film's answer print, "in my film, time is shattered."[55] This shattering of space and time does not preclude the abandonment of aesthetic experience to nonsense. Here, through the film form, we undergo the configuration of a certain theme and recover it, without providing ourselves with an object of contemplation and its original aura of ontological identity. The sequence follows the most rigorous lesson of Eisenstein's montage and juxtaposes different images in order to create a sense that cannot be brought back to any of the elements at play.[56] No single sequence or word apart from the whole montage sequence could situate us in that space of love, horror, and indeterminate need, in that fresh and anxious experience in our flesh. It is the film form—what Benjamin calls the mode of production that makes possible this aesthetic experience.

Hiroshima, a Politics of Art

The sequence from *Hiroshima Mon Amour* affords us the undergoing of a transformation in our sense of the disaster, not by giving another interpretation of the facts, or another moral lesson for humanity, but, rather, by bringing the audience to undergo a transformation in the flesh. In undergoing this experience, Hiroshima is no longer a name that indicates a place at a distance from us, a series of facts available for analysis, ready to be hanging in museums, or to become subject to moral evaluation. In undergoing the unsettling aesthetic experience of a montage that does not give us the object that may release us from, and put at a distance the horror, the film situates in the flesh the disaster that cannot be said or represented, that is, in a certain aesthetic experience that must be undergone and carried in inseparable moments of despair and love, in a situation that without releasing us from our historical situation renders that memory flesh, desire, anxiety, and perhaps even, as Duras suggests, fresh. Here, the politics of art do not give us new idols, or banners to carry. They do not afford us the comfortable possibility of inscribing experiences that mark the limit of what can be said in the praxis of political ideologies or socioeconomic political analyses or moralizing judgments. Furthermore, such experience in the flesh is no longer the property of an individual subject. In the undergoing of the aesthetic experience we are discussing, subjectivity is only secondary to the immediacy of an irrecoverable disaster that cannot be held at a distance. This does not mean that Hiroshima does not call for reflection, but one might speak here of a reflection in the flesh. At the same time, this does not mean that subjectivity vanishes. Rather, in its configuration, the subject is always already a figure of the disaster. In terms of sensibility and touch, one might say that in light of this aesthetic experience even the subjective touch bears the sharp traces of the disaster in the very texture of experience. In this short sequence, through the film form, we undergo an aesthetic experience in which we find a political place in the flesh, in the undeniable monstrous experience of being in our time, of being of this time, and of being in exquisite exposure to the freedom that such living politics affords us beyond and towards our subjectivity.

Conclusion

In closing our discussion let us return to Adorno's reception of Benjamin's essay on mechanical reproduction. Adorno's first reaction to the essay is immediately critical. In a letter written in march of 1936, immediately after first receiving and reading the essay, Adorno writes to Benjamin:

> When I spent a day in the studio of Neubabelsberg a couple of years ago, what impressed me most of all was how *little* montage and all the advanced techniques were actually used; rather, it seems as though reality is always constructed with an infantile attachment to the mimetic and the 'photographed.' You underestimate the technical character of autonomous art and overestimate that of dependent art; put simply this would be my principal objection.[57]

As Buck-Morse points out, whereas Adorno sees the transformation of art as a dialectical praxis between artist and the historical development of his or her techniques, Benjamin, in focusing on the mode of production, concentrates on the objective forces of the superstructure.[58] Indeed, Adorno's complaint seems to be that, in emphasizing the mechanical means of production, Benjamin has failed to see its dangers and shortcomings for the proletariat, who seems to remain passive under the force of production. Benjamin does not see the evident possibility and reality of the fetish objects produced by the same mechanical reproduction, and the stupidity rather than revelatory absent-mindedness of the passive public.[59] As Adorno puts it, "The laughter of a cinema audience—I have discussed this with Max and he has probably related this to you already—is anything but salutary and revolutionary; it is full of the worst bourgeois sadism instead."[60] But, as we saw through our discussion, Benjamin's analysis never advocates the subject's passivity. Ultimately, Adorno's criticism is that Benjamin fails to carry out the task of a critical dialectic to its necessary extreme. Adorno introduces his principal objection by saying that what he would want is "more dialectics."[61] As Adorno sees it, without the dialectic articulation of subject and work the subject remains a mystery while work becomes an ontological force over it.[62] To paraphrase the main point of the final passage from Adorno's letter, Benjamin as an intellectual has idealized mechanical reproduction, and instead of serving the proletariat's transformation, has made the work's and his own necessity into a virtue of the proletariat. In light of this Adorno closes his criticisms by writing, "I am convinced that the further development of the aesthetic debate which you have so magnificently inaugurated, depends essentially upon a true evaluation of the relationship between intellectuals and the working class."[63]

Given the role of mass reproduction in today's capitalist society, and its passive audience, Adorno's reservations about Benjamin's essay are more than justified.[64] However, the disagreement can be traced a step further, to another letter written to Benjamin a few months later, on September 6th of the same year. This time Adorno refers to Benjamin's work "On the Story-teller," and writes:

> For all those points in which, despite our most fundamental and concrete agreement in other matters, I differ from you could be summed up and characterized as an *anthropological materialism* that I cannot accept . . . if I am not mistaken, a certain *overexertion* of dialectic, in the sense of an overly hasty acceptance of reification as a behaviouristic 'test' for the body, is merely the inverted image of the undialectic ontology of the body which emerges in this work (it is the same objection which I made against the essay on 'Art in the Age of Mechanical Reproduction').[65]

Here Adorno articulates the issue of the ontologizing of the mechanical reproduction further, and ultimately identifies the difference between his thought and Benjamin's in terms of a certain anthropological materialism. For Adorno, Benjamin's analysis of mechanical representation never questions the assumed body of the subject. This can be rephrased in terms of our discussion, and we can say that, here, Adorno goes so far as to recognize Benjamin's reliance on tactility and aesthetic experience for the claim of a politics of art that serves as emancipation from capitalism. For Adorno, the sensibility Benjamin has for aesthetics in the sense of tactility and an immediate physical experience of the work of art in the flesh is an overly hasty acceptance of reification, where critical thought fails because it dwells too close to the somatic, to a body which, for Adorno, will always require a critical dialectical discussion.

In our discussion, I have wanted to point out Benjamin's singular insight regarding the dialectic critique of the work of art: Where it becomes apparent that, what for Adorno is a rarefying overexertion of dialectics, turns out to be an opening for thinking through the ephemeral and concrete experience of the moment of political transformation. For Adorno, Benjamin's engagement with aesthetic experience is ultimately a reliance on an idealized and critically naïve (bourgeois and self-serving) sense of body. However, as we have seen, Benjamin's engagement of the physical shock and tactility of the work of art through film does not rely on an already defined sense of body or subject, but exposes us to the concrete dynamics of their configuration. Although not subject to Adorno's rationalist dialectical requirement, through Benjamin's analysis of mechanical reproduction, a certain aesthetic experience emerges, in light of which all relations, including the configuration of bodies, can be reinterpreted and transformed.

In the horizon of Benjamin's thought, we find the undergoing of a political and social experience in the flesh, an unsettling political experience that occurs in our exposure to what is indeterminate, indescribable, and yet vibrant, and occurs in fragile passages in which power, wealth, and marketable goods are not yet the guiding issue for how self, work, community, and the work of art are encountered. This is not a matter of preserving or cultivating an aura, but rather it is a matter of having the rigor to undergo the moment in its transformative ephemeral movement. Are lives not transformed in undergoing such intense and intensifying passages as the aesthetic experience we have been discussing in *Hiroshima Mon Amour*? Can we really say that the exposure to our finitude in the flesh comes down to the goods produced? What is the value of goods for one who undergoes the aesthetic experience of the beginning sequence of *Hiroshima Mon Amour*, or for the dead that configure our memory in our flesh and yet without possible representation?

Throughout the discussion of aesthetics in this chapter, my aim has not been to inscribe it into some laconic lyricism or poetry of the cinema, or to lose the difference between philosophical thinking and the experience of art works. In this discussion I have wanted to regain a sense of the aesthetic experience at play in a genuine politics of art, in order to begin to articulate the critical moment opened by such aesthetic experience.[66] As filmmakers well know, film is not only a matter of effects accomplished by lenses and montage. Its material is a most fragile medium; not only is it difficult to handle without damaging, but its ruin is also only a matter of time. No symbol, no matter how marketable, will survive the fading of the oxidized silver grains, the scratching of the celluloid, and the exposure to a light that, in its vibrancy, burns, consumes, exposes images, and never preserves. What will be the value of a critique that speaks in terms of values for what in its moment has no time, except for its distinct and violent material passage? Perhaps, in Benjamin's materialist thought, we begin to engage the concrete immediacy of the disaster without making of it the readymade and comfortable subject of an operation of dialectic critical reasoning at a distance, or a commodity, without making of it an infernal passage under the name of machination, and even, without turning it into a secret preserved in a constant figuration of death, or a gift that never arrives.

CHAPTER 10

Unbounded Spirits

From Solitude to Ethical Words in Hegel, Fanon, and Gabriel García Márquez

To Jim Risser, friend in dialogue

The interpretation of our reality through patterns not our own serves only to make us ever more unknown, ever less free, ever more solitary.

(Gabriel García Márquez)

The theme of the following discussion is a certain ethical sensibility that opens in part in the work of Hegel, and that once broached will serve as an introduction to two diversifying figures of spirit in their ethical sense.[1] This chapter introduces a thinking sensibility, that is, not a thinking that gives sense to experience through abstract propositions or concepts but a thought that from its specificity and singular situatedness unfolds diverse senses of being. In the most general terms, we might say that by ethical we will understand precisely the opening of such situated senses of being in each of the three authors we will discuss, taking each in his specificity and singular word. To speak of a conceptual ethics in departure from Hegel, on the one hand, indicates our intention to search for Hegel's sense of ethical human freedom without abandoning the lightness of his thought in its taking flight. On the other hand, in speaking of ethics and human freedom, we get ourselves into some of the densest, heaviest, and harshest spaces in contemporary philosophy; since the proposition of a fundamentally ethical character of thought leads to the need to think with the other. As Derrida indicates, the other is already here with us, among us, she is an inarrestable element in the very determination of contemporary thought's many and fluid identities. Furthermore, the other is a figure of our memory (voluntary or involuntary) of genocides and the cultural destruction accomplished by colonialism, all exercised by the

139

same culture that seeks through rationalism the ethical and ontological sense of humanity. Hence, the almost suprahuman dilemma in which philosophy encounters (itself) today; a dilemma that we cannot seek to resolve, but we must instead traverse, precisely in order to discover through the most intense passages of thought in its situated living and latent specificity the ethical sense and freedom of human consciousness. This last sentence, almost heroic, or ridiculous, undoubtedly inviting, requires a brief clarification if it is to give us a sense of the central problem I want to take up in the following pages.

When, in 1982, Gabriel García Márquez received the Nobel Price for Literature, the Colombian writer explained to the academy that the reason behind the misery, abandonment, and solitude that Latin American has experienced for hundreds of years is not so much the result of a conspiracy engineered three thousand kilometers from the South, but rather, "a lack of conventional means to render our lives believable."[2] In other words, the poverty and oppression of the other has as much to do with economic and political interests, as with certain aphasia, a lack of expressions that would make possible the partial recognition of the other in her lived specificity. If such is the case, the encounter of Western culture with the other, and our discovery of "the other" in Western philosophical discourse, is not about making room for the foreigner in our discourses: the crucial point for us is not to re-cognize the other, define her, or recover her, through her incorporation into our conceptual figurations of existence, be they the artifice of metaphysics or the laborious strategies of deconstruction. Instead, we are speaking of going beyond deconstruction and of giving a twist, a push to Western thought towards the specificity and pulse of experiences of being that occur beyond the determinate grasp of the Western tradition: We are speaking of rushing in and leaping into incommensurable languages and difficulties. We are speaking of learning to listen. In these pages I seek an introduction into that incommensurable leap. By incommensurable, I indicate experiences that in their specific difference cannot even be juxtaposed as direct or dialectical opposites to rational grasping and ordering. In our discussion, this leap will occur in departure from a certain overflow (not excess) in Hegel's concrete idealism, and through the discussions of Fanon and García Márquez. I emphasize here that this leap is not gratuitous; rather, without an opening to the diversity and living specificity of our times, philosophy becomes a stone monument to a past that sustains its indifference by claiming its sense in light of an impermeable past that never was, or must follow the dictum and fashions of that normalizing, pseudoemotional, pseudopolitical religious culture that rules today. Finally, without undergoing the direct contact with her living specificity and diversity, not only the South, the other, but also the philosophical tradition in general, slowly, tacitly become victims of a growing deep solitude, as we find ourselves further and further submerged in our tautological and aphasic discourses, undaunted in our solitary solipsism.

In terms of what has already been said, two difficulties inseparable from our task become apparent: the necessary unfolding of the other's expression, and the impossibility of setting out towards contacting her with the certainty of a presupposed discourse of recognition. The conceptual specificity we seek is already lost if we begin by supposing that the difficult thematic of the other in her specificity, by definition and necessity, is based primarily on and must be studied through multiculturalism, perspectivism, or comparative linguistics. This chapter is not about this, but it is about a conceptual specificity given in certain registers of words in which open senses of being irreducible to a single ruling knowledge, rationalism, or discourse. This is a fundamental point in which I agree with Dennis Schmidt's idea that my thinking is thinking in translations. This phrase indicates a thinking that unfolds in specificity and otherness that overflow and ultimately do not refer to a self-same identity. One could say that we are speaking of thinking in translations without a possible resolution into originals. In this sense the following discussion intends to situate us in a conceptual space between the three author's registers, without forcing the traditional resolution of differences into one rational consciousness. At the same time, as we will see, this is only possible if we do not abandon the singularity characteristic of philosophical thought. This means that in our discussion we will have to develop a discipline that may let the diverse discourses and cultures converse out of their singular eventuation, and without the supposition of a logical, conceptual, teleological, or linguistic necessity that may determine a concordance between Hegel, Fanon, and García Márquez. As we see, the contact with the other and the passage towards an open Western thought, in its exposure with the other, are experiences much more intense and radical than those presupposed by rationalism and its forces.

Hegel: Overflowing Spirit

In Hegel's *Phenomenology*, spirit doubles and twists, and through the mutual and fluid negation between specific singularities and universals arise the figures of consciousness that represent it. These lead us to the absolute concept, in which all difference seems to be internalized in order to find recognition in relation to a whole and absolute identity. Through this movement Hegel points us towards a reflexive human consciousness that goes beyond conceptual subjectivism, and that in doing so takes flight towards a sense of humanity fundamentally ethical and free. But the *Phenomenology* does not end there. As is well known, within Hegel's works, the book also offers a kind of passage or introduction to his later works, to his *Logic*. As we will see in what follows, the *Phenomenology* not only opens a path towards the rest of Hegel's thought, but leads us towards a thinking sensibility that from its situatedness in its lived specificity opens spirit to diversified and diversifying, unexpected

senses of being, a thinking which overflows all ontological figurations based
on the idea of resolution into a single and absolute identity. To say it formally: The idealism that sustains Hegel's thought in the *Phenomenology* slips
and ends up opening towards a thought in difference, an experience that
overflows it, and which opens ontology to the unfolding of senses of being
in differences without a teleological recourse to an identity or history that
may internalize the differences and in this way resolve them and contain
them. Certainly, one would have to be an inept reader not to realize Hegel's
driven idealism; therefore, with this last proposition we are going beyond
Hegel's intentions in order to point out something in his thought that passes
beyond it, as we attend to what I call a situated conceptual sensibility. I add
that we are not speaking of an overflow of Hegel's idealism that will stand
against or as a kind of excess to Spirit; we are speaking of a transformation
in thought, a transformation that will situate thought in its lived specificity
without recourse to a dualist sense of something that may be extant, outside
or inside spirit. I find this situated sensibility of thought already indicated
by that figure at the closure of the *Phenomenology* that marks the passage
from it to the *Logic*. I mean those lines that Hegel appropriates from the
end of Schiller' s *Die Freundschaft*, as he writes at the end of the section on
"Absolute Knowledge" in the *Phenomenology*: "Only from the chalice of this
realm of spirits foams forth for Him his own infinitude."[3] I think that in a
sense, what I will say in this section is nothing more than an introduction
to the thought intimated by these words as they indicate a certain overflow
or foaming forth of spirit.

The ethical sense of the knowledge of spirit is explicit in the *Phenomenology*. Hegel writes that spirit is the, " 'I' that is 'We' and 'We' that is 'I.' "[4]
And yet, this sentence does not say anything to us if we do not understand
in what sense absolute knowledge of spirit comes to pass. On this issue the
three fundamental points we will have to discuss are:

1. specific alterity as fundamental negativity in the dialectical move-
    ment;

2. the movement of internalization (*Er-innerung*) of difference or nega-
    tivity in its double sense: On the one hand, as the internalization of
    all differences under one absolute identity; on the other hand, this
    internalization as the unfolding of a more intensified sensibility of
    consciousness situated by the specific differences of other beings.
    Along with this last point, and as the last main sections of the
    Phenomenology indicate, we will have to emphasize that this inten-
    sification of the lived sense of difference is given in the undergoing
    of reason and spirit in human action.

3. This series of observations will lead us to uncover an overflowing movement in Hegel's idealism, that is to say, they will lead us to the indication of a conceptual experience that can not be defined or contained by the internalization (*Er-innerung*) of all difference and by knowledge of a single and totalizing identity or being.

The ethical sense of spirit opens with the movement of spirit as self-consciousness, that is, beyond sheer sense-perception and the relationship of consciousness to nature. This does not come to pass as the apotheosis of subjective reason in itself, but when consciousness engages its other in living flesh. As Hegel explains in his famous section, On Lordship and Bondage, "A self-consciousness exists for a self-consciousness. Only so is it in fact self-consciousness; for only in this way does the unity of itself in its otherness become explicit for it."[5] Here it is not enough to have an internal self-consciousness; it is not enough for me to think, I am. As the quote indicates, we are speaking of a reflexive self-consciousness in which consciousness recognizes itself; it is for itself, appears to itself: but this happens only if and when that consciousness encounters itself as an other given to it. What is crucial for this moment of consciousness or spirit is that a sense of identity should appear that is given and is recognized through and as an other. As is well known, to arrive at such sensibility of being requires a struggle to death between two opposing consciousnesses. Through that struggle the two annihilate each other and as a result effect a double negation: On the one hand, the battle occurs because the other and my consciousness mutually negate each other. On the other hand, in that violent negation and mutual destruction their difference is internalized, and it is in this way that self-consciousness arises in its opening for other consciousnesses or human beings.[6] This occurs as the two consciousnesses in their intense negations come to recognize each other in a universal identity. At this crucial moment self-consciousness becomes universal, as it leaves its sole obsession with itself and recognizes itself in a world that has the weight and sense consciousness only could see in itself up to this point. Hegel explains that:

> With this, we already have before us the Notion of Spirit. . . . It is in self-consciousness, in the notion of spirit, that consciousness first finds its turning-point, where it leaves behind it the colorful show of the sensuous here-and-now and the night-like void of the supersensible beyond, and steps out into the spiritual daylight of the present.[7]

So that no matter where Hegel's thought will lead from here, its ethical opening occurs with the unfolding of universal self-consciousness, which unfolds through the undergoing of a specific and lived experience of alterity.

At the same time, a certain difference has been internalized in order to get to universal self-consciousness. Hegel writes, "negativity or diversity, like free being, is also the Self...."[8] We are speaking here of the general movement of consciousness in its unfolding towards absolute spirit, or of the *Aufhebung*. At each turn in the fluid movement of consciousness toward absolute spirit, negativity or difference is internalized. First, all affirmation encounters a movement of difference—an externalization of spirit in the form of negation. Then this encounter leads to a second negation, in which the opposition or exteriorization of spirit is internalized and consciousness finds itself in its newborn form. Through this process of internalization (*Erinnerung*) all negativity and difference ends up being appropriated by the movement of spirit. As the quote above indicates, this is because the difference or negativity is always proper to spirit, and a manifestation of it. Given this movement, although recognized, ultimately all differences should be claimed and explained in terms of one central identity and absolute knowledge. But such absolute resolution depends on how we understand the coming to pass of this movement.[9] If we go beyond the section of self-consciousness in the *Phenomenology* and take up some specific points in the experience of spirit, we see that the internalizing of differences only leads towards a more concrete, specific, and lived sense of universal difference, and particularly in terms of human action. This is why, in his famous course on the *Phenomenology*, Hyppolite refers to Hegel's thought as a "concrete idealism."[10]

In the section on Spirit, Hegel writes that self-consciousness has actuality "only in so far as it alienates itself from itself."[11] This alienation takes the form of works and culture. As Hyppolite indicates throughout his commentary, and as Kojève also emphasizes, spirit occurs for Hegel through the experience of the world, understood through culture and specific human action. For example, when we arrive at the moment of reason in consciousness, reason's idealism is not sufficient as spirit's knowledge and requires the undergoing of human action and works. Here is where Hyppolite speaks of concrete idealism. As he explains, this is clear in the *Phenomenology* where the spiritual world is the world of culture and alienation, as figured by the case of the slave's production of goods, which in its dialectic sense can be the alienation from self that sets him free; and also, as well, as figured by the case of the lacerating function of language in the world of culture.[12] As Hegel writes, "in speech, self-consciousness, qua independent separate individuality, comes as such into existence, so that it exists for others."[13] Thus, the experience of spirit in light of self-consciousness will lead us towards a more concrete experience of conceptual understanding, one that requires the undergoing of the specificity and differences of human life.

If we return to the end of the *Phenomenology*, we find a further sense of the specificity of spirit in Hegel's thought, and a step beyond its idealist articulation in terms of the dialectic of spirit towards the absolute. Immediately before the passage that opened our discussion Hegel writes:

> The goal, Absolute Knowing, or Spirit that knows itself as spirit, has for its path the recollection of the Spirits as they are in themselves. . . . Their preservation, regarded from the side of their free existence appearing in the form of contingency, is History; but regarded from the side of their [philosophically] compre-hended organization, it is the Science of Knowing in the sphere of appearance: the two together, comprehended History, form alike the inwardizing and the Calvary of absolute spirit, the actuality, truth, and certainty of his throne, without which he would be lifeless and alone.[14]

As a transition or introduction to his later works this last quote from Hegel indicates a thought that goes beyond the different moments of con-sciousness figured in the *Phenomenology*. But to where does this intimation point us? History and its formal sense have been seen in the *Phenomenology* through a language of images, a language that allows us to recall (*erinnert*) each step of consciousness and to undergo the movement of spirit in it. And yet, absolute knowledge must go beyond this, because if spirit is to think itself in its self-movement, the reflexive space established by representational language as the space for the undergoing of spirit must also be overcome.[15] This is because we are no longer looking for the formal moments and histori-cal contingencies in absolute knowledge. But if not that, what are we talking about? And how are we to speak? I think that it is precisely at this point that we can begin to understand the sentence from Hegel that opened our discussion, a sentence that announces the overflowing of spirit over a cup that can not contain it.

The *Phenomenology* leaves us at the edge of a fluid thought that would not treat or seek an object or movement from a distanced position of knowl-edge.[16] But if nothing rests to be grasped or explained from a reflexive distance, this does not mean that we are now beyond life, in a kind of metaphysical trance. The fluid movement of thought intimated at the closure of Hegel's work refers us to a word that unfolds in and from a state of consciousness in which life and knowledge are spirit, and in which, for this very same reason, the word is life. That is to say, Hegel's work leads us to a point where thought is not only reflexive, but also where all reflexivity and senses of being may only occur out of a thought undergone and arisen in its living specificity.[17] In this sense, thought figures a certain sensibility in which unfolds our con-sciousness of living, a consciousness found in the word. At the same time, as Hegel's paraphrasing of Schiller indicates, such thought overflows the form and content accomplished by the *Phenomenology's* concrete idealism. How is one to understand then this sensibility of being that is neither universal proposition—formal abstraction, nor pragmatic fact? How to think that overflowing fluidity that is not even an excess, but sheer spirit? Curiously, at this point in the *Phenomenology*, Hegel seems to be speechless, because the intimation of the radical opening to a living fluid thought is found in words stolen from a poet.

Conclusion: Toward Identities beyond The Other *of* Spirit

As we see, in the *Phenomenology* Hegel proposes that we situate conceptual knowledge, its possibility and sense, in the specificity of life, and as a universal knowledge that is inseparable from ethics and human freedom. But we can not engage this aspect of Hegel's thought without recognizing its internal conflict. On the one hand, the knowledge of which we speak does not abandon a certain appropriative self-sufficiency of spirit figured by the internalization of differences in each movement of consciousness towards a universal absolute identity.[18] Furthermore, given this appropriative manner of internalization of all differences, we should begin to be aware of the possible impossibility of hearing other discourses as other if all otherness is ultimately under one universal principle of identity. As Gadamer reminds us at the end of "Hegel's Dialectic": "The path of mankind to universal prosperity is not as much the path to the freedom of all. Just as easily, it could be a path to the unfreedom of all."[19] This danger is heard in its specific imperialistic connotations when one considers that for Hegel the history of spirit is Western rationalist and Judeo-Christian history. On the other hand, as we have heard, Hegel's thought leads towards a conceptual sensibility that can situate us precisely in an overflow of all conceptual or historical internalization of alterity under one single and absolute principle of identity. In this sense, the thought that is anticipated by the end of the *Phenomenology* suggests a thinking from the specificity of difference, since in being situated in the overflowing of spirit thought would begin to unfold ethical and political discourses and community out of its lived specificity. But here we encounter an indication towards a radical shift in thought that we must underline before going on to the next section.

Perhaps the definitive characteristic of Western thought in its constructed identity, from ancient Greek philosophy on, is the ontological difference between self and other which serves as ground for the determination of all identities. As we have seen, in Hegel this differentiation takes the form of a dialectic of identity, in which all experiences of being are understood as universal singularities, that is, as being through an otherness that ends up belonging to a single absolute identity. In speaking of otherness in the tradition through

Hegel, we are speaking of the other *of* a self-same identity. However, in recognizing in our discussion of Hegel a certain overflowing of such structure of identity, we have sought an opening towards a thinking that takes up the issue of identity in other ways: that is to say, we have sought a thought that goes beyond the understanding of otherness or alterity as the other of a certain absolute identity or first principle. This means that at this point we are seeking other ways of articulating senses of being, ways which do not take as the only possible way of thinking identities the relationship between the self-same identity and its other or otherness. In short, to paraphrase Rodolphe Gasché: *the problem is to think otherness (alterity) in departure from the other of the self-same identity.*[20]

This issue brings with it a series of implications that serve as a passage to the next section of our discussion. First of all, we are speaking of thinking in and from alterity and not in terms of an absolute self-same identity and its other. If this is the case—although it was necessary for us to recognize philosophy's characteristic way of understanding identity—we are now not necessarily looking for a traditional philosophical thought. But, to go beyond such philosophical thought does not mean not thinking. On the contrary, the point is to open our work beyond that ontology of self-sameness, towards possibilities for thinking and unfolding senses of being through other dynamics and movements of thought. Note that I am not speaking here of a thought that appears in excess of rationalism, idealism, or the history of metaphysics; rather, we are speaking of thought as an intensification of consciousness in which the senses or ontological character of experiences are configured in and from specificity and differences. Lastly, although I think it is crucial to the very possibility of our discussion, it would not be sufficient at this point to deconstruct the tradition and its other if we intend to engage in such thought, because the point is to think beyond the identification of otherness with a central figure of identity, and this means Western culture and its tradition, including the self-critiques and deconstructions of that tradition.[21]

Fanon: Others beyond Dialectic Spirit

In Frantz Fanon's *Black Skin White Masks* (*Peau noire masques blancs*) the other is the white man and woman, the colonizer, Western culture. This already announces a radical change in the situation of thought, that is, the situation from which one begins to think the sense of being of humanity in its ethical possibility, alterity, and towards freedom. Indeed, one of the most powerful aspects of the book is its transposition of the human situation to an experience outside, beyond Hegelian reflexive dialectic, and therefore outside the dominant insistence in situating the sense and sensibility of being human under and in terms of a central identity that translates all otherness into the discourse of rationalism and the Western Judeo-Christian canon with its version of the Greeks. At the same time, Fanon does not abandon the ideal of a fundamentally ethical sense of being for humanity. But before discussing these points, we must at least have a general idea of Fanon's aim in his book.

Fanon's book is not written against whites or the West. As Fanon himself explains in reference to Nietzsche, his is not a reactive book but rather a call for action.[22] He writes in his introduction, "I believe that the fact of the juxtaposition of the white and black races has created a massive psycho-existential complex. I hope by analyzing it to destroy it."[23] In his work, Fanon offers a prognosis of an ill society that situates the colored human being in terms of a vicious cycle figured by two fundamental elements: The false idea of superiority of whites, and the complex of inferiority in the part of the men and women of color, which sustains an almost total existential dependency on whiteness. As Fanon explains: "The negro enslaved by his inferiority, the white man enslaved by his superiority alike behaves in accordance with a neurotic orientation."[24] He concludes, "The black man wants to be white. The white man enslaves to reach a human level."[25] The problem is that, although not symmetrically, both sides live and suffer a lie that ends up alienating them from their own sense of existence and from their possible humanity. "I am speaking here, on the one hand, of alienated (duped) blacks, and, on the other hand, of no less alienated (duping and duped) whites."[26] Fanon's work focuses on the situation of the colored men and women within this pathology, and explores their sense of identity in departure from their inferiority complex. This sense of inferiority resides in the fact that in contrast to the white person who is content with his/her whiteness, the colored person has only one horizon for her destiny and possible identity: "For the black man there is only one destiny. And it is white. Long ago the black man admitted the unarguable superiority of the white man, and all his efforts are aimed at achieving a white existence."[27] This is what Fanon seeks to destroy, and why the final goal of his book is, "the desalienation of the negro."[28]

The final aim of desalienation is the liberation of the colored person in order that he or she can be recognized as a human being: "what is truly to be done is to set man (*l'homme*) free."[29] Fanon's work is about, "restoring man (*l'homme*) to his proper place."[30] For Fanon the issue is not ultimately the Negro, the Jew, or the white man, but it is "*l'homme*," the human being. But in what sense? As Fanon concludes at the end of his book:

> Superiority? Inferiority? Why not the quite simple attempt to touch the other, to feel the other, to explain the other to myself? Was my freedom not given to me then in order to build the world of the

You? At the conclusion of this study, I want the world to recognize, with me, the open dimension of every consciousness.[31]

L'homme of which Fanon speaks refers to an experience of a sense of being that goes beyond the vicious cycle between the black skin and white masks, beyond the personification of the person of color and Western Judeo-Christian culture as her master and judge. We are speaking of raising consciousness to an ethical dimension of human freedom, and of human existence as such consciousness: This is what Fanon seeks when he speaks of *l'homme*. At this point, we hear Fanon's proximity to Hegel, and we are reminded of the primary importance the German philosopher has for Fanon.[32] As is the case for Hegel, it is as a certain state of consciousness that we may arrive at a sense of ethical being and human freedom, specifically in the sense of a consciousness that overcomes its narcissism. For both thinkers, humanity depends on being with and for others. However, we should not leap at the conclusion that in speaking of *l'homme* Fanon's thought follows Hegel's idealism.

Fanon explains his intention precisely in contrast to empty idealism:

> Ah, yes, as you can see, by calling on humanity, on the belief in dignity, on love, on charity, it would be easy to prove, or to win the admission, that the black is the equal to the white. But my purpose is quite different: What I want to do is help the black man to free himself of the arsenal of complexes that has been developed by the colonial environment.[33]

Indeed, Fanon distances himself from idealism to the point of indicating in his conclusion that his project is situated from the outset outside the ideal expectations of the universal categorical imperative of Kantian ethics.[34] Fanon's aim is the uncovering and recognition of the ethical being and freedom fundamental to being human, but this is not an idealist endeavor. Fanon's way is concrete. He will work out of the specific situatedness of the colored person, and in departure from colonialist consciousness. Through his situated understanding of the pathology of colored consciousness he aims to make a leap towards a state in which a mutual self-recognition with others is possible. In order to understand this leap we will have to discuss first how this situated analysis uncovers a sense of being that does not fit in the internalizing movement of Hegel's dialectic; and then, how this same analysis opens a sensibility of thought in difference that does not abandon the issue of the sense of being of humanity, but rather situates it in its immediate specificity.

Fanon writes in his introduction, "Man is not merely a possibility of recapture or of negation."[35] If, in Hegel's case, spirit points towards a conceptual experience that goes beyond an absolute concept that internalizes all differences and makes them part of the absolute that contains them, in Fanon's engagement with Hegel we find in the experience of the person of color senses of being that do not have place within the dialectic of identity that understands otherness as the other of the self-same identity. Fanon writes of his experience as a colored man in the Western world, "I came into the world imbued with the will to find a meaning in things . . . and then I found that I was an object in the midst of other objects."[36] The problem is that the colored person appears as an object and does not have a sense of being an independent and therefore human consciousness. Given this lack of recognition of the colored man as an independent consciousness among others, Fanon concludes that, "Ontology—once it is finally admitted as leaving existence by the wayside—does not permit us to understand the being of the black man."[37] The point is not to make a general attack against all conceptual understanding of being. Here, ontology refers to the principle of identity that, as we said above, sustains the philosophical tradition. The problem is that there is a discrepancy between the encounter of consciousnesses that according to Hegel grounds and leads to a possible mutual recognition between them and the specific and situated experiences of being of the colored person in a colonialist culture.

As Fanon explains, "The black man has no ontological resistance in the eyes of the white man."[38] In the section titled "The Negro and Hegel," he elaborates this problem:

> Man is human only to the extent to which he tries to impose his existence on another man in order to be recognized by him. As long as he has not been recognized by the other, that other will remain the theme of his actions.[39]

In a footnote in the same section he writes:

> I hope I have shown that here the master differs basically from the master described by Hegel. For Hegel there is reciprocity; here the master laughs at the consciousness of the slave. What he wants from the slave is not recognition but work. . . .[40]

Concerning the slave, he goes on to indicate in the same note, "In Hegel the slave turns away from the master and turns towards the object [production, culture, etc.]. Here the slave turns toward the master and abandons the object."[41] First of all, what fails is the encounter between the two consciousnesses: The colonizer does not see the colonized as an opposite consciousness, but only sees the laborer's production. It is precisely this blindness that dupes the white man into believing to be superior to the colored person. At the same time, the colonized does not recognize his labor, but only recognizes himself in and through the image of his creator. Fanon explains that this happens even when the white man frees the colored person.[42] Even the encounter in which freedom is granted to a slave lacks a certain des-encounter, that is, it lacks the tension in which the two consciousnesses end up destroying each other and in that passage come to recognize each other. "There is no open conflict between white and black. One day the White master, *without conflict*, recognized the Negro slave."[43] Without resistance, in the indifference of a consciousness that serves itself of the other without recognizing him as an opposite equal, the possibility of being recognized as a human being vanishes: "it is just this absence of wish, this lack of interest, this indifference, this automatic manner of classifying him, imprisoning him, primitivizing him, decivilizing him, that makes him [the black man] angry."[44] Furthermore, without the tension of a des-encounter, the desire for recognition does not arise.[45] This lack of desire is crucial for Fanon's analysis: The point is precisely not to define the situation of the colored person in terms of the white colonizer, to blame him or her would be useless and would once again put the colored person in a passive position of nonrecognition. The leading problem is that the colonized never has enough self-consciousness to have the desire for recognition as an independent and autonomous consciousness, and, therefore, never recognizes the possibility of being equally productive of culture and meaning as the white person. Ultimately, Fanon's analysis leads him to a drastic conclusion: the lack of dialectic tension and its result in the absence of a desire for full recognition make the colonized non-existent. Fanon asks rhetorically, "A feeling of inferiority?" His reply: "No, a feeling of nonexistence."[46] We are ultimately speaking of lives degraded to the point of being inexistent as human beings: The colored person has the value of an object for the other, and the other dazzles his workers with a narcissistic presence.[47] Given this last point, we can see that the non-dialectic specificity of the colored person also figures the impossibility of arriving at an ethical sense of human freedom, since, as we saw above, according to Hegel it is through this des-encounter that self-consciousness comes into its ethical openness. But where does this analysis lead beyond indicating a negativity lost to its senses of being?

By pointing to the lived specificity of the colored man and the impossibility of fitting this experiences in Hegel's dialectic of identity, Fanon's work exposes us to experiences of being that can not be situated in accordance with the history of being as a history determined by Western idealism and Judeo-Christian thought.[48] Given this separation of the specific experiences Fanon analyzes from the dialectic history of Europe, the experience of humanity that Fanon seeks can not take as its point of reference the concepts of identity that sustain Western and European modern philosophy, specifically the fictitious relationship between a self-same central and unified identity and its "other." But this does not mean that we must abandon the attempt to articulate that

specific existence of the colonized, rather, we will have to seek an ontological thought that unfolds out of experiences that overwhelm and overflow the
traditional ideas of identity. As we will see now, Fanon's analysis focuses on
the specific living situatedness of the colored person, in order to open from
those experiences towards a sense of humanity beyond the colonialist neurotic
pathology, and as he himself puts it, he does so by "digging through his own
flesh to find a meaning."[49]

Although the experience of being colored has neither place nor value
in Hegel's dialectic movement towards humanity, for Fanon this is an experience of sense in its lived specificity that can be analyzed, and through which
a person of color may move towards her ethical sense and human freedom.
In the chapter titled, "The Fact of Blackness," immediately after his discussion
of Hegel, Fanon goes on to give a phenomenological account that explains in
what way the person of color encounters herself in her specific lived situatedness. As Fanon explains, under the white gaze, the colored being is configured
through a specific *epidermic schema*:

> And then, the occasion arose when I had to meet the white man's
> eyes. . . . A slow composition of my self as a body in the middle
> of a spatial and temporal world—such seems to be the schema.
> It does not impose itself on me; it is, rather a definitive structur-
> ing of the self and the world—definitive because it creates a real
> dialectic between my body and the world.[50]

The issue is not what the white man does to the colored man, but the configuration of a consciousness as a specific body, a configuration that happens
out of and in the experience of the colored man. As Fanon indicates, with this
relationship between body and world, the colored man finds himself locked
in his colored body and skin.[51] This epidermic schema is configured through
various levels of consciousness, such as, "legends, stories, history, and above
all, historicity."[52] Fanon does not leave out the economic situation that leads
to this experience, but it is through the specificity of the epidermic experience that the situation of the colored man takes hold and comes to give full
sense to being the colored other.[53] For Fanon the sense of being colored in its
specific situatedness is found throughout the various levels that we recognize
as concrete experiences of being, and these concrete experiences are the ones
that end up making the colored man responsible for "his body, race, and his
ancestors"; a trinity that repeats and assures the impossibility of the recognition of the colored person as a human being, that is, as the schema sustains
the reduction of possible human beings into human-objects.[54] But in what
direction are we moving with this analysis, if not towards the euphoria or

aggressive feelings Fanon does not accept as fundamental dispositions that will lead to the release from such situation?[55]

In the same chapter we have been discussing, amid his relentless critique, Fanon writes, "if I were asked for a definition of myself, I would say that I am one who waits; I investigate my surroundings, I interpret everything in terms of what I discover, I become sensitive."[56] In closing this chapter let us take up for a moment this sensibility in its affirmative and positive sense. In the book's conclusion, Fanon writes: "I find myself—I, a man—in a world where words wrap themselves in silence; in a world where the other endlessly hardens himself."[57] As he explains, the cultural setup in which the colonized are caught occurs through words, "A man who has a language consequently possesses the world expressed and implied by that language. . . . Every colonized people in other words, every people in whose soul an inferiority complex has been created by the death and burial of its local cultural originality finds itself face to face with the language of the civilizing nation: that is the culture of the mother country."[58] The transformation that Fanon seeks depends then on the uncovering of a word in which a space will open for the articulate unfolding of that experience of being that is denied its recognition under the pathological cycle of colonialism. But how should such word unfold?

Fanon's aim is not towards abstract propositions or political theories. Rather, he seeks our specific decisions.[59] As Fanon writes, we stand towards "One duty alone: That of not renouncing my freedom through my choices."[60] It is on this choice, and its decisive word that depend ethical being and human freedom. Furthermore, such decisive word must transcend the epidermic schemata into which history fixes us: "I am not a prisoner of history. . . . I am part of being to the degree that I go beyond it."[61] This does not mean that Fanon calls for abandoning lived specificity and memory. Rather, this departure from historically assigned identities only emphasizes Fanon's dynamic sense of lived specificity, and leads us to his sense of articulate lived specificity as a decisive moment: decisive because of its transformative character. As he explains, "I am a man, and what I have to recapture is the whole past of the world. . . . In the world through which I travel, I am endlessly creating myself."[62] In our realization of our immediate situation, and of our memory, history, and lineages, we may come to recognize ourselves. But this only happens if and when we are able to overcome them. In other words, when we follow his concrete analysis, we find that Fanon calls us to take flight towards ethical human freedom in light of the living pulse in which we are situated. But this is a radical realization, since in following him we are situated in a temporal disposition or sensibility that cannot wait for its sense of being. Nor can we answer to spirit in order to be given a place in history. Fanon writes in his conclusion to *Black Skin White Masks*, "I should constantly remind myself that the real *leap* [*saut*] consists in introducing invention into existence [*l'invention dans l'existence*]."[63] Here invention indicates the transformative character of an active consciousness that in light of its situation finds force to leap beyond it. Ultimately, Fanon's words invite us to make a creative leap out of our situation or time, understood in its transformative movement, in its overflow of all historical figurations, in an inventive leap out of and towards our senses of humanity.

As we see, in Fanon we find an analysis of a negativity that can not be internalized under the dialectic of the absolute and the identity based on this idealism which distinguishes Western philosophy. In contrast to the traditional dialectic of identity as the other of the self-same principle, Fanon's analysis leads one to conclude with a call for a transformative leap towards a sense of humanity found in a transformative passage offered by a future that arises from and in departure from the situated specificity of experiences of difference, alienation, and oppression. We close this brief and introductory discussion of Fanon with an inviting proposition: The seeking of a word that arises in its situated specificity, beyond the dialectic ordered by a single identity as is the case in Western idealism. The next and last section of this chapter offers a short discussion of an author whose work is a fine example of such leap towards senses of ethical humanity and freedom in their lived specificity and differences.

Gabriel García Márquez and the
Words of a Stupendously Immeasurable Reality

Few of us today fail to have at least a general idea concerning that apparently incredible world that began to open half a century ago with the so-called boom of Latin American literature, and particularly through such works as *One Hundred Years of Solitude* by Gabriel García Márquez. The movement was also named magic realism, given the events and orderings that often occur in those works. At the same time, the same works, often written in Paris and other cities in Europe, gave voice and presence to what is today a strong part of Latin America's identity. *One Hundred Years of Solitude* opens with the son's memory of the originator of that genealogical impossibility that is the Buendias lineage, when Aureliano recalls the day his father took him to see ice. The work closes after the last of the Buendias has seen his son, born with a pig's tale, die, and carried away and eaten by ants. At that point, Aurelio locks himself in a room away from all spirits in order to decipher his destiny, written one hundred years before in Aramaic. While he deciphers the text, Macondo, that world contained in the one town that locates the Buendias' stories, flies away in a whirlwind and disappears, only for us to be left to hear the closing words of the book, "the races [*estirpes*] condemned to one hundred years of solitude did not have a second opportunity on the earth."[64] It is precisely against this last sentence of the book that we may place García Márquez' Nobel Peace Prize speech: The author closes it with a hopeful indication towards the unfolding of a world in which, "the races condemned to one hundred years of solitude will have, at last and forever, a second opportunity on earth."[65]

But in what way will these races find their opportunity? We find an indication in something almost as incredible or at least as difficult to accept as the stories García Márquez tells in his books, that is, in what the author says in his interview with his friend Plinio Apuleyo Mendoza in *The Scent of Guayaba*. When Apuleyo asks him about his stories, García Márquez replies, "There isn't one line in my books not based on reality."[66] I do not doubt that this reply may cause one to grin precociously or that it may sound like mere hubris. And yet, this sentence is crucial to understanding in what way according to García Márquez the solitary races may be heard and recognized in their specific ways of being. As we will see now, the key to this recognition is a conception of language as a word that arises in its specific reality: The theme we will pursue at this point is how in the word unfolds a thinking of the senses of being as lived consciousness in its specificity and difference.[67]

In the same interview, and in relation to his most famous novel, the author explains, "the discovery that allowed me to write *One Hundred Years of Solitude* was simply that of a reality, our reality, observed without the limitations imposed to them by rationalists and Stalinists in order to make their understanding easier."[68] Beginning from a reality that is ours is fundamental for the author, and this is because of the character of such reality. As he tells Apuleyo, "Our reality is unbounded (*desmesurada*) and often offers us writers very serious problems, that of the insufficiency of words."[69] The lack of conventional means to make oneself heard that condemns Latin America refers precisely to a lack imposed by experiences or a lived specificity that require a certain language that we do not have at hand. As the citation above indicates, to a large extent this lack occurs because reality does not fit within the delineations and fields of experience acceptable to rationalism, that is, to the ordering of the Western rationalist tradition. García Márquez insists on this throughout his interview and Nobel Speech.[70] That for him Latin American reality is *desmesurada*, literally means that we are faced with an incommensurable reality, a reality beyond measure; it means that this reality cannot be explained or for this mater internalized through a rational principle of identity (dialectical or quantitative). Furthermore, if García Márquez begins to unfold such reality, this articulation and reality must also figure outside the parameters of a rationally explainable European history, be it as a logical or rational movement of spirit or as its factual process. This is because, as we find from factual histories as well as the stories born from them, reality in Latin America occurs in an overflow of ideas that do not hold to a single principle of identity, such as the ones that sustain Western philosophy and its rational ordering and logic. In simple terms, one can recall that, since 1492, Latin America exists in a double history that makes impossible the claim of one distinct identity. Just as it occurs when one begins to trace the encounters and des-encounters that sustain the so called *estirpe* (race) of the Buendias' in *One Hundred Years of Solitude*; or to take another familiar example, when one looks for the definitive text or word in the stories of Jorge Luis Borges, only to end up like Foucault, situated by an inspiring fit of laughter given in the discovery of the insurmountable space of differences out of which claims to identities in pure sameness make their claims.[71]

As García Márquez points out, this overflowing reality is not a senseless chaos, a negativity lost to nonsense for being incommensurable in relation to a logical dialectic that may allow us to situate identity. As he explains concerning what he finds in Latin American reality, "Within the greatest seeming arbitrariness there are laws. One can take off the rational vine leaf, with the condition of not falling into chaos, in total irrationalism."[72] In its lived specificity, Latin America has sense and order, although these may not fit or refer to the requirements of a rationalist Western canon. García Márquez recalls for example that when the railroad of Panama was constructed under European tutelage, the European agreement included the strict measure that the railroads could not be built from iron because of its cost, so that, given its location, the most practical choice of material was gold. The author also reminds Apuleyo of those deluges in Central America that escape the word rain in a European context, and of those people, who, by means of prayers take away worms from animals' ears. The point is not the strangeness of reality in general, but the singularity and sense of a specific reality. Furthermore, for García Márquez the way that reality is engaged is crucial, that is, through concrete imagination rather than through the volatile production of fantastic rational images and their empty ideals. As García Márquez explains, "With time I discovered . . . that one can not invent or imagine what ever one wants, because one risks telling lies . . . I think that imagination is but an instrument of elaboration of reality. But at the end, the source of creation is always reality. And fantasy, that is invention pure and simple, a la Walt Disney, without any footing in reality, is the most detestable that there can be."[73] The function of imagination is crucial: the author understands it as an instrument that works out of its specific lived situatedness, and beyond rationalism, in order not to abandon sense and order in their specificity. We are not speaking of imagination as the making of images that may be invented or as the rationalist function that may provide projections of order. Also, we are not speaking of confusing literary fiction with reality. For García

Márquez literature and language occur from and through a necessity imposed by their lived specificity, and from that incommensurable but concrete experience weave senses of being. As he indicates in his discussion with Apuleyo, language unfolds a necessity imposed by its lived specificity, i.e., as a word arisen with its specific situatedness.[74]

Conclusion: Remedios la Bella that Rises to Heaven

If Fanon invites a leap towards a sense of humanity and freedom found in the creative specificity of a lived word, Gabriel García Márquez's works figure that experience. Both authors agree on the need to unfold senses of being in departure from the lived specificity in which they arise, and as a result of this in their works they lead us beyond the Western rationalist delimitation of senses of humanity and freedom. Without doubt Fanon and García Márquez invite us to enter territories of which we have little knowledge and to encounter issues we cannot control, and for which we can not simply propose solutions at a distance or a single historical horizon.[75] In the case of García Márquez it is impossible to define life in its specificity as the other of a single rationalist principle of identity and with a view towards such identification of origins. But this does not mean that we must forgo the possibility of engaging the sense of that lived specificity: a lived specificity that in García Márquez even slips between God's fingers. In *One Hundred Years of Solitude* Remedios la Bella ends up rising to heaven. As García Márquez tells in the interview, such levity is not easy to accomplish:

> No, she did not rise. I was desperate for making her rise. One day, thinking about the problem, I went out in the patio of my house. There was much wind. A very large and beautiful black woman that came to wash our clothes was trying to hang sheets on a line. She could not, the wind kept taking them away. Then I had the illumination. . . . Remedios la Bella needs sheets in order to rise to heaven. In this case, the sheets were the element offered by reality. When I returned to the type writer, Remedios la Bella rose, rose and rose without difficulty. And there was no God that could stop her.[76]

This story gives us an example of the specific relation between story and reality in García Márquez. Furthermore, as a point of distinction between the three authors we have been discussing, the story makes us understand that there often is certain lightness in the situated and overflowing word of a spirit stupendous and immeasurable in its time. I find in such experience or time a specificity that is not translatable into philosophical discourses of identity, and that precisely because of this, may offer us a site for thinking the other in departure from the other of the self. It has been my intention throughout our discussion to lead us to such space of des-encounter and to give you a sense of an experience of thought and of senses of being in trans-lations, that is, in the impossibility of translating our being in difference into a single absolute identity or discourse of spirit and its history and destiny. Perhaps in such des-encounters we might begin to encounter histories in their unbounded realities and play. I am referring to our being there exposed in that which does not belong to us, in that which does not own us and that we do not need to internalize completely—to own, in order to understand each other and find spacings towards our senses of being in their specificities, differences, and stupendous histories . . .

CHAPTER 11

Towards a Politics of Lightness

A Roberto e Claudia

The Uruguayan writer Eduardo Galeano opens his famous book, *The Open Veins of Latin-America*, with the following quote, "We have kept a silence close enough to stupidity. . . ."[1] These words exemplify the painful discovery of postcolonial peoples, who find that they have survived and subsisted throughout modern history to date by learning to insert themselves in the economies and values of other more powerful states and their discourses. With this realization, a need arises for other ways of thinking and for voices that would free us from economies of domination that secure our silences. There is little doubt that because of the political and economic injustices perpetuated by this economy of insertion the issue in its most immediate forms would take the path of political and economic discourses that attempt to overcome the structures of domination in place. These first reactive impulses take the form of strategies of empowerment in contemporary philosophy. With this politicization of the task of thinking comes a paradoxical problem. The understanding of the task of philosophy as inseparable from the calculative reasoning of politics and economy that is suggested by the thematization of thought as a struggle for power and domination often repeats the very approaches to our human condition that sustained the colonial and imperialist strategies of domination we are trying to overcome. Furthermore, in spite of its liberating task, the interpretation of the possibility of a diversified community and of giving voice to alterity in terms of power structures makes the other, the voiceless, the powerless, still dependent on structures that, although they might make space for their voice, still demand a certain repetition of an economy of insertion. The issue here is one of a discourse that remains always within the self-certainty of its interpretation of the human condition as essentially determined by its version of politics and economy as founded primarily on issues of power. This means both that the concrete material condition of communities are always accounted for in terms of larger interests, and that the political is always understood in terms of a sovereign conceptual structure that situates all singularities under its own interests. Indeed, one characteristic of the politics of power and rationalism is the perpetual denial of any other possibility of understanding our situation. At the same time, one should be clear about the almost comical irony of attempting to apply some of the strategies of deconstruction in the Latin American context: For example, speaking of silent reservedness (Heidegger) or deferrals of meaning in which the saying slips (Derrida) to peoples who have been oppressed and precisely denied their voice and word for centuries. One marked difference between Heidegger's and Derrida's questioning of the traditions and the needs of Latin Americans is that in contrast to the crowding and erasing of horizons in the production of discourses of power, which happens with the machination and capitalism of Western tradition in Latin America, we have kept silent for too long.

In the first pages of his last work, *Six Proposals for the New Millennium*, which remained unfinished due to his untimely death, Italo Calvino asks himself: "how could we hope to be saved by that which is most fragile?"[2] This question already suggests an approach to the question of the political and alterity essentially different from that of power based strategies. In this chapter, we see how Calvino replies to this question, and we open up an alternative approach to the thinking of the concept of the political. This is not to argue against the relevance of empowerment in the question of the political—this would make little sense at the practical level. Rather, our task is to indicate a certain essential aspect of the political that remains outside the question of empowerment, although it belongs essentially to the gravity of the concept of the political. As we will see, Calvino's lectures open towards a different approach to the question of the political. In his lectures, Calvino develops his engagement of our human condition through an idea of lightness that opens the possibility for thinking the political out of its essential alterity.

Calvino and the Political

Calvino's work is entangled with the question of our human condition from the start. The Italian author begins his career in the wake of neorealism in Italy after the war. Much like Fellini, Calvino finds his style out of his attempt to confront the harsh social and political issues of this time. His concern with these issues is further corroborated by his participation in the Italian Communist Party (PCI) from 1945 to1957, and then, many years later, when in the seventies he contributes to *Il Corriere della Sera*[3] with articles on the overwhelming political corruption and governmental turmoil of the time. As well, he contributes with articles that touch the heart of Italy's culture, a culture that at the time is undergoing the change from being a diversified gathering of regional dialects and traditions to the homogeneous socio-cultural standard common to the rising technological discourse of the West. Indeed, at this time, next to Calvino's articles in *Il Corriere* one finds the famous political and social critiques of another great figure of Italian literature and film, Pier Paolo Pasolini.[4] Pasolini's painfully clear readings of the development of Italian society, at the time lead him to announce that with the change from diversified dialects and traditions to the homogeneous discourse of technology and worldwide communications Italy is suffering a cultural genocide.[5] This statement might seem somewhat exaggerated to us, yet, it does shed light on Calvino's work. The two authors share the sense of urgency in light of the homogenization of culture and the loss of diversity to technological standards and the single minded language of such economy. We hear Calvino's concern as background throughout his *Six Memos for the Next Millennium*, that is, when he speaks of the imagination and the diversifying character of the word as values that must be defended, or when he directly attacks the loss of articulatedness and inventiveness we seem to be suffering in everyday language today. Yet, Pasolini approaches the political with a social critique that focuses on politics, economy, and strategies of empowerment through the analysis of cultural symbols, whereas Calvino's work is concerned with the engagement of the incalculable and ephemeral relations that underlie these issues.

As late as 1980, Calvino explains in *La Republica* his break with the PCI and politics, "I think today that politics record with much delay things that, through other channels society manifests, and I think that often politics exercises operations that are abusive and mystifying."[6] Calvino abandons programmatic ideological politics, but he does so in a move towards a further engagement with the human condition. The author's commitment to the question of the political is exemplified by his *Invisible Cities*, a work that the author himself understands as "a dream born out of the heart of the unbelivable cities" of our times.[7] In the same lecture where the author makes this statement, he says that the book explores that which allows human beings to construct and live in such cities. For him these essential elements at the heart of the city are "exchanges that are not mercantile but of desires, memories, and words."[8] Here we find that for him cities are not constituted by dreams but by certain concrete aspects that stand beyond ideological politics and purely economy concerns. As Pier Paolo Pasolini puts it in his review of *Invisible Cities*, "It is always a 'bases' of sensibility for the real that gives the material for Calvino's poetical and ideological heights."[9] In short, to close this first part: Calvino's works are always concerned with the political. The question is that of his approach to the political, an approach that, after what we have seen thus far, we rightly expect to be different from that of the struggles for power wrought by a politics and economy driven by calculative thought alone.

Another Approach

Calvino's concern with our human condition throughout his career is unmistakable, and calls for a reading of his works that does not assume him to be a fantasist. Rather it suggests that there is a particular approach to the political that is essential to his writings. This observation seems necessary for us today in light of the insistence of many of our critics in categorizing authors like Calvino, Borges, and, in fact, the whole of Latin-American contemporary fiction as fantastic-realism, which suggest a certain flight of fancy in the part of the authors, and thus ignores or covers over the direct insight and radical diversity in their understanding of the political in their works. Needless to say, the closer we put these works to the fantastic the less threatening their different approach to our human condition is to our common and homogeneous interpretation of the political as the real hard facts of technology, science, economy, and politics. Indeed, these observations are called forth by Calvino himself, who is clear in his *Six Memos for the Next Millennium* that his work, as that of the other writers I have mentioned, involves the closest aspect of concrete language. For Calvino these works are eicastic works and not phantastic works.[10] They are works that involve a most intense engagement of the world by the written or spoken word. They are works that sustain in a most concrete and existential manner the engagement of the word with life's direct finitude through the event of writing and thinking. The question is now, what kind of engagement of the political does Calvino's work enact?

As the author states in the first of his *Six Memos for the Next Millennium*, titled "Lightness," his writing is always concerned with an "extraction of weight." He says, "I have sought to take away weight at times from human figures, at times from the celestial bodies; most of all I have tried to take away weight from the structure of story telling and from language."[11] Calvino goes on to say in the same section, "I am not speaking of escaping into dreams or irrationality. I mean to say that I have to change my approach, I have to look at the world with another vision, another logic, another method of knowledge and verification."[12] His writing is not a form of escapism from the hard facts of life. Rather, he enacts a different approach that seeks to engage our human condition in its full gravity by acknowledging not only the unavoidable heaviness of life but also its essential lightness.

A figure Calvino chooses to illustrate his approach is that of the Italian troubadour Guido Cavalcanti. He recalls the way Boccaccio, in the *Decameron*, presents the Florentine poet's lightness. While walking in a cemetery Cavalcanti finds himself in danger when he is accosted by a group of cavalieri; he manages to escape by literally leaping out of the situation, and thus leaving his pursuers behind. Immediately after recounting the story Calvino says:

That which strikes us is the visual image Boccaccio evokes: Cavalcanti that frees himself with a leap, "since he was so light."

If I chose a wishful symbol for our coming to the new millennium, I would choose this one: the sudden agile leap of the philosopher poet that rises above the heaviness of the world, demonstrating that his gravity contains the secret of lightness.[13]

In Calvino's reading of Cavalcanti we find lightness as the essential approach to our human condition. But we have to ask now, what would this mean? How would we understand a thinking of the political in such leap, that is, in terms of its essential lightness?

In the lecture on *Invisible Cities*, Calvino himself gives an indication concerning the question of lightness and the political.

As a reader among others I can say that in chapter five, which develops at the heart of the book a theme of lightness strangely associated with the theme of the city, there are some pieces I consider the best as visionary evidence, and perhaps these most filiform figures ("citta sottili" e altri) are the most luminous zone of the book.[14]

It is in those sections at the heart of the book where lightness and the political are found together that we would find Calvino's strongest vision. Furthermore, these are the most luminous sections of the book, not because they make a political statement, or because they solve the difficulty of our human condition. These luminous moments are found in the subtlest figures, in the most filiform pieces, in that which is lightest in the book and also most fragile, as Calvino's own words indicate at the beginning of section five of *Invisible Cities*: "in cities that grow in lightness."[15]

For Calvino, the most fragile, the filiform, holds at the heart of the city. We are speaking of exchanges beyond mercantilism, and relations outside politics, that is, at the heart of the city appear those spaces of finitude in which we find "exchanges of words, desires, memories."[16] We can see that this is the case when we think back to Calvino's works, to the kinds of experiences and engagements that constitute the fabric of his stories: From an inexistent knight who pleases Charlemagne by letting the ruler's own voice echo back from an empty white suit of armor,[17] to a man obsessed with calculating the ocean's waves,[18] or a man who grows up and lives only in the trees,[19] or the conversations of Marco Polo with the Khan, a conversation began by one conqueror and an explorer who do not speak the same language.[20] All of these predicaments speak to our situatedness, to our human condition with a certain insurmountable lightness, as our understanding of our condition arises in the rising awareness of essential aspects of our existence that in their inherent incalculability, diversity, and indeterminateness operate in a disarming way. I say disarming because in light of our own diversified and ephemeral ground our discourses and our positions can never claim the self-certainty of political ideologies, or the certainty claim of the causality at work in calculative thinking.

In a sense, Calvino's approach demands a certain attunement to that which is most fragile, and indeed ephemeral. If we were to enter with lightness into the heart of the political we would have to engage the incalculable and unpredictable spaces of those words, desires, and memories that sustain politics, calculation and struggles of power. This is not a matter of engaging only hard fact, but the ephemeral, the passing, the incalculable. This means that even the ground of struggles for power bears a certain ungrounding quality in the fragile character of its unavoidable passage. Thus, our task becomes one of listening and speaking in light of the passing character of voices and discourses, and in attunements in these passages; the rigor of a thought that in its situatedness begins to engage the essential thinking of the political.[21] Indeed, this is most difficult, since it puts us outside the calculative and affirmative self-certainty of politics, and yet it places us ever so close to the political in terms of our human condition, that is, in the uncanny event of cities arisen out of diversified memories, desires, and words. I am suggesting that in the latter sense we are political. But here the register of the political has changed.

A Politics In Lightness

When Calvino recognizes Cavalcanti's lightness, he does so particularly in Cavalcanti's writing.[22] Lightness is possible and occurs in the text and discourses of writers, poets, and philosophers.[23] In order to begin to understand the lightness essential to our circumstances and thought, we can engage the question of how, for Calvino, the political might be opened to its essential alterity and diversified event by words.

For Calvino, words have a particular temporality. He reminds us, in his second lecture, titled "Quickness," that Sicilian poets have the expression "*lu cuntu nun metti tempu,*" "the story does not take time."[24] Ultimately, stories do not occur in an already determinate time. The storyteller always has the freedom to leap from time to time, for example passing in a moment from present to past, or in an even more dramatic leap, from historical time to ahistorical times of creation. According to Calvino this freedom is itself temporal, since the telling of stories arises and is sustained by the patterns of repetition that give it its momentum. Ultimately what sustains all discourses is rhythm, that is, meter in verse, and in prose the effects that keep us interested in listening for what comes next.[25] These observations situate words in their essential temporality: the word is a temporal event not because it occurs in time but in so far as it arises temporally, in that it is sustained by repetition and rhythm. This temporalizing character of words opens the question of language and discourses to the fragility of the passing of words. For Calvino, words occur in passage, in the rising and falling of the sounding out, in the rhythm and repetition of our breath. Ultimately, they occur in the breath-turn, in light of our singularity or finitude.

What is sustained is a passing that appears and fades, and this passage calls for a certain velocity of mind. As we speak, as we listen, we rise along with our words, we remain ever so lightly on top of the voice as its sounding out comes peaks and fades. In this quickness Calvino discovers that words are never unidimensional, of one meaning. In the rushing of the saying and listening, many ideas are at play at once. It is to this plural character of words that Calvino attributes their force and possibility. The words of philosophers or poets occur as "the excitement of simultaneous ideas."[26] This means that there is never only one meaning been said, but multiple meanings that are opened and sustained in the saying (one always says more, and less, than one intends.)[27] This certainly decentralizes the discourses of philosophers and poets, as language does not serve primarily as the tool for fixing ideologies or positions towards power; rather, language appears here as an occasion for openings that remain already from their very occurrence beyond themselves and their ideological or calculated intentions. In other words, for Calvino words occur as a diversifying event, which could never claim to be of one mind.

This decentering character of the word is figured in at least two other evident and significant ways in the *Six Memos for the Next Millennium*. In his lecture on visibility Calvino discusses images and the imagination. For him words arise out of the forging of images by the imagination. But this imagination is for Calvino "a repertoire of potentials, of the hypothetical, of that which is not has not and perhaps will never be but that could have been."[28] If words arise with the imagination, they arise out of an event that remains beyond determinate images, an event that is only accounted for as pure possibility. Here we enter a world of play between infinite forms of the possible and the impossible, a play that as such cannot be fixed but remains essentially a freeing event, open to the arising of uncanny diversity.[29] Furthermore, in writing or speaking, as well as in interpretation and reading, images superpose each other, and, indeed, they must if they are to make sense. For example, in encountering any text or work of art, the artist's world, the reader's world, and the text must all gather in a kind of vertical simultaneity in order for reading/interpreting to occur. Thus, writing or speaking can be understood as an intensifying task.[30] This superposition of images necessary for the understanding of the text or discourse, together with the infinite possibility of imagining in its event, indicate how the words of writers, poets, or philosophers in their arising and their interpretation have always already invited readings that remain beyond any single calculative intention.

In his lecture, "Multiplicity," Calvino expands on his idea of intensive writing or the superposition of images, and goes on to discuss writing as an "extensive" event.[31] This last term indicates a kind of writing or saying that would go beyond itself. Calvino differentiates between four forms of this kind of writing. The single text that can be interpreted at diverse levels; the dialogical text, to use Backhtin's term, which is constituted by a multiplicity of voices, themes, views of the world . . . ; the work that in its attempt to contain all that there is always goes beyond its own form and design; and, finally, a kind of thought that Calvino recognizes in philosophy as a non-systematic thinking.[32] These various ways of understanding words indicate a certain characteristic of our times: we are caught in the writing of an "open encyclopedia."[33] Our knowledge and our desire to know are caught in an expansive movement that always leads beyond what is intended. Thus, in the saying of philosopher or poet, as well as in their writings, we can only ultimately find a certain expansiveness that will challenge and eventually overcome the limits or intention of the particular text or discourse.

For Calvino, the very event of the word of philosophers, poets, and writers, spoken or written, marks an event essentially diversifying and open to possibilities beyond its immediate intention. This is because, in every case, the saying proves to be a diversifying event, since the very event of the word is in itself a call for an opening of multiplicity and diversity.

In light of Calvino's understanding of words, no discourse could occur as a self-certain ground for strategies of empowerment, either as calculative implementation or as the granting of a space for the same kind of self-certainty for the other. Rather, the discourses' words always arise in the fragile lightness of their coming to pass and in their diversifying event; characteristics of words that may interrupt the discourses of inflexible political ideologies and the self-certainty of calculative reasoning and their strategies of empowerment. This awareness of the essential alterity of words places all discourses in exposure to their otherness, as words always occur in a motion outside their intended signification, that is, as they enact the opening of a diversified field of possibilities. Was one then to address in thinking this interruption of self-certainty, one's discourse would open to the essential alterity of the political, a dynamic arising of discourses that in the awareness of their essential otherness could not claim nor invite the insertion of its other. In this opening without recourse to a self-closure, we find a path towards the understanding and formation of communities in difference. Along these lines, on the question of the understanding of community and the political in this openness I should at least mention Derrida's work on hospitality as well as *The Community of Those Who have Nothing in Common* by Alphonso Lingus.[34] Both works explore how community may hold together in alterity, rather than through a universal claim to relationships held under a sense of language as the operation of homogeneous identity in its recognition of its negativity, or other.

Conclusion

I am afraid in this discussion we have already failed Calvino and the project we have introduced, since we have added weight to the lightness of Calvino's own words. Such difficulty sustains the interpretation of Calvino's text in this chapter, because at every turn we have fixed our attention on particular aspects of his lectures, aspects that the author touches upon in his quick and exact movement. There is something of the lightness and elegance of an ice skater in Calvino's text that is always slowed down if not frozen by the attempt to develop further specific points. This tells us something about the relation between thinking and telling stories. It tells us that it might be almost impossible to sustain lightness and quickness when we begin to think through the exactitude and plurality of words. This indicates that the task of thinking in lightness is always put in danger by the very character of the task of thinking. Furthermore, this also indicates that the very lightness of the political is itself always in danger of being lost to thought. But perhaps this very realization already echoes the work of lightness in our understanding of the task of thinking the political, since we now find thinking already placed in its own uncertain ground, thus called to go on with a certain pause[35] and hesitation in its touching on the political.

I take this hesitation and sense of danger to be what we would gain in stopping to think through Calvino's idea of lightness. Indeed, it would be this sense of uncertainty that would enact our entrance towards thinking the political. It is clear from our discussion that thinking in its discourse is always political, since it leads itself in its saying towards its own otherness, as it leads always outside its saying, and, furthermore, since in this motion it always occurs as the very possibility of engaging diversity and alterity. As my friend Claudia interjects at this point in her reading, "speaking never occurs without relatedness, without non-self-coincidence, without openness to the irreducible."[36] I also think that Calvino is right in indicating that the political is essentially constituted by what is almost invisible, by the most fragile, by those relations, those attunements that in their passage form webs of filiform moments that hold the city together, and that hold the space of the political open. Indeed, in beginning to understand the thinking of the political as an event of lightness, we would always remain not only opened to the other, but in the essential play of the political in its alterity, and this would mean that the other would not have to wait to be empowered to have a voice, since our own voice would only rise in the same fragile passage and alterity from which the powerful (be they individuals or institutions) have always distanced themselves by attributing it to the other while remaining in their strange self-certainty.

I close with a story: A story told by the Italian poet Edoardo Sanguineti in a beautiful little essay published under the suggestive title, *How One Becomes an Historical Materialist*.[37] I say suggestive because today so many of us think that historical materialism has disappeared along with its caricature, that is, the imperialist Russia of Stalin. Today, so many claim and hold on to the belief that a social political consciousness outside the parameters established by the capitalist market and its institutions cannot exist. In this little essay, published as a pamphlet, inexpensive and circulated without meeting the requirements of the large and important publishing houses, Sanguineti recalls the moment when he came to have class-consciousness. This happened before the Second World War, in one of those closed quarters of Torino. It was one of those close middleclass neighborhoods where everyone knew each other. He remembers a boy, a worker, who one day appeared and, in the way children do, began to play soccer with him and his friends. Later, the stranger spoke with them, and at a certain moment, Sanguineti realized that there was another race, that of the workers, who not only came to his house to fix things. He realized in that encounter, *en passant*, that there were people different from him, and that those people had worlds he did not know, worlds unsuspected as long as he had not engaged those seemingly faceless, grey, lifeless workers.

I find the story moving because it affirms a genuine awareness of political consciousness. It affirms the unfolding of political consciousness out of singularity, and not as a requirement of institutions. Whereas, one who lives in a Hobbessian modern capitalism, between God and the law, will certainly take Sanguineti's account to be an exception, the great poet is simply asking us to notice—to mark the way we encounter each other, to mark the singularities and chance-ridden circumstances in which we touch and begin to form those webs we call political. Sanguineti's story exposes us to the simplicity, and hence, the difficulty of living politically. Living in light of possible and impossible singular encounters that always require our utmost attentiveness and discipline as we find ourselves with others exposed and claimed by unsuspected sensibilities, in dis-positions, encounters, des-encounters, even silences as fine and far reaching as the filiform designs of a seemingly innocuous spider web. There are no guarantees in such encounters, no sanction beyond the fleeting touch in which something opens up to give us a place—us. Fortunately, I can say that I know such encounters and people—I have lived with them all my life. I have watched them persecuted, executed, and many still speak, work, love, and create today. I meet such people almost every day. I can even say I know a major and a town where politics rises to such sense of humanity—where the streets are paved with the childhood drawings and memories of their citizens—some would call this idealistic, art, poetry, but as Roberto, the major, and that little town keep reminding me, such is also the space of politics.[38]

Notes

Introduction

1. This is something I have learned from the fine work of Linda Alcoff. Vide Linda Martín Alcoff, *Real Knowing: New Versions of the Coherence Theory* (Ithaca, NY: Cornell University Press, 1996).
2. Paul Celan, *L'Ephémère*, 26 March 1969, number 14 (1970), 184.

Chapter 1

1. Throughout the book *Seyn* is translated as beyng in order to preserve the indication made by the spelling. This also means that I have changed the spelling when quoting the translation by Parvis Emad and Kenneth Maly, who translate Seyn as be-ing. I have also replaced "the essencial sway of be-ing" with "essencing of beyng," *Wesung des Seins*.
2. Indeed in *Contributions to Philosophy* Heidegger's thought engages the discloseness of events of beings and thought in their concrete finitude by thinking these events out of the time-space (*Zeit-Raum*) that belongs to essencing of being (*Wesung des Seins*), or, in other words, to the disclosure or presencing of beings and thought. See, Friedrich-Wilhelm von Herrman, "*Wahrheit-Zeit-Raum*," *Die Frage Nach der Wahrheit*, ed., Ewald Richter (Frankfurt am Main: Klostermann, 1997), Part III. "*Wahrheit des Seyns und Zeit-Raum in der seinsgeschichtlichen Fragebahn*," 249–56.
3. Friedrich-Wilhelm von Herrman, "Way and method: hermeneutic phenomenology in thinking the history of being," *Martin Heidegger Critical Assessments*, ed., Macann (London: Routledge, 1992), 328.
4. David Farrell Krell, *Intimations of Mortality* (State College, PA: Pennsylvania State University Press, 1991).
5. Ibid., 4; 111.
6. Ibid., 1.
7. Ibid.
8. Ibid., 7 and 8; ch. 11.
9. John Sallis, *Double Truth*, "Deformatives: Essentially other than Truth" (Albany: State University of New York Press, 1995), 105.
10. Ibid.

11. Vide, David Farrell Krell, "Contributions to Life," *Heidegger towards the Turn: Essays on the Work of the 1930s*, ed., James Risser (Albany: State University of New York Press, 1999).

12. "Again—and yet, not simply again—it would be a matter of the beautiful: Being shining forth in the midst of the sensible, Being shining in and from the shining of the sensible." "Twisting Free—Being to an Extent Sensible," *Echoes After Heidegger* (Bloomington: Indiana University Press, 1990), 96.

13. Daniela Vallega-Neu, *Heidegger's Contributions to Philosophy* (Bloomington: Indiana University Press, 2003); and *Die Notwendigkeit der Gründung im Zeitalter der Dekonstruktion* (Berlin: Duncker und Humblot, 1995).

14. *Companion to Heidegger's* Contributions to Philosophy, ed., Scott, Schoenbohm, Vallega-Neu, and Vallega (Bloomington: Indiana University Press, 2001).

15. "Die Seinsverlassenheit ist die erste Dämmerung des Seyns als Sichverbergen aus der Nacht der Metaphysik. . . ." 207/293. The first refers to *Contributions to Philosophy (From Enowning)* and the latter to the original edition *Beiträge zur Philosophie (Vom Ereignis)*, GA, 65.

16. 76/108–9. "Gesagt sei vom *Zeitalter der völligen Fraglosigkeit*, das seinen Zeitraum unterzeitlich über das Heutige hinaus weit zurück und weit nach vorne erstreckt. In diesem Zeitalter ist nichts Wesentliches—falls diese Bestimmung überhaupt noch einen Sinn hat—mehr unmöglich und unzugänglich. Alles ‚wird gemacht' und ‚läßt sich machen,' wenn man nur den ‚Willen' dazu aufbringt. Daß aber dieser ‚Wille' es gerade ist, der im voraus schon gesetzt und herabgesetzt hat, was möglich und vor allem notwendig sein darf, wird schon im voraus verkannt und außer jeder Frage gelassen. Denn dieser Wille, der alles macht, hat sich im voraus der *Machenschaft* verschrieben, jener Auslegung des Seienden als des Vor-stell-baren und Vorgestellten. Vor-stellbar heißt einmal: zugänglich im Meinen und Rechnen; und heißt dann: vorbringbar in der Her-stellung und Durchführung. Dies alles aber aus dem Grunde gedacht: das Seiende als solches ist das Vor-gestellte, und nur das Vorgestellte ist seiend. Was der Machenschaft scheinbar einen Widerstand und eine Grenze setzt, ist für sie nur der Stoff zur weiteren Arbeit und der Anstoß in den Fortschritt, die Gelegenheit zur Ausdehnung und Vergrößerung. Innerhalb der Machenschaft gibt es nichts Frag-würdiges, solches, was durch das Fragen als solches gewürdigt und allein gewürdigt und damit gelichtet und in die Wahrheit gehoben werden könnte."

17. 92/131 and 88/126.

18. ". . . das Seiende als solches ist das Vor-gestellte, und nur das Vorgestellte ist seiend." 76/109. Heidegger also writes, "Machenschaft als Herrschaft des Machens und des Gemächtes." 92/131.

19. "Order and progress" is the positivistic phrase that marks the project of reason away from reality that accompanies the liberation and foundation of Latin American countries.

20. 83/119 and 84/120.

21. I agree with Claudia Baracchi, who has pointed out the difference between Heidegger's analysis of technology and the concrete Marxist analysis of capital. On this relation vide, Carlos Estrada and Rodolfo Kusch. Vide, for example Carlos Astrada, *Existencialismo y Crisis de la Filosofía* (Buenos Aires, Argentina: Devenir, 1963); Rodolfo Kusch, *Obras Completas*, Volumes II and III (Santa Fe, Argentina: Editorial Fundación Ross, 1999 and 2000, respectively).

22. "da hat die Not der Seinsverlassenheit gar keinen Zeit-Raum." 86/125.

23. "In modern thought, there are rare but significant attempts to conceive of being beyond the principle of sovereignty. . . . In the Heideggerian idea of abandonment and the *Ereignis*, it seems that Being itself is likewise discharged and divested of all sovereignty." Giorgio Agamben, *Homo Sacer: Sovereign Power and Bare Life*, trans., Daniel Heller-Roazen (Stanford, CA: Stanford University Press, 1998), 48; *Homo Sacer: Il potere sovrano e la nuda vita* (Torino, Italia: Einaudi, 1995), 55–56. Furthermore, in the same book, Agamben indicates how he finds this insight already in *Being and Time*, in a manner that links Heidegger situating of *Dasein* in its facticity with the attraction of his thought for fascism (Ibid., page 150 in English and 167 in Italian.)

24. 76–77/109.

25. Themes that are used as much by television shows, priests, and politicians, as by educators and parents!

26. Michel Haar, "Empty Time and Indifference to Being," *Heidegger Towards the Turn*, ed. James Risser (Albany: State University of New York Press, 1999), 312–13.

27. "da alle wesentlichen Titel durch die Vernutzung aller Grundwörte und die Zerstörung des echten Bezugs zum Wort unmöglich geworden sind."3/3.

28. 86/124; graphic, 91/130.

29. 89/127.

30. 76/109.

31. 79/113; cf. 81/115, *Ver-wesung des Seyns*.

32. "Versagung aber ist nicht nichts, sondern eine ausgezeichnete ursprüngliche Art des Unerfüllt-, des Leerlassens; somit eine ausgezeichnete Art der Eröffnung."

Chapter 2

1. "Die Seinsverlassenheit: sie muß als das Grundgeschehnis unserer Geschichte erfahren und ins Wissen—das gestalterische und führende—gehoben werden." *Beiträge zur Philosophie (Vom Ereignis)*, 78/112.

2. "Die Seinsverlassenheit ist die erste Dämmerung des Seyns als Sichverbergen aus der Nacht der Metaphysik. . . ." 207/293.

3. Echo of the essencing of beyng
Out [*aus*] of the abandonment of being:
Through [*durch*] the distressing distress
Of the forgottenness of beyng. 75/107

4. 65/95.

5. Dominique Janicaud, *The Powers of the Rational*, trans., Peg Birmingham and Elizabeth Birmingham (Bloomington: Indiana University Press, 1994), 16–21 and 176–86.

6. "Seynsverlassenheit ist im Grunde eine Ver-wesung des Seyns." 81/115; cf. "Above, the decomposition of truth," *Zerfall der Wahrheit*, 79/113.

7. Heidegger will take this theme of overcoming as the task of *Contributions* immediately after the composition of this work. Vide, "Die Überwindung der Metaphysik," *Metaphysik und Nihilismus*, GA 67. On the issue of overcoming also see Dominique Janicaud's "Overcoming Metaphysics" and "Heidggeriana," in *Heidegger: From Metaphysics to Thought*, trans., Michael Gendre (Albany: State University of

New York Press, 1995), 1–37. Vide, also Françoise Dastur's "La fin de la philosophie et l'autre commencement de la pensée," en *Heidegger, questions ouvertes* (Paris: Osiris, 1998), 137.

　　8. Heidegger writes, "Versagung aber ist nicht nichts, sondern eine ausgezeichnete ursprüngliche Art des Unerfüllt-, des Leerlassens; somit eine ausgezeichnete Art der Eröffnung. 265/379.

　　9. 96/138; and, "This awareness dare not get bogged down in either the word or in an initial elucidation of what is meant [by nihilism] in Nietzsche. Instead this awareness must recognize the abandonment of being as essencing." 98/141.

　　10. Martin Heidegger, "The Grounding Question and the Guiding Question of Philosophy," *Nietzsche*, Vol. I, trans., David Farrell Krell (San Francisco: Harper, 1991), 67.

　　11. 96–97/139–140. Here I am using Heidegger's differentiation between the grounding and the leading question (question of being) as is appears in Martin Heidegger, "The Grounding Question and the Guiding Question of Philosophy," *Nietzsche*, Vol. I, trans., David Farrell Krell (San Francisco: Harper, 1991), 67–68.

　　12. 79/113; cf. 81/115, *Ver-wesung des Seyns*.

　　13. 97/137. As Derrida indicates in "De l'esprit," in Heidegger *Verwesen* figures a move against Platonism, which in turn can be seen as a repatriation of the strange (*fremd*). Jacques Derrida, "De l'esprit Heidegger et la question," *Heidegger et la question* (Paris: Flammarion, 1990), 107.

　　14. 76/109.

　　15. 76/109.

　　16. 89/127.

　　17. "Within machination there is nothing questionworthy, nothing that could be esteemed through enactment of questioning as such, simply esteemed and thus lit up and elevated into truth." 76/109.

　　18. "Die Entscheidungslosigkeit als Bereich der Ungebundenheit der Machenschaften, wo das Große in der Ungestalt des Riesigen und die Klarheit als Durchsichtigkeit des Leeren sich aufspreizen." 84/120.

　　19. 84/121.

　　20. 84/121.

　　21. 85/121.

　　22. This latter term will later also refers to the transformative overflowing always already operative with all conceptual configurations of beings.

　　23. "Warum das Riesenhafte nicht den *Überfluß* kennt?" 96/137.

　　24. *Überfluß*, 96/137.

　　25. "Die Innigkeit dieser Erzitterung bedarf der abgründigsten Zerklüftung, und in dieser läßt sich die Unerschöpflichkeit des Seyns ahnend erdenken."173/244.

　　26. The term can be directly contrasted with the emotional adventure (*Erlebnis*) that is real life under the workings of machination.

　　27. We can think of the shift in thought from machination to thinking in the overflowing finitude of thought as the movement that Heidegger marks in the playful difference between the words *Ver-lassenheit* and *Ge-lassenheit*.

　　28. "Das seynsgeschichtliche Erfragen des Seyn ist nicht Umkehrung der Metaphysik. . . . Dieses soll anzeigen, daß das Sein hier nicht mehr metaphysisch gedacht wird." 307/436; Vide: 122/173; 129/184.

29. 130–31/186.

30. "Greek *peras*. A boundary is not that at which something stops but, as the Greeks recognized, the boundary is that from which something *begins in presencing*." "Building, Dwelling, Thinking," *Poetry, Language, Thought*, trans., Albert Hofstadter (New York: Harper and Row, Perennial Classic Edition, 2001), 152. "Bauen Wohnen Denken," *Vorträge und Aufsätze*, Fünfte Auflage (Neske, 1985), 147.

31. "Das Da-sein im Sinne des anderen Anfangs ist das uns noch ganz Befremdliche, das wir nie vorfinden, das wir allein erspringen im Einsprung in die Gründung der Offenheit des Sichverbergenden, jener Lichtung des Seyns, in die der künftige Mensch sich stellen muß, um sie offen zu halten." 210/297.

32. "Weil im philosophischen Erkennen jedesmal alles zugleich . . . in die Verrückung kommt und somit nie ein unmittelbares Vorstellen von etwas Vorhandenem möglich ist, bleibt das Denken der Philosophie befremdlich." 10/14.

Chapter 3

1. ". . . *vom Ereignis er-eignet ein denkerisch-sagendes Zugehören zum Seyn und in das Wort "des" Seyns*." My translation, cf. 3/3.

2. "Das Denken im Übergang stellt das erste Gewesene des Seyns der Wahrheit und das äußerste Zukünftige der Wahrheit des Seyns in die Zwiesprache und bringt in ihr das bisher unerfragte Wesen des Seyns zum Wort" 5/5–6. 75/107.

3. Abyssal refers to the face to face with the emptiness of machination, as well as to the overflowing fecundity of thought in its release from the illusion of rational domination of all configurations of beings.

4. 170/241

5. "das Sein hier nicht mehr metaphysisch gedacht wird." 307/4366.

6. "Keine Gegenbewegung . . . ," 130–31/186; "alle Versuche, die *gegen* die Metaphysik, die überall—auch als Positivismus—idealistisch ist, *r*eagieren, eben re-aktiv und damit von der Metaphysik grundsätzlich anhängig und somit selbst Metaphysik bleiben." 122/173; "Jetzt aber ist not die *große Umkehrung*, die jenseits ist aller 'Umwertung aller Werte. . . .'" 129/184.

7. Hans Ruin, "Origin in Exile: Heidegger and Benjamin on Language, Truth, and Translation," *Research in Phenomenology*, vol. xxix, 1999.

8. Ibid., 154.

9. Ibid., 153. For reasons of space and emphasis this is not the place for a discussion of will, in relation to *Stimmung*. For a fine study of and introduction to the issue vide Bret W. Davis's *Heidegger and the Will: On the Way to Gelassenheit* (Evanston, Il: Northwestern University Press, 2007).

10. 10–11/14.

11. "Weil im philosophischen Erkennen jedesmal alles zugleich . . . in die Verrückung kommt und somit nie ein unmittelbares Vorstellen von etwas Vorhandenem möglich ist, bleibt das Denken der Philosophie befremdlich." 11/14. As I have already indicated in the previous meditation, Derrida indicates in "De l'esprit" that Heidegger's rethinking of the tradition also suggests a repatriation of the strange (*Fremd*). Jacques Derrida, "De l'esprit Heidegger et la question," *Heidegger et la question* (Paris: Flammarion, 1990), 107.

12. As Agamben shows, Heidegger's concern with *Stimmung* occupies a central part of his 1929–1930 lecture course. Giorgio Agamben, *L'Aperto: L'uomo e l'animale* (Torino, Italia: Bollati Boringhieri, 2003), 60–74. And this only goes to repeat Krell's point in *Intimations of Mortality*, that Heidegger's thought is sustained by an intense sense of the modality of thought in thought that goes beyond the kind of methodological turn or shift of focus assigned him on the 1930s. (David Farrell Krell, *Intimations of Mortality* (State College, PA: Pennsylvania State University Press, 1991).) I mean that it is not a matter of other thought but of a modal change, a transformation in dis-position, where disposition is still the issue.

13. 11/14.

14. 11/14.

15. 75/107.

16. 119/169; 161/227.

17. "aber entspringend je der Grund-stimmung der Verhaltenheit." 75/107.

18. 15/21.

19. 17/23.

20. "Allein, die Grundstimmung *stimmt* das Da-sein und damit das *Denken* als Entwurf der Wahrheit des Seyns im Wort und Begriff." 16/21.

21. "Die Grundstimmung des Denkens im anderen Anfang schwingt in den Stimmungen. . . ." 11/14.

22. 16/21–22.

23. "Die Ahnung legt die anfängliche In-ständigkeit in das Da-sein." 16/22.

24. "Diese Entschiedenheit aber ist als erahnende nur die Nüchternheit der Leidenskraft des Schaffenden." 17/22–23.

25. The echo of being is only heard through undergoing the refusal of being, later understood as the call of being, and this double passage requires that thought be exposed to the fury of being.

26. This is a point central to the delineation of the limit of Heidegger's thought, which I owe to Claudia Baracchi.

27. Jacques Derrida, "Différence sexuelle, différence ontologique (Geschlecht I)," and "La main de Heidegger (Geschlecht II)," *Heidegger et la question: De l'esprit et autre essays* (Paris: Flammarion, 1990). In the latter text, we should note that Derrida's first footnote, attached to the title, makes direct mention of Heidegger's reading of Trakel, the poet that according to David Farrell Krell indicates Heidegger's engagement with singularity. *Intimations of Mortality* (State College: Pennsylvania State University Press, 1991), 7–8; ch. 11.

28. "Stimmung ist die Versprühung der Erzitterung des Seyns als Ereignis im Da-sein." My translation. 16/21.

29. Heidegger indicates this sense of being exposed in the fecund overflowing of beings when he writes that being conscious of this abyssal fecundity is only a preparation for a disposition that is not intentional: "die von Grund aus ein Zu-fall bleiben muß." 16–17/22.

30. "dessen Hoheit im Freimut der Begeisterung für die unausdenkbare Schenkung der Verweigerung die Entschiedenheit findet. . . . In dieser Entschiedenheit muß alle Wächterschaft des Da-seins Fuß gefaßt haben. . . ." 17/22–23.

31. "Die Entschiedenheit aber ist als erahnende nur die Nüchternheit der Leidenskraft des Schaffenden." 17/23.

32. "A Dialogue On Language," *On the Way to Language*, trans., Peter D. Hertz (San Francisco: Harper, 1971), 6–8.

33. "Die Verhaltenheit: das schaffende Aushalten im Ab-grund." 26/36.

34. Ibid.

35. "dies nicht als gelegentliches Vorkommnis, wobei eine vollziehbare Rede und Aussage unterbleibt, wo nur das Aus- und Wiedersagen des schon Gesagten und Sagbaren nicht vollzogen wird. . . ." 26/36.

36. "Die Verschlagung ist die anfängliche Bedingung für die sich entfaltende Möglichkeit einer ursprünglichen—dichtenden—Nennung des Seyns." 26/36.

37. "das anfängliche Denken als unbegriffliches." 26/36.

38. "de faire venir le silence à la parole." Françoise Dastur, "La fin de la philosophie et l'autre commencement de la pensée," en *Heidegger, questions ouvertes* (Paris: Osiris, 1998), 137.

39. "Die Sprache gründet im Schweigen." 359/510.

40. "Das Schweigen ist das verborgenste Maß-halten. Es hält das Maß, indem es die Maßstäbe erst setzt. Und so ist die Sprache Maß-setzung im Innersten und Weitesten, Maß-setzung als Erwesung des Fugs und seiner Fügung (Ereignis)." 359/510.

41. "die Sprache Grund des Da-seins." 359/510. Giorgio Agamben offers a fine and enlightening interpretation of the concept of the open in Heidegger in *L'aperto*. (Giorgio Agamben, *L'Aperto: L'uomo e l'animale* (Torino, Italia: Bollati Boringhieri, 2003).)

42. "Aufklang der Erde, Widerklang der Welt. Streit, die ursprüngliche Bergung der Zerklüftung, weil der innigste *Riß*. Die *offene Stelle*." My translation. 358/510.

43. "Sucher des Seyns ist im eigensten Übermaß sucherischer Kraft der Dichter, der das Seyn 'stiftet.' " 9/11.

44. Ibid. 9/11, 14/19.

45. For a thorough discussion of the issue see Friedrich-Wilhelm v. Herrman, *Wege ins Ereignis*, ch. 3 (Frankfurt am Main: Vittorio Klostermann, 1994).

46. "Darnach ist die Philosophie jetzt zuerst Vorbereitung der Philosophie in der Weise der Erbauung der nächsten Vorhöfe, in deren Raumgefüge Hölderlins Wort hörbar wird, durch das Da-*sein* beantwortet und in solcher Antwort zur Sprache des künftigen Menschen gegründet." 297/421–22.

47. For my discussion of poetry and the work of art in Heidegger Vide, Alejandro A. Vallega, "Concrete Passages," *Heidegger and the Issue of Space: Thinking on Exilic Grounds* (University Park: Pennsylvania State Press, 2003)

Chapter 4

1. "Die Wahrheit als Grund gründet aber ursprünglich als Abgrund." 267/383.

2. "die Nüchternheit der Leidenskraft der Schaffenden . . . die der Wesensgewalt des Seiendes die Stille eröffnet, aus der das Seyn (als Ereignis) vernehmbar wird." 17/23.

3. "Dieser aber bedarf einer höheren Kraft des Schaffens und Fragens, zugleich aber der tieferen Bereitschaft zum Leiden und Austragen im Ganzen eines völligen Wandels der Bezüge zum Seienden und zum Seyn." 129/184.

4. Respectivamente: 278/397; 9/11, cf. 77; 279/397.

5. 11/14.

6. "die Verhaltenheit ist die Mitte für das Erschrecken und die Scheu. Diese kennzeichnen nur ausdrücklicher, was *ursprünglich* zu ihr gehört. Sie bestimmt den Stil des anfänglichen Denken im anderen Anfang." 12/15.

7. Heidegger is clear that this is not a heroic task, a rational project, or a simple matter of living real life in thoughtless projections of the immediate. 11/14 Furthermore, we should also keep in mind that here is not the case that we can simply apply the false dialectic of machination between rational calculative production and emotions. "Die Zusammengehörigkeit beider wird nur begriffen aus dem Rückgang in ihre weiteste Ungleichzeitigkeit und aus der Auflösung des Scheins ihrer äußersten Gegensätzlichkeit. Wenn die denkerische Besinnung (als Fragen nach der Waherheit des Seyns und nur als dieses) zum Wissen von dieser Zusammengehörigkeit gelangt, dann ist zugleich der Grundzug der Geschichte des ersten Anfangs (die Geschichte der abendlandischen Metaphysik) bereits aus dem Wissen des anderen Anfangs her Begriffen." 89–90/128.

8. Jacques Derrida, "Différence sexuelle, différence ontologique (Geschlecht I)," "La main de Heidegger (Geschlecht II)," and "De L'Esprit Heidegger et la question," *Heidegger et la question:De l'esprit et autre essays* (Paris: Flammarion, 1990). Giorgio Agamben, *Homo Sacer* (Torino, Italia: Einaudi, 1994), 168 on *Dasein* and 69 on *Contributions*. English *Homo Sacer* (Stanford, CA: Stanford University Press, 1998), 151 on *Dasein* and 59 on *Contribution*. *L'Aperto: L'uomo e l'animale* (Torino, Italia: Bollati Boringhieri, 2003).

9. "Darnach ist die Philosophie jetzt zuerst Vorbereitung der Philosophie in der Weise der Erbauung der nächsten Vorhöfe, in deren Raumgeüge Hölderlins Wort hörbar wird, durch das Da-sein beantwortet und in solcher Antwort zur Sprache des künftigen Menschen gegründet." 297/421–22.

10. "Darnach ist die Philosophie jetzt zuerst Vorbereitung der Philosophie in der Weise der Erbauung der nächsten Vorhöfe, in deren Raumgefüge Hölderlins Wort hörbar wird, durch das Da-sein beantwortet und in solcher Antwort zur Sprache des künftigen Menschen gegründet." 297/421–22. I have replaced essential swaying with essencing.

11. See *Germanien* y *Der Rhein*, in his course about the poet (GA39). Also see Daniela Vallega-Neu, *Heidegger's Contributions to Philosophy* (Bloomington: Indiana University Press, 2003), 75.

12. "Keiner sei heute vermessen und nehme es als bloßen Zufall, daß diese drei, die je in ihrer Weise zuletzt die Entwurzelung am tiefsten durchlitten haben, der die abendländische Geschichte zugetrieben wird, und die zugleich ihre Götter am innigsten erahnt haben, frühzeitig aus der Helle ihres Tages hinweg mußten." 143/204.

13. F.-W. von Herrman's *"Die Blume des Mundes" Zum Verhältnis von Heidegger zu Hölderlin," Wege ins Ereignis* (Frankfurt am Main: Klostermann, 1994): 246–63. " 'The flower of the mouth': Hölderlin's hint for Heidegger's thinking of the essence of language" from *Martin Heidegger: Critical Assessments*, ed., Christopher Mac Ann, vol. iii (London: Routledge, 1992).

14. Hans Ruin, "Origin in Exile: Heidegger and Benjamin on Language, Truth, and Translation," *Research in Phenomenology*, vol. xxix, 1999.

15. 297/422.

16. 143/204.

17. "Die Gefährlichkeit der Frage, wer wir sind, ist zugleich . . . der einzige Weg, um zu uns selbst zu kommen und damit die ursprüngliche Rettung, d.h. Rechfertigung des Abendlandes aus seiner Geschichte, anzubahnen." 38/54.

18. "Soll noch einmal uns eine Geschichte beschieden sein, die schaffende Ausgesetztheit in das Seiende aus der Zugehörigkeit zum Sein, dann ist unabwendbar *die* Bestimmung: Den Zeit-Raum der letzten Entscheidung—ob und wie wir diese Zugehörigkeit erfahren und gründen—*vorzubereiten.*" 10/13.

19. Jacques Derrida, De L'Esprit Heidegger et la question," *Heidegger et la question: De l'esprit et autre essays* (Paris: Flammarion, 1990), 134–43.

20. The whole of my work on exilic thought is a preparation for engaging Heidegger at its limit and beyond it, in its borders and transgressions. Vide *Heidegger and the Issue of Space: Thinking On Exilic Grounds* (University Park: Pennsylvania State University Press, 2003).

21. "um so dem Geschichtlichen Menschen noch einmal ein Ziel zu geben. . . ." 12/16.

22. 24/33; 278/396. The lectures were published in GA39.

23. 278/396.

24. "der Gewähr der Größe, nicht der leeren und riesigen Ewigkeit, sondern der kürzesten Bahn." 285/406.

25. "Dasein ist die *Krisis* zwischen dem ersten und dem anderen Anfang." 208/295.

26. "Nur in der unmittelbaren Überspringung des ,Historischen' wird Geschichte." 8/10.

27. 210/297.

28. "Das Denken im Übergang stellt das erste Gewesene des Seyns der Wahrheit und das äußerste Zukünftige der Wahrheit des Seyns in die Zwiesprache und bringt in ihr das bisher unerfragte Wesen des Seyns zum Wort." 5/5–6.

29. He writes of his thought in the outline of *Cotributions* as, "*Vorbereitung des Übergangs . . .*" 5/6.

30. "Die Zeit der Erbauung der Wesensgestalt des Seienden aus der Wahrheit des Seyns ist noch nicht gekommen." 4/5.

Chapter 5

1. Scott, Charles, *The Time of Memory* (Albany: State University of New York Press, 1999). All references will be marked only by page number.

2. 254.

3. 254–55.

4. 9.

5. 7.

6. 30–35.

7. Nietzsche, "On the Use and Abuse of History for Life," *Untimely Meditations* (Cambridge: Cambridge University Press, 1997); Jorge Luis Borges, "Funes el Memorioso," *Ficciones* (Buenos Aires, Argentina: Emecé, 1992).

8. 34.
9. 33.
10. 36.
11. 9.
12. 9.
13. 11.
14. 11.
15. 7.
16. 7.

17. For Scott's treatment of Heidegger's understanding of *aletheia* see "Adikia and Catastrophe: Heidegger's 'Anaximander Fragment,' " in *Heidegger Studies*, volume 10/1994, 127–42.

18. 79.
19. 80.
20. 248.
21. 254.
22. 272.

23. "An art that unites those knots of insistence that so often compose the obsessions of thought that are centered on an image of something unifying and unchanging and continuously, unceasingly repeating in all appearances." (272)

24. 21.
25. 60.
26. 32.
27. 31.
28. 57.
29. 56.
30. 57.
31. 57.

32. This is the crucial term for Scott in his interpretation of Nietzsche. Also, I believe David Krell is pointing to such a moment in Heidegger, when he discusses his conversation with him and the way Heidegger spoke of *lichtung* in registers attuned to lightness, weightlessness. Krell's keen ear hears this in the expression "*viel-**leicht***." Vide David Farrell Krell, "The Transitions of Lichtung," *Intimations of Mortality* (State College: Pennsylvania State University Press, 1991), 94.

33. Scott treat this point in "All Truth—Is that not a Compound Lie?; The Ascetic Ideal in Heidegger's Thought," *The Question of Ethics: Nietzsche, Foucault, Heidegger* (Bloomington: Indiana University Press, 1990), 202–10.

Chapter 6

1. "*ainos athanateisi theeis eis hora eoiken*," *The Iliad*, III, 158.
2. Juan José Saer, "En Linea," *Lugar* (Buenos Aires: Seix Barral, 2000), 40.
3. 243b.
4. Longinus, *On the Sublime*, trans., A. O. Prickard (London: Oxford at the Clarendon Press, 1961), 30 and 31.

5. This is particularly the case for Greek thought, and in this sense marks a difference with modernity, a point made by Heidegger in terms of the change from the concept of space as place to a mere quantifiable being, *History of the Concept of Time*, trans., Theodore Kisiel (Bloomington: Indiana University Press, 1985), 234–36. GA20, 321–25. Jacob Klein specifically develops the issue of the concreteness of the Greek concept of number and its transformation in modernity in *Greek Mathematical Thought and the Origin of Algebra*, trans., Eva T. H. Brann (Cambridge, MA: MIT Press, 1968).

6. In this sense, I suspect that in part what is uncanny and disturbing in beauty as well as in the appearing and the intelligibility of beings is that translucence in which they shine.

7. Jacob Klein, *A Commentary on the Meno* (Chicago, IL: University of Chicago Press, 1989), 3–4.

8. Jacob Klein, *Greek Mathematical Thought and the Origin of Algebra*, trans., Eva T. H. Brann (Cambridge, MA: MIT Press, 1968). "It can be shown that *arithmos never* means anything other than 'a definite number of definite objects.'" Introduction, 6.

9. "*For Plato, however, it is precisely his unmathematical use of the* arithmos *structure that is essential.* For the *arithmoi eidetikoi* are intended to make intelligible not only the inner articulation of the realm of ideas but every possible articulation, every possible division and conjunction—in short, all *counting.*" (*Greek Mathematical Thought and the Origins of Algebra,* 92) Along these lines, although Klein recognizes the dramatic import of the logos in the dialogue, he differentiates mimetic playfulness from dianoetic seriousness. (*A Commentary on the Meno,* 27.) Cf. Oskar Becker's treatment of geometry in *Beiträge zur phäenomenologischen Begründung der Geometrie und ihrer physikalischen Anwendung,* 2. unveränderte Auflage (Tübingen: Max Niemeyer Verlag, 1973).

10. Jacques Derrida, "Plato's Pharmacy," *Dissemination*, trans., Barbara Johnson (Chicago, IL: University of Chicago Press, 1981).

11. "In the end 'Plato's Pharmacy' is much less about Plato's dialogue than about the possibilities for reading the dialogue . . . the possibilitiy of receiving it at the limits of a theory of intention." Michael Naas, *Taking On the Tradition: Jacques Derrida and the Legacies of Deconstruction* (Stanford, CA: Stanford University Press, 2003).

12. Vide comments by the editor in *A Derrida Reader: Between the Blinds*, ed., Peggy Kamuf (New York: Columbia University Press,1991), 112–13.

13. "The *khairein* takes place in the name of truth: that is, in the name of knowledge of truth and, more precisely, of truth in the knowledge of the self." Jacques Derrida, "Plato's Pharmacy," *Dissemination*, trans., Barbara Johnson (Chicago, IL: University of Chicago Press, 1981), 69. Gadamer's passing remark that in the *Phaidros* the soul appears as "a many headed monstrosity" seems to me to be more fruitful in terms of understanding the dialogue, in as much as it recognizes the impossibility of reading the dialogue as the matter of one central way of understanding philosophical logos. (Hans-Georg Gadamer, *Dialogue and Dialectic: Eight Hermeneutical Studies on Plato*, trans., Christopher Smith (New Haven, CT: Yale University Press, 1980), 88. In fact, Derrida insists on the fractured thematic of the dialogue in order to show the impossibility of gathering language into one self-knowing discursive consciousness; while perhaps in the various accounts of the dialogue's theme in Diogenes Laertius

we find indications of a simplicity almost lost to us moderns, namely, the unfolding of philosophical thought in the density of experience rather than from the distance of rational discourse. As Diogenes Laertius indicates, the dialogue seems to have been understood as a dialogue primarily on love, and also ethics (from Thrasylus, 328), as a practical instruction of the ethical (320), and, most important for us, on the movement of letters (reading and writing), *"tes grammatikes ten dunamin"* (298). (Diogenes Laertius, *Lives of Eminent Philosophers*, volume I (Cambridge, MA: Loeb Series, Harvard University Press, 1966)). The difficulty with understanding how its themes relate and its seemingly abrupt structure is indicated by Paul Friedländer in his essay on the Phaidros. Paul Friedländer, *Plato*, volume III (Princeton, NJ: Princeton University Press, 1969), 241. Cf, Diogenes Laertius on the beauty of the dialogues: *Lives of Eminent Philosophers*, vol. I (Cambridge, MA: Loeb Series, Harvard University Press, 1966), 318.

14. Cf. Claudia Baracchi's discussion of Derrida in "Words of Air: On Breath and Inspiration:" *Epoché*, vol. 11, no. 1 (Fall, 2006), pages 40 and 41. Notice that this critique is based on the reading of Socrates as not primarily a matter of transcendental subjective consciousness, rather as a figured ecstatic (35) and as a "surface and appearance through which voice resounds." (37) Also on Derrida's understanding of the voice as transcendental, see Françoise Dastur's "Derrida and the Question of Presence," *Research in Phenomenology*, vol. 36 (2006), 45–59.

15. A fine example of this third way of looking at the dialogue is found in Claudia Baracchi's "Words of Air: On Breath and Inspiration:" *Epoché*, Vol. 11, no. 1 (Fall, 2006). The idea of a *mathesis universalis* in Descartes' *Rules for the Direction of the Mind* is one of the places where knowledge becomes mind, separate from body. Descartes, *Rules for the Direction of the Mind*, *The Philosophical Writings of Descartes*, vol. I, trans., Dugal Murdoch (Cambridge: Cambridge University Press, 1988), 19.

16. Interestingly, the plot thickens in relation to the central figure of the dialogue, and its theme, *philia*, since Diogenes Laertius in the *Lives of Eminent Philosophers* claims that Plato was in love with Phaidros, to whom he even wrote a few lines of poetry. The closing lone of the passage quoted by Laertius is particularly interesting: "Was it not thus that we lost Phaidros?" Diogenes Laertius, *Lives of Eminent Philosophers*, vol. I (Cambridge, MA: Loeb Series, Harvard Press, 1966), 304–5.

17. Although much of the discussion in the dialogue is about *philia* I believe that ultimately it is the erotic sense of *philia* and of the madness behind *philosophia* that is central to the text, as is the case throughout Plato's dialogues. On the fundamental role of *eros* in relationship to the philosophical logos and the ideas see Stanley Rosen, *The Quarrel Between Philosophy and Poetry* (New York: Routledge Press, 1988), for example 80; and, Eva Brann, *The Music of the Republic* (Philadelphia: Paul Dry Books, 2004), 240.

18. 227a–230e., all quotes follow the numeration of Plato, vol. I, trans., Harold North Fowler, Loeb Series (Cambridge, MA: Harvard University Press, 1990.) The quotes are from William S. Cobb, *Plato's Erotic Dialogues* (Albany: State University of New York Press, 1993).

19. For this vide, Cicadas, 259a–259e. Also see Claudia Baracchi's "Words of Air: On Breath and Inspiration:" *Epoché*, vol. 11, no. 1 (Fall, 2006): "In being there Socrates is present in and to the place—not *in* and *to* himself. But present *outside*

himself, ecstatically." Also "Socrates exposed to the environs, its voices, the moods and registers of the living . . . ," (35); and, "Socrates shows himself, then, as *persona*, as surface and appearing *through* which voice *resounds*" (37).

20. Unlike the sophist's speech, which contorts and disfigures what is by nature by fixing its gaze on what seems to be true in speeches alone.

21. Socrates constantly alludes to this sense of the name with phrases that identify his interlocutor, as for example, golden (235e), handsome (244a), and beautiful (252b).

22. 234d; Cf. "Well, you my beautiful boy, for whom my speech is given. . . ." 252b. *Ganasthai*, from *ganao*, to shine, glitter, gleam; Lat. *Nitere*. English "nitid," bright, lustrous. The term "*nítido*" is used in Spanish to indicate clarity, in the sense of visibility and definition.

23. 236e.

24. The issue of this leeway is fundamental to the thought of the dialogue, and it is introduced from the start by the word "*scholē*" (leisure). "You shall hear if you have the leisure to come along and listen," 227b. Here, leeway is also inseparable from a certain temporality required for thought. This is again indicated in the early sections of the dialogue in contrast with the word "*diatribē*," a slow passing away or even delaying of time associated with Phaidros' listening to Lysias' speech, 227b5.

25. 257b.

26. 231a–234c.

27. 231a–234c.

28. As Baracchi point out, this does make sense for the sophist. "Words of Air . . . , 32.

29. 231d.

30. This is present in statements about the true friend as one who makes plans in terms of one's own interest, 231e; cf.231b; for future benefit not love, not slave to love but one's own master, 233c.

31. Vide ft. not 12.

32. 237a–241d.

33. 237a; cf.243b.

34. The word for the difficulty Sócrates may encounter if he looks at Phaidros is *diaporomai*, and refers us to *aporia*, which means literally a break in the road, a point one cannot pass. 237a.

35. "I'll attempt to render my recantation to him, with my head bare not hidden as before out of shame," 243b. Socrates' second speech goes from 244a to 257b.

36. In this speech, Socrates begins by discussing three ways in which madness is not interpreted as destructive by public opinion. (244b–245a) After this, he gives an argument for the immortality of the everchanging soul, and he follows this argument with the well known image of the two horses and the charioteer for the structure of the soul. (245b–246b) He then goes on to tell the story of the journeys of winged souls to the limits of the heavens, and of how souls lose their wings, fall to earthly life and come to have mortal bodies. (246c–247c) His story then comes to its central point, as Socrates explains on the basis of what he has already stated, there exists a fourth kind of madness, this is the recollection of what the soul experienced

in the company of the gods before falling to earthly and bodily life. (249a–250e) He will then conclude by giving an account of desire, the lover, and love on the basis of recollection. In this lengthy final argument love is called forth as one encounters the image of the beautiful in the world, the bearable form of wisdom to the senses, and in relation to recalling the beautiful and true as such, as the soul has seen them before falling to earth. (251e–257a)

37. "In language and in other ways it was forced to be somewhat poetical because of Phaidros." 257b. In this sense, the third story can be read in terms of the discussion which almost immediately follows it, in which Socrates states that in order to be fully persuasive one must know the soul of the interlocutor and the kind of speech that will be most fitted to that particular soul. (271d–272b) Thus, Socrates tells stories, and stories fitting to the nature of the interlocutor, stories fitting to Phaidros.

38. 247c–e.

39. 275d–275e.

40. 275e.

41. 276a.

42. "*lógon légeis zönta kaí émpsuchon . . . ,*" 276a.

43. 276a.

44. 278a.

45. 276a.

46. A number of times in this part of his conversation Socrates likens his speech to a dissemination, a transformative spreading. Socrates speaks of this speech as a planting of seeds, of the writer watching the shoots grow, and even as speeches that "are not barren but contain a seed from which others grow up in other abodes, such that its process is rendered eternal and immortal." 276c; 276d; 277a; cf. 278b.

47. Indeed, in this sense, one might say, that it is a *pharmakon*; a *pharmakon* that aims to transform the soul of Phaidros, rather than merely appropriating his life without regard for the soul.

48. "Every soul is immortal. For that which is everchanging is immortal." 245c.

49. Thus, Socrates will speak about the many journeys of the soul in its progress, while sustaining that ultimately the friends of wisdom experience a kind of madness or love that arises from recollecting what their souls have already seen of the good, being, and the beautiful. 249d–250d.

50. In this sense translucent in undergoing the resounding of voice. Cf. "Socrates shows himself, then, as *persona*, as surface and appearing *through* which voice *resounds*" (Claudia Baracchi's "Words of Air: On Breath and Inspiration," *Epoché*, vol. 11, no. 1 (Fall, 2006), 37).

51. That is to say, if Phaidros will shine, this intelligibility will occur with and through the motion of the soul as figured in the word or turning.

52. 48c.

53. It is curious, and perhaps accents Derrida's forceful reading of the *Phaidros* in terms of writing as the site of the slippage of discursive transcendental consciousness, that Derrida never speaks of the *Phaidros* in his book on *philia*: Jacques Derrida, *Politics of Friendship*, trans., George Collins (London: Verso, 1997).

54. 266b; 269b.

55. 265d and 265e.

56. Vide Cobb, *Phaedrus*, footnote 91,199. Although it might sound as stating the obvious, I might add that the very form of Plato's works suggests that dialectic should not be severed from its dialogical sense, i.e., from being understood as a thinking that occurs *through* conversation.

57. As Rosen points out, "In the *Phaidros*, Socrates or Plato proceed by indirection and dramatic enactment, but these are not less eloquent than logical symbolism." Stanley Rosen, *The Quarrel Between Philosophy and Poetry* (New York: Routledge Press, 1988), 98.

58. 275d–e. This is clear in many instances in Plato's dialogues, certainly in Socrates' critique of the poets, a critique, I might add, echoed at the turning point of his third discourse in the *Phaidros*, 247c.

59. 244a.

60. 270b. According to Socrates, the best speeches call for something more than merely technical ability to cause a desired effect.

61. 243a–b. In Euripides' *Helen*, she even appears as a ghost, while the real Helen is eventually found in Egypt.

62. Juan José Saer, "En Linea," *Lugar* (Buenos Aires: Seix Barral, 2000), 39–42.

63. 36.

64. 37.

65. 37.

66. Again, one can see the relationship to Baracchi's understanding of Socrates' figure in the dialogue in "Words of Air . . . ," 37.

67. 41.

68. Wallace Stevens, "Of Modern Poetry," *The Collected Poems* (New York, Random House, 1990), 239.

69. In having ventured thus far towards the nature (*phúsis*) of the translucence (*phaidros*) of beings, we have often spoken of the soul (*psuche*). This last term can only be for our discussion an indication of what now remains to be thought, i.e., of the task of learning to speak in those words with which in their translucence beings may shine.

70. One finds an indication as well as the neglect of this insight in Blanchot's remarks on the unsayability of death in Plato's cave analogy: "*Dans la cave de Platon, nul mo pour signifier la mort, nul rêve ou nulle image pour en fair pressentir l'infiguralite.*" *L'écriture du desastre* (Gallimar, 1980), 60. Our discussion does not only engage this impossibility operative in the logos as fundamental to the shine of beings, as does Blanchot. According to what we have said, in order to engage language beyond its merely descriptive sense in metaphysics, we do not need to follow Blanchot's strategic interpretation of the logos as an operation of self-undoing or nothingness. In what we have said of translucence the presentment of "l'infiguralite" is precisely what is at play in the writing in the soul, and this writing occurs through "l'infiguralite." The point is that through our discussion we gain insight into experiences of the word that free us from the infinite deferment of senses of being in thought forced by Blanchot's strategy. If in order to free writing to its transgressive being one must say with Blanchot that nothing occurs, in Plato we find a word that is already engaged in its transgression without deferment.

Chapter 7

1. Paul Celan, *Atemkristall*, bibliophile edition, 75 copies (Paris: Brunidor, 1965). (Republished. Frankfurt am Main: Suhrkamp, 1990). *Atemwende* (Frankfurt am Main: Suhrkamp, 1982). *Paul Celan die Gedichte, Kommentierte Gesamtausgabe* (Frankfurt am Main: Suherkamp, 2003), PCG 175–217. All page numbers here refer to the latter, and as *PCG*. All English translations are from Paul Celan, *Selected Poems and Prose of Paul Celan*, trans., John Felstiner (New York W. W. Norton, 2001), and will be indicated by SPPC.

2. Hans-George Gadamer, *Wer bin Ich und wer bist Du?* (Frankfurt am Main: Suhrkamp, 1973). *Who Am I and Who Are You?* trans., Heinemann and Krajevwski (Albany: State University of New York Press, 1997). *Äesthetik und Poetik II*, Gadamer Gesammelte Werke, vol. 9 (Tübingen: Mohr, 1993), 383–451. All page numbers will refer to the GW, and then to the English translation as "*Who. . . .*"

3. "*Es gibt offenbar auch andere Weisen des Sprechens, in denen sich das hermeneutische Grundverhältnis von Frage und Antwort eigentümlich modifiziert. . . . Sie bilden eine hermeneutische Anwendungsproblematik, der ich mich seit dem Erscheinen von "Waherheit und Methode" zunehmend mehr gewidmet habe.Von zwei Seiten aus glaube ich der Sache nährgekommen zu sein . . . und sodann von moderner hermetischer Dichtung her, wie ich sie in einem Kommentar zu Paul Celans "Atemkristall" zum Gegenstand gemacht habe.*" Gadamer, "Selbstdarstellung," GW. vol. II, 508.

4. Vide also Jean Grondin, "Gadamer and the Universe of Hermeneutics," 120.

5. An implicit question throughout this discussion is that of the relationship between poetry and philosophy. For a guiding discussion on the issue, specifically in Hermeneutics, see, Risser, James "The Voice of the Poet," *Hermeneutics and the Voice of the Other: Re-Reading Gadamer's Philosophical Hermeneutics* (Albany: State University of New York Press, 1997), 185–208.

6. This speech was given by Celan in the occasion of accepting the Büchner Prize in 1960. *Paul Celan, Ausgewählten Gedichte* (Frankfurt am Main: Suhrkamp, 1968), 133–48. Paul Celan, *Selected Poems and Prose of Paul Celan*, trans., John Felstiner (New York: W. W. Norton, 2001), SPPC, 47–48. Although not yet available in English, I should mention the fine and important work on Gadamer and also on Celan by the Italian philosopher and scholar Donatella Di Cesare.

7. GW, 133–34; *Who . . .* , 146.

8. Jean Grondin, "Gadamer and the Universe of Hermeneutics," *Introduction to Philosophical Hermeneutics*, trans., Weinsheimer (New Haven, CT: Yale University Press, 1997), 108.

9. From Gadamer's *Truth and Method*, 7–8: GW, vol. I (Tübingen: Mohr, 1990), 13; in Grondin, "Gadamer and the Universe of Hermeneutics," 108.

10. From Gadamer's *Truth and Method*, 7–8: GW, vol. I (Tübingen: Mohr, 1990), 13; in Grondin, "Gadamer and the Universe of Hermeneutics," 108.

11. When I use sensuousness, I only mean to indicate this issue of the experience of the configuration of concepts and language understood in light of Gadamer's broad hermeneutical overture.

12. Although this chapter is on Gadamer and Celan, I will punctuate it by introducing a third voice, that of Jacques Derrida, from the collection of essays on Celan titled *Sovereignties in Question: The Poetics of Paul Celan*, ed., Thomas Dutoit and Outi Pasanen (New York: Fordham University Press, 2005). As the careful reader will notice, the contrast will serve to make the direction of my discussion clearer.

13. For a reading of the poem that seems to touch on the same issues but at a more literary level, see Jerry Glenn, *Paul Celan* (New York: Twayne Publishers, 1973.)

14. The work was republished by Suhrkamp in 1990.

15. Concerning the first, Gadamer is brief and clear, "every poem in this sequence is a configuration of ambiguous precision." (GW, 383; *Who* . . . , 67) He sees in this precision a need for reading the poems first word by word, and, by situating the sense of each word in terms of the unity of the figure formed by the speech. (GW, 429; *Who* . . . , Epilogue, 129) Such discipline serves as an introduction to Celan's poems in their polyvalent complexity. But ultimately, in his characteristic simplicity and directness, he states that one must, "simply try to keep listening." (GW, 383; *Who* . . . , 67)

16. GW, 388; *Who* . . . , 73.

17. *DU DARFST mich getrost*
Mit Schnee bewirten:
Sooft ich Schulter an Schulter
Mit dem Maulbeerbaum schritt durch den Sommer,
schrie sein jüngstes
Blatt. PCD, 175.

18. GW, 388; *Who* . . . , 73.

19. GW, 391; *Who* . . . , 78.

20. GW, 421; *Who* . . . , 118.

21. PCG, 178–79.

22. GW, 414; *Who* . . . , 108.

23. "Die eigentliche Aussage ist vielmehr, daß es 'Wundgelesens' ist, das so nach oben kommt"). GW, 413; *Who* . . . , 107.

24. "Words are not necessarily transparent, hermeneutics cannot escape non-transparency and the word that may be untranslated." James Risser, *Hermeneutics and the Voice of the Other*, 198.

25. PCG, 178; SPPC, 237.

26. GW, 411–12; *Who* . . . , 105.

27. "Sinn und Sinnverhüllung bei Paul Celan," GW, 452; "Meaning and Concealment of Meaning in Paul Celan," in *Who* . . . , 167.

28. "Phänomenologischer und semantischer Zugang zu Celan," GW, 462; *Who* . . . , 180.

29. Cf. Breath as a figure of the rift in thought that is wonder in philosophy, in Rodolphe Gaché's "Thinking, Without Wonder," *Epoché*, vol. 10, no. 2 (Spring 2006), 333.

30. Vide footnote 14.

31. GW, 413; *Who* . . . , 107.

32. "Ansprache anläßlich der Entgegennahme des Literaturpreises der Freien Hansestadt Bremen," Paul Celan Ausgewählte Gedichte," 128; "Speech on the Occasion of Receiving the Literature Prize of the free Hanseatic City of Bremen," *Paul Celan: Collected Prose*, 34.

33. See John Felstiner's "Loss and the Mother Tongue," *Paul Celan: Poet, Survivor, Jew* (New Heaven, CT: Yale University Press, 1995).

34. For a very interesting and well informed discussion of Celan, Heidegger and Derrida around the issue of temporality and the *Augenblick* in Celan's "Meridian" see Outi Pasanen's "Notes on the *Augenblick* in and Around Jacques Derrida's Reading of Paul Celan's 'The Meridian,'" *Research in Phenomenology*, vol. 36 (2006), 214–37.

35. "Ansprache anläßlich der Entgegennahme des Literaturpreises der Freien Hansestadt Bremen," Paul Celan Ausgewählte Gedichte," 141; "Meridian," *Selected Poems and Prose of Paul Celan*, trans., John Felstiner (New York: W. W. Norton, 2001), 47.

36. See Fóti, Veroníque, "Meridians of Encounter," *Heidegger and the Poets* (New York: Humanities Press, 1992), 99–110.

37. "Ansprache anläßlich der Entgegennahme des Literaturpreises der Freien Hansestadt Bremen," Paul Celan Ausgewählte Gedichte," 142; "Meridian," *Paul Celan: Collected Prose*, 47.

38. Vide Derrida's "Majesties," *Sovereignties in Question . . . ,*" 108.

39. "Edgar Jené and The Dream About The Dream," *Paul Celan: Collected Prose*, 4.

40. For a general discussion of the history of this text, and a literary interpretation of it that parallels my discussion, see Jerry Glenn, *Paul Celan* (New York: Twayne Publishers, 1973), ch. 2.

41. "Edgar Jené and The Dream About The Dream," *Paul Celan: Collected Prose*, 6. *Edgar Jené und der Traum vom Traume* (Vienna: Agathon, 1948). I shall at least indicate here that this emphasis On a certain sense of interruption and loss behind the experience of words is meant to set up an opening for the engagement of the word as a prelinguistic sensuous experience. This is a step which requires that the understanding of word as encased and determined by a system ruled by logic and syntax, and as a matter of representation, be at least placed in question.

42. Ibid.

43. "Edgar Jené and The Dream About The Dream," *Paul Celan: Collected Prose*, 6–7.

44. For Celan's early life and works see Israel Chalfen, *Paul Celan: Eine Biographie seiner Jugend* (Frankfurt am Main: Insel Verlag, 1979).

45. Letter, May 20, 1965, in *Die Welt*, 20 May, 1990.

46. The proximity of Gisèle's graphic works to Celan's word and well-being is again apparent in 1967, when after seven month of clinic treatment Celan writes again and dedicates the poem to his wife. The poem is later published along with a print by her. Vide Felstiner, *Paul Celan: Poet, Survivor, Jew*, 231.

47. An example of the impossibility of taking such differentiation for granted can be seen in the works of Cy Twombly, for example his well known "Goethe in Italy," part of the Kunsthalle collection in Zürich.

48. Felstiner, John, "Etching and Alchemy" and "Crossing into Hebrew," *Paul Celan: Poet, Survivor, Jew* (New Heaven, CT: Yale University Press, 1995).

49. PCG, 177; SPPC, 233.

50. The first image from *Selected Poems and Prose of Paul Celan*, 214; the second from *Paul Celan: Poet, Survivor, Jew*, 234.

51. "Sinn und Sinnverhüllung bei Paul Celan," GW, 452; "Meaning and Concealment of Meaning In Paul Celan's Work," *Who . . .* , 167.

52. "Phänomenologischer und semantischer Zugang zu Celan," GW, 462; "A Phenomenological and Semantic Approach to Celan?," *Who . . .* , 180.

53. As Derrida affirms, Celan's poetry does not answer to the idea of "a previously existing art of writing." Jacques Derrida, *Sovereignties in Question: The Poetics of Paul Celan*, ed., Thomas Dutoit and Outi Pasanen (New York: Fordham University Press, 2005), 65. However, I do not see that this should mean that there is a secret which sustains the word. I think the word is undergone by Celan in its finitude or temporality, not deferred. As I argue through out the book, the opening of temporality does not require a deferral of meaning unless this is understood as a strategy over against the traditional understanding of philosophy as the task of a transcendental subject. This leads me to a second point. Speaking of Celan's struggle in his relationship with the German language, Derrida writes, "what I suggest is that one never appropriates a language, but rather to carry on a hand-to-hand, bodily struggle with it. What I try to think is an idiom . . . and a signature in the linguistic idiom. . . ." ("Language is Never Owned," *Sovereignties in Question . . .* ," 99) And again, speaking about Celan, "He wakes up language, and in order to experience the awakening, the return to life of language, truly in the quick, the living flesh, he must be very close to its corpse." (Ibid., 106). But how does Derrida engage this physicality? To what extent? See chapter 8; and also on this question Françoise Dastur's "Derrida and the Question of Presence," *Research in Phenomenology*, vol. 36 (2006), 45–62.

54. *Paul Celan: Poet, Survivor, Jew*, 217.

55. *Paul Celan, Ausgewählten Gedichte* (Frankfurt am Main: Suhrkamp, 1968), 144.

56. PCG, 175; SPPC, 225.

57. WORD-DEPOSIT, VOLCANIC / sea-overroared. // Above, / the surging mob / of anti-creatures: it / hoisted a flag-image and after-image / cruise vainly timewards. // Until you hurl / away the / Word-moon. From which / The miracle ebb originates / And the heart- / Shaped crater / Nakedly bears witness to the beginnings, / to the king- / births. Wordaufschüttung, vulkanisch, / meerüberrauscht. // Oben / Der flutende Mob / Der Gegengeschöpfen: er / Flaggte—Abbild und Nachbild / Kreuzen eitel zeithin. // Bis du den / Wortmond hinaus- / Schleuderst, von dem her / Das Wunder Ebbe geschieht / Und der Herz- / Förmige Krater / Nackt für die Anfänge zeugt, / die Königs- / geburten. (PCG, 180.)

58. PCG, 180.

59. GW, 388; *Who . . .* , 73.

60. PCG, 177; SPPC, 231.

61. Vide footnote 41.

62. PCG, 175. In this as in other poems in the series the erotic overtones are clear, a small indication that these poems are indeed a series of love poems.

63. *Collected Prose*, trans., Waldrop, 6.

64. *Collected Prose*, trans., Waldrop, 6.

65. How will our concept of language resist this insight, so that one may begin to engage language before language, before words, i.e., that sensuous experience which configures the word, and that as such may perhaps be called language, all though now the word will have carried us well beyond logic, syntax, and representation?

66. The play of eye, finger, and mouth indicates that the sensuous experience of the summoning of the word is not a matter of the mouth as taste, a sense separate from sight and hearing.

67. *L'Ephémère,* 26 March 1969, no. 14 (1970), 184.

68. Again, I agree with Derrida, that the issue of reading Celan is that of engaging that singular word that his breath unfolds, i.e., as it unfolds a "spacing that does not pertain to meaning." (Sovereignties in Question. . . ." "The Truth that Wounds," 163.) However, this spacing is not a secret, it may be engaged in its physicality, in its silences, in ways that let the opening temporality of thought undo the centrality of discourses founded on the idea of a transcendental subjectivity without having to read physicality in light of signification, i.e., in light of (strangely) what seems a response to a proper language in Derrida's insistence on the strategies of *Différance.* I take these issues up directly in the chapter on Derrida's reading of Artaud, as well as in the appendix on *Différance.* The point is not to refute or diminish the masterful opening Derrida accomplishes for thought. Indeed, the reader should keep in mind that the difference I have marked arises in light of Derrida's work!

Chapter 8

1. *Artaud le MOMA* (Paris: Galilée, 2002).

2. "*le* front, un sorte de guerre incessant qui, comme la antipathie même, fair pour moi d'Artaud une sorte d'ennemi privilégié, un ennemi douloureux que je porte et préfère en moi, au plus près de tout les limites sur lesquelles me jette le travail de ma vie et de la mort. Cette antipathie résiste mais elle reste une alliance, elle commande une vigilance de la pensée. . . ." (*Artaud le Moma,* 19–20)

3. "Privi-lege" already points to various registers or tones that will play out in our discussion: the unleashing of the *privus,* the singular, at play in the *lege* and *logos,* in the text, the writing, the speaking, and the interpreting of the word in Derrida's encounter of that name: Artaud. *Privus* also in its verbal form, *privo,* meaning to steal, to rob, also to strip, and at the same time, to release. I am speaking here of various dynamics I find in Derrida's various and singular encounters with Artaud.

4. "La parole soufflé," *Writing and Difference,* trans., Alan Bass (Chicago, IL: University of Chicago Press, 1978), 194–95. All quotes from this work will be indicated by the page number from the English translation from the University of Chicago Press edition.

5. Julio Cortazar, "The Death of Antonin Artaud," trans., Alfred Mac Adam, *Review* 51 (1995): 40–41. Originally published in *Sur* 163 in 1948.

6. "La parole Soufflé" was first published in 1965 in *Tel Quel.*

7. "Le théâtre de la cruauté et la clôture de la representation," a lecture first given in Parma Italy, and first published in *Critique,* 230, July 1966.

8. First published in Germany in 1986, then in English, together with an essay by Paule Thévenin, *The Secret Art of Antonin Artaud*, trans., Mary Ann Caws (Cambridge, MA: MIT press, 1998).

9. First delivered as a lecture in 1996 at the MOMA, in the occasion of the retrospective of Artaud's paintings and drawings, later published as a book by the same title. Vide footnote above.

10. "to unsense the subjectile," *The Secret Art of Antonin Artaud* (Cambridge, MA: MIT Press, 1998), 67. I must add for the sake of clarity, that, in the following discussion, the brief interpolations of other texts do not indicate any intention in my part to present a general theory about Derrida or Artaud, any more than the discussion of specific texts wants to treat them as case studies or examples of such theory. Vide footnote 44.

11. "La différance," was first given as a lecture at the French Society of Philosophy in 1968. In the same year, it was published simultaneously in *Bulletin de la société française de philosophie* and in *Théorie d'ensemble* (*Tel Quell*). Then it appeared in *Marges de la philosophie* (Paris: Minuit, 1972).

12. This extends to the very configuration of experience in consciousness as figured through the system/play of *différance*.

13. Ibid., 27.

14. La parole soufflé," *Writing and Difference*, 175.

15. Ibid., 175.

16. Ibid., 175.

17. Ibid., 175: "spirited away" is a fortunate translation, because it catches the play of souffler, to blow, and the Greek word for spirit, *psyche*, which not only means also breath, but in its verbal form means literally to cool or warm by blowing. One might relate this directly to another figure of the word in its concrete undergoing in Celan's *Atemwende*, literally, "breath-turn."

18. "Lifting" should also be heard as a substitution for Derrida's translation of *aufheben* in Hegel as "relever." *Margins of Philosophy*, "Tympan," (Chicago, IL: University of Chicago Press, 1982), x.

19. Ibid., 175.

20. Ibid., 175.

21. Ibid., 176.

22. Ibid., 176.

23. Ibid., 176.

24. Ibid., 177. More specifically in terms of *différance* we can say that: The forgetting does not forget something, nor is this the withdrawing of being. The lifting figures a movement that has no place, a movement that is not, and that at the same time, is always disseminated in the interminable significations that arise in the theft. In other words, this lifting or *soufflé* figures *différance*. Later on in the essay Derrida calls this gesture "furtive différance." (Ibid., 192) This is an indication that for Derrida the lifting and forgetting ultimately are not other than the play of *différance*. This will be a crucial distinction between Derrida's reading of Artaud, and Artaud's understanding of the theft as different from his speech and body.

25. Ibid., 176.

26. Ibid., 176.
27. Ibid., 178.
28. Ibid., 178.
29. Ibid., 179.
30. Ibid., 179.
31. Ibid., 179.
32. Ibid., 180.
33. Ibid., 181.
34. Ibid., 182.
35. Ibid., 183.
36. Ibid., 183.
37. Ibid., 183.
38. Ibid., 183.
39. Ibid., 183.
40. Ibid., 186–87.
41. And even, as Derrida indicates later, an erection that in becoming an inflamed member may become for Artaud a figure of castration. Ibid., 186.
42. Ibid., 183.
43. Derrida's essay opens by speaking of two discourses that traditionally situate Artaud, the clinical and the critical, and by pointing towards "the common elements of their origin and their horizon." (Ibid., 169) And, the essay closes by indicating the transgression and double play of the two discourses. Derrida concludes: "The concepts of madness, alienation, or inalienation irreducibly belong to the history of metaphysics. Or, more narrowly: they belong to the epoch of metaphysics that determines Being as the life of a proper subject" (Ibid., 193).
44. "La parole . . . ," 184.
45. Ibid., 184.
46. Ibid., 185.
47. Ibid., 185–86.
48. "But what we call organic differentiation had already raged within the body, before it had corrupted the metaphysics of the theater" Ibid., 186.
49. Ibid., 186. I must at least mention that here mind is not prior to the body's theft and the appearing of the body as organs or as divided into sensing faculties.
50. Ibid., 186–87.
51. Ibid., 187.
52. Ibid., 187.
53. Ibid., 187.
54. Ibid., 188.
55. Ibid., 188. As Martin Esslin explains in *Antonin Artaud*, poetically speaking, Artaud develops a new vocabulary. Martin Esslin, *Antonin Artaud* (New York: Penguin Modern Masters, 1976), 3; chapter 3, "The Limits of Language."
56. Ibid., 188.
57. Ibid., 188.
58. "The Theater of Cruelty," *Writing and Difference*, trans., Alan Bass (Chicago, IL: University of Chicago Press, 1978), 234.
59. "La parole . . . ," 189.

60. "The Theater of Cruelty," 240.

61. "The Theater of Cruelty," 240.

62. "La parole . . . ," 190.

63. Ibid., 191. At this point we come to an explicit crossing with the essay I use to supplement our discussion of Artaud's return to speech and writing, "The Theater of Cruelty and the Closure of Representation," in which, as its title indicates, Derrida develops his an engagement with Artaud's thought through the problem of representation.

64. Ibid., 191.

65. Ibid., 191.

66. "The Theater of Cruelty," 240.

67. "The Theater of Cruelty," 241.

68. We find a figure of this language in Artaud's word play in the title, *Artaud le Momo*, which Derrida brings to bear in his essay at the MOMA, an essay on the museum and the idea of the work of art, *Artaud le Moma*, a title that figures the cruelty of metaphysics and representation, the institutionalization of Artaud, as well as the unsettling that the play of the name may cause in the institution. The MOMA resisted the title and replaced it with an institutional formality: "Jacques Derrida . . . will present a lecture about Artaud's drawings." *Artaud le Moma*, 11–12.

69. "La parole . . . ," 193.

70. Ibid., 194.

71. "La parole . . . ," 193.

72. "The Theater of Cruelty," 245.

73. "La parole . . . ," 192.

74. Ibid., 194.

75. "One entire side of his discourse destroys a tradition which lives within difference, alienation, and negativity without seeing their origin and necessity." Ibid., 194.

76. "Artaud affirms the cruel law of difference; a law that, this time, is raised to the level of consciousness and is no longer experienced within metaphysical naïveté." Ibid., 194. Artaud, "has denounced, with a gesture that does not give shelter to another metaphysics, the *other* metaphysics, as the metaphysics that lives within difference, within metaphor and the work, and thus within alienation. . . ." Ibid., 193.

77. Ibid., 194.

78. Ibid., 194.

79. On the way to my final remark I should mention the dynamics that I think make Artaud Derrida's "privileged enemy." Derrida finds in Artaud a metaphysical desperation that leads it to its closure . . . a closure that situates thought over against a transgressive limit, i.e., in its simultaneous exposure to the cruelty of presence and necessary risk of metaphysics in the almost hidden desire for non-difference. Artaud's extreme closure leads Derrida to the other side of the metaphysical delimitation of word and thought, thus, Artaud accompanies thought as much in its life as in its death.

80. Ibid., 195.

81. "to unsense the subjectile," *The Secret Art of Antonin Artaud*, trans., Mary Ann Caws (Cambridge, MA: MIT press, 1998).

82. The other two dates are 1946 and 1947. *The Secret . . .* , 61.

83. *The Secret* . . . , 78.
84. *The Secret* . . . , 77.
85. *The Secret* . . . , 78.
86. *The Secret* . . . , 78.
87. *The Secret* . . . , 80.
88. *The Secret* . . . , 80.
89. *The Secret* . . . , 80.
90. *The Secret* . . . , 80.
91. Vide Alejandro A. Vallega, "On the Tactility of Words: Gadamer's Reading of Paul Celan's *Atemkristall*," *Internationales Jahrebuch für Hermeneutik*, Band 3/2004.
92. *The Secret* . . . , 82, 113, and 114.
93. *The Secret* . . . , 128.
94. Hans-George Gadamer, *Wer bin Ich und wer bist Du?* (Frankfurt am Main: Suhrkamp, 1973). *Who Am I and Who Are You?* trans., Heinemann and Krajevwski (Albany: State University of New York Press, 1997), 105. *Äesthetik und Poetik II*, Gadamer Gesammelte Werke, vol. 9 (Tübingen: Mohr, 1993), 411–12.
95. *The Secret* . . . , 139.
96. *The Secret* . . . , 139–42.
97. As Gasché rightly points out, deconstruction's infinity hinges on finitude. (Vide *Inventions of Difference: On Jacques Derrida* (Cambridge, MA: Harvard University Press, 1994), 148. My point is that in the strategic concern thought does not engage its physicality beyond making such engagement possible.
98. Here I find a response to David Wood's concerns about the transcendental character of deconstruction, in "Différance and the Problem of Strategy" (in *Derrida and Différance* (Evanston, IL: Northwestern University Press, 1988), 63–69. *Différance* seems to have to be transcendental because its strategic character requires a deferral in any undergoing of language, since the strategic movement is that of the unsettling of presence and representation by virtue of a pause that marks the interruption, delay, loss, erasure operative in consciousness and the metaphysics of presence. Therefore, because a deferral is required, that very deferral figures a seemingly transcendental moment.
99. This is not the end of philosophy: As Rodolphe Gasché explains in an essay in memory of Derrida, "Only on condition that the shock that triggers thinking is not immediately supplanted by an effort to achieve knowledge about its cause, but threatens thinking in its very possibility, does thinking have a chance to occur." Vide Rodolphe Gasché, "Thinking, Without Wonder," *Epoché*, vol. 10, no. 2 (Spring 2006), 329–30.
100. Artaud's last work for La voix des poétes, titled "Pour en finir avec le jugement de Dieu," was rehearsed and recorded between the 22nd and 29th of November, 1947, and reworked in January, 1948. The broadcast was schedule for February 2, 1948 but was cancelled a day before by the Director General of Radiodiffusion Française. Not only was the material of the broadcast inflammatory in its themes and language, even today when one hears Artaud's voice, the dissonant sound of his sharp screams and glottal utterances are physically assaulting to the listener . . . but the issue is if this assault does not call us from and towards senses of language in the flesh. Vide Martin Esslin, *Antonin Artaud* (New York: Penguin Modern Masters, 1976), 65; chapter 3, "The Limits of Language."

Chapter 9

1. Adorno's statement is not a theory but a critical situation from which his thinking occurs. The trail of this problem can be seen in the various formulations of it: In 1939, he writes that "Actually, it is no longer possible to say anything. Action is the only form left to theory." (*Can One Live after Auschwitz ?* Introduction, 11, ed., Rolf Tiedemann (Stanford, CA: Stanford University Press, 2003.) In 1949, in "Cultural Criticism and Society," he writes the famous statement, "To write poetry after Auschwitz is barbarie." (*Can One Live . . .* , 162; *Gesammelte Schriften* Bd.10.1, 11–30 (Frankfurt am Main: Suhrkamp, 1970–1986). And, in 1967, in "Art and the Arts," he amends the statement by situating it in relation to art: "While the present situation no longer has room for art—that was the meaning of the statement about the impossibility of poems after Auschwitz—it nevertheless has need for it." (*Can One Live . . .* , 387; *Gesammelte Schriften* Bd.10.1, 432–53 (Frankfurt am Main: Suhrkamp, 1970–1986).

2. "Art and the Arts," *Can One Live . . .* , 386; *Gesammelte Schriften* Bd.10.1, 452–53 (Frankfurt am Main: Suhrkamp, 1970–1986). As Howard Caygill indicates, there are at least three versions of this essay, one from 1935, one from 1936, and a final version worked out from 1936 to 1939, which is the last version. I refer in my discussion to this last one. Caygill's commentary on the essay is as informative as it is insightful. Vide, *Walter Benjamin: The Color of Experience* (New York: Routledge, 1998), 97–117. Vide also Susan Buck-Morss on a 1938 version, *The Origin of . . .* , 149, footnote 127.

3. Benjamin, Walter: "Das Kunstwerk im Zeitalter seiner technischen Reproduzierbarkeit," *Illuminationen* (Frankfurt/Main: Suhrkamp, 1977). Benjamin composed the essay during 1934, when he was already in exile, and it was first published in 1936 in the *Zeitschrift für Sozialfroschung* 5, under the title, "L'ouvre d'art à l'epoque de sa reproduction mécanisee." The quotes in English are from *Illuminations*, ed., Hannah Arendt (New York: Schocken Books, 1969); I have indicated wherever I altered the translation. All references from it will be indicated by "I" followed by the page number, and will be followed by the German edition page number. The same order of page numbers will be observed for other texts.

4. I, 218; 137. The French title of Benjamin's essay gives a stronger character of this, because it emphasizes the relation of work of art and reproduction with the possessive "*sa*": "L'ouvre d'art à l'epoque de sa reproduction mécanisee."

5. Adorno writes in "Art and the Arts," "As the antithesis to empirical reality, by contrast, art is one. Its dialectical nature consists in the fact that it can carry out its movement toward unity simply and solely by passing through multiplicity. Otherwise, its movement would be abstract and futile. Art's relation to the empirical stratum is vital to it." I might add that this means that we should find the articulate sense of the work of art through the specific form of the particular art, a point that goes along with Benjamin's inquiry into film as mechanical representation and its aesthetic sense. "Art and the Arts," *Can One Live After Auschwitz?* ed., Rolf Tiedemann (Stanford, CA: Stanford University Press, 2003), 383.

6. As Susan Buck-Morss indicates, they do disagree on the way this is understood: for Adorno it is an issue of dialectic between subject and production, for Benjamin in his essay on mechanical reproduction the emphasis is on production alone.

Ultimately, the issue will be the understanding of dialectic in relationship to the status of history. Susan Buck-Morss, *The Origin of Negative Dialectic: Theodor W. Adorno, Walter Benjamin, and the Frankfurt Institute* (New York: The Free Press, Macmillan, 1977), 146–50; and chapter 3.

7. "process reproduction can bring out those aspects of the original that are unattainable to the naked eye and yet accessible to the lens. . . . ," I, 220; 140. Cf. "Evidently a different nature opens to the camera than to the naked eye. . . ." I, 236; 162.

8. I, 218; 136–37.

9. I, 241; 168.

10. I, 241; 168.

11. I, 241; 168.

12. As Benjamin explains, in a passage that stands directly against futurism, this is a system that must result in war, since its production does not bare transformation but the inadequate need and use of production distilled from any natural relation between production, technology and humans. This is an observation that I believe can contribute to the understanding of the internal need for continuous war that we find today along with the development of global capitalism. I, 241; 168.

13. I, 223–24; 143–44.

Here is worth noting Giorgio Agambens observation about the concept of the aura and its decay. Agamben argues that Benjamin takes up this concept not only from mystical-esoteric texts, but from the work of Léon Daudet, in *La Melancholia*, circa 1928. The relationship seems direct when one considers Daudet's work on Baudelaire as "poet of the aura," and Benjamin's study of Baudelaire. Also, the passage on the aura and photography in "The Work of Art in the Age of Reproduction" seems to be predated by Daudet's discussion of photography and the cinema as "transmitters of aura." Giorgio Agamben, "The Absolute Commodity," *Stanzas*, trans., Ronald L. Martinez (Minneapolis: University of Minnesota, 1993), 44–45. (Besides his own work in philosophy, Giorgio Agamben is the editor of Benjamin's complete works in Italian.)

14. Agamben makes a similar association in "Marx; or, The Universal Exposition" in *Stanzas*, 36–40.

15. I. 224, footnote 5; 143, footnote 7.

16. "*Dagegen sind sie zur Formulierung revolutionärer Forderungen in der Kunstpolitik brauchbar.*" I, 218; 137.

17. "One might subsume the eliminated element in the term "aura" and go on to say that: that which withers in the age of mechanical reproduction is the aura of the work of art." I, 221. Cf. I, 222, wherein Benjamin equates aura "with the unique phenomenon of a distance." This will be important later in our discussion. I, 223–24, aura in relation to ritual: "It is significant that the existence of the work of art with reference to its aura is never entirely separated from its ritual function."

18. This transformation happens then as "logic of the matter," in the sense that objects change through a kind of transformative translation in moving from matter into words. Vide Buck-Morss, *The Origin of . . .* , 82–87.

19. Benjamin, Walter, "Über die Wahrnehmung," Gesammelte Schriften, Bd. VI, (Frankfurt am Main: Suhrkamp Verlag, 1980), 33–38.

20. Benjamin writes, "Philosophy is absolute experience deduced as language in a systematic symbolic context. Absolute experience is, for the philosopher's intuition, language; language, although, understood as symbolic systematic concept. It (experience) is specified in modalities of language, one of which is perception . . ." (Gesammelte Schriften, Bd. VI, Frankfurt am Main: Suhrkamp Verlag, 1980), 33–38.

21. We should at least keep in mind that Benjamin does not say that perception is language but that perception is a modality of language, and this leaves open the question of how we can understand language, because we are speaking of perception as a modality of language, rather than in terms of linguistic signs as determining perception. This at least suggests that the work of art in its particular form configures an articulate although not conceptual sense.

22. Benjamín writes: "The film makes the cult value recede into the background not only by putting the public in the position of the critic, but also by the fact that at the movies this position requires no attention. The public is an examiner, but an absent minded one (*ein zerstreuter*)." I, 240–41; 167.

23. "The film form" is Sergei Eisenstein term to define film in terms of its technical production, particularly as montage. Vide Sergei Eisenstein, *Film Form: Essays in Film Theory*, ed. and trans., Jay Leyda (New York: Harcourt, 1977).

24. This ruin occurs through the relentless destruction of the aura of the creator; Benjamin speaks of the loss of the aura that happens when the actor becomes a reproduced image in film (I, 229; 152), or in the Dada Art Works (I, 237; 163).

25. *"zum resten Mal—und das ist das Werk des Films—kommt der Mensch in die Lage, zwar mit seiner gesamten lebendinge Person aber unter Verzicht aus deren Aura wirken zu müssen."* I, 229; 152.

26. I. 239; 165.

27. I think that Riefenstahl's incapacity to see her work as fascist comes from the fact that she creates an aesthetic that becomes a style, fascist style. At the same time, the fascist practice of giving a false sense of activity to the public while keeping an unchanging content, thus alienating all subjects, occurs widely today and is sustained in the name of being something other than Riefenstahl's fascist style: where fascism is concealed by appealing to looks rather than to the movement or absence thereof, arisen with the image.

28. I, 236; 162.

29. I, 236–37; 162.

30. I, 235; 161.

31. From manuscript A of Kant's *Critique*: "The Synthesis of Recognition in a Concept," The Deduction of the Pure Concepts of Understanding, *Critique of Pure Reason*, trans., Norman Kemp Smith (New York: St. Martin's Press, 1965), 136. Kritik der reinen Vernunft, Kant Werke, vol. II (Darmstadt: Wissenschaftliche Buchgesellschaft, 1998), 167–68.

32. I, 237–38; 164

33. I, 238; 164.

34. "die physische Chockwirkung . . . ," I, 238; 165.

35. I, 238; 164. The understanding of tactility as the primary experience of sense perception at least goes back to Aristotle's *De Anima*, where touch appears as

the primary sense without which no other sense experience (*aisthesis*) is possible (*De Anima*, 414b33; 435a20). Aristotle goes as far as to state that we can only have a sense of having a body if we are able to touch (*De Anima*, 434b9). Finally, unlike all other sense experiences, touch is the sensing that does not happen at a distance from the sensed. In touch the medium is the touch (*De Anima*, 423b12). It is also interesting for our discussion that as Aristotle points out, unlike all other senses, touch refers us to more than one specific sense experience, for example, both taste and density involve touch (*De Anima*, 422b17). Lucretius in the *Rerum Natura* will go as far as to identify vision with touch. I should add that, for filmmakers like Eisenstein, the cinema gathers all the other senses, while remaining a singular aesthetic experience, make an analogous argument to that of Aristotle.

36. I, 238; 165.

37. I, 222; 142.

38. The word "habit" translates "*Gewohnheit.*" I, 240; 166.

39. "For the last time the aura emanates from the early photographs in the fleeting expression of a human face." I, 226. It is worth mentioning that this identification of the aura with the face invites an engagement with Levinas, under the question of the import of the face as aura for his ethics of alterity.

40. I, 236–37; 162.

41. "Die bilder, die beiden davontrangen, sind ungeheuer verschieden. Das des Malers ist ein totales, das des Kameramanns ein vielfältig zerststückeltes, dessen Teile sich nach einem neuen Gesetze zusammen finden." I, 234; 158.

42. As Buck-Morss indicates Benjamin's relationship to history shifts between the composition of his essay on mechanical representation (1934–1939) and his "Thesis on the Concept of History" (1940). *The Origin of . . .* , 168. However, as we see in this discussion, the theme of tactility we begun to discuss goes to the heart of Benjamin's discussion of history's temporality.

43. "Theses on the Concept of History," original translation title: "Theses on the Philosophy of History," *Illuminations*, ed., Hanna Arendt (New York: Schocken Books, 1969), 262. "Über der Begriff der Geschichte," *Illuminationen,* 260. I have altered the English title slightly in order to emphasize the "*Begriff*" which can be easily overlooked if one follows the standard English translation.

44. "Theses on the Philosophy of History," *Illuminations*, ed., Hanna Arendt (New York: Schocken Books, 1969), 262–63; 260.

45. I agree with Adorno, as well as with Derrida, that Heidegger's emphasis on ontology limits his engagement with the concreteness of thought (vide Adorno, "Art and the Arts," *Can One Live after Auschwitz?*, 379–81). This is already clear in *Being and Time*, as well as in his later work. One might also consider the criticism of Enrique Dussel and of Rodolfo Kusch.

46. "Theses on the Philosophy of History," *Illuminations*, ed., Hanna Arendt (New York: Schocken Books, 1969), 263; 260.

47. I, 238; 165.

48. *Hiroshima Mon Amour*, "Synopsis," trans., Richard Server (New York: Grove Press, 1961), 9.

49. Ultimately we are speaking of a transformation of aesthetic sensibility that would affect how we view all works of art, and not only film. Film is the medium of

transformation, rather than the only form of the work of art which bares the imme-diacy Benjamin is indicating. From the experience of the work of art in the flesh that we are beginning to articulate, a whole new aesthetics opens, in which the sense of the work of art is rediscovered. This is Benjamin's point along with the uncovering of the politics of art, which are given in such immediate experience of the work. At the same time, this does not say that we can abstract the work of art from its particular form and mode of production. On the contrary, the change that occurs is that we may begin to see works of art in light of their contrast with the film sense-form.

50. When I speak of sensibility, I am not speaking of the internal experience or intuitions of an already constituted subject or subjective consciousness, or of those feelings and emotions so often juxtaposed with the subject's reason and offered as its irrational alternative. As Benjamin suggests, there is much we have to learn about the configuration of the subject, and this must include our sense of self through the analysis of the experience of film. "The enlargement of a snapshot does not simply render more precise what in any case was visible, though nuclear: it reveals entirely new structural formations of the subject." I, 236; 162. Also, that we aim to articulate the immediate experience of the work of art given in film means that we are not interested in preserving mysteries. And yet, it does not suppose that film will represent aesthetic experience: to speak of being exposed to certain experience or finitude, or of undergoing such singular experience, is not synonymous with either signification or representation. Also, that we might undergo a certain sense through experience does not mean that work and sense must be transparent to reason; or, that because they are not thoroughly subsumable under reason and presence they must be irrational. Let me suggest that our task will be that of making apparent an experience that by its very character, as an experience outside the metaphysical and subjectivist aura and immediate in its shock, must challenge the idea of articulation as the representation of an original or essence, and the modes that accommodate experience and even language within the logic of representation and its ontological aura. In other words, given the matter to be thought, we cannot yet give a conceptual status to works of art as if they are there already constituted and open to analysis, but we can at least give a critique of the experience in which we encounter the work, as well as a critique of its sense—that is, in attentively marking the delimitations of work and sense in the singular experience of their material arising.

51. *Hiroshima Mon Amour*, "Synopsis," trans., Richard Server (New York: Grove Press, 1961), 9.

52. Ibid.

53. Ibid., "Scenario," 15.

54. Ibid., "Synopsis," 9.

55. Kent Jones recounts this story in his notes to the film DVD edition in the Criterion Collection, 2003.

56. Vide footnote 23.

57. Theodore W. Adorno and Walter Benjamin, *The Complete Correspondence 1928–1940*, ed., Henry Lonitz, trans., Nicholas Walker (Cambridge, MA: Harvard University Press, 1999), 131.

58. Susan Buck-Morss, *The Origin of . . .* , 147.

59. Susan Buck-Morss, *The Origin of . . .* , 149.

60. Ibid., 130. This point questions Benjamin's idea of a certain distraction as a central disarming element in the disintegration of the aura of the work of art.

61. Ibid., 131.

62. In contemporary terms, could Benjamín not see that Warhol's reproductions could also become a commodity regardless of their irony concerning the market?

63. Ibid., 132.

64. In one of the most important works on aesthetics written in Latin America in the last century, *Operatory Aesthetic in its Three Directions* (*Estética Operatoria en sus tres direcciónes*), in a reflection on the cinema based on Benjamin's essay, Luis Juan Guerrero writes: "Let us say, on the one hand, that the cinema is the most formidable auto-alienating enterprise man can have invented; but, on the other hand, it also promotes certain unexpected productive springs in that alienating process." (*Estética Operatoria en sus tres direcciónes*, Volume III (Buenos Aires, Argentina: Losada, 1967), 232–33.) Guerrero closes his study on aesthetics with a reflection on film based on the French version of Benjamin's essay. Unfortunately, in spite of its importance for aesthetic theory in Latin America, this work has not been translated into English (the quote above is my rendition of the Spanish text).

65. Ibid., 146–47.

66. As Pier Paolo Pasolini explains in 1965 in "Il cinema di poesia," "Poetic Cinema," the poetic language of the cinema attributed to such filmmakers as those of the French New Wave can be seen as a neo-capitalist product: "To sum up, in a general schema, the formation of a tradition of a "poetic language of the cinema" turns out as the spy of a strong and general boosting of formalism, i.e., the average and typical production of neo-capitalism.... That is, all of this, in the part of bourgeois culture, is part of the general recovery of the turf lost to Marxism and its possible revolution." (Pier Paolo Pasolini, "Il cinema di poesia," *Empirismo Eretico,* 2nd Ed. (Milano, Italia: Garzanti, 1995), 186–87 (my translation). In identifying the experience of the political in the flesh we have not made a leap over the critique of the work of art, but rather uncovered another disposition for such critique.

Chapter 10

1. An earlier version of this chapter was delivered as a conference at the Collegium Phaenomenologicum in 2005. I have tried to keep the candid tone of the exchange and the atmosphere in which and for which I wrote the original piece.

2. Gabriel García Márquez, *The Solitude of Latin America* (Nobel Lecture 1982).

3. All references to the *Phenomenology of the Spirit* come from *Phenomenology of Spirit*, trans., A. V. Miller (New York: Oxford Press, 1977), and will be indicated as *Phenomenology* followed by the paragraph number. In this case: *Phenomenology*, para. 808.

4. *Phenomenology*, para. 177.

5. *Phenomenology*, para. 177.

6. "Thus the relation of the two self-conscious individuals is such that they prove themselves and each other through a life-and-death struggle. They must engage

in this struggle, for they must raise their certainty of being for themselves to truth, both in the case of the other and in their own case." (*Phenomenology*, para. 187).

7. *Phenomenology*, para. 177.

8. *Phenomenology*, para. 805.

9. *Phenomenology*, para. 808.

10. Hyppolite, Jean, *Genesis and Structure of Hegel's* Phenomenology of Spirit, trans., Cherniak and Heckman (Evanston, IL: Northwestern University Press, 1974), 296–317.

11. *Phenomenology*, para. 488.

12. Hyppolite, 415.

13. *Phenomenology*, para. 508.

14. *Phenomenology*, para. 808.

15. *Phenomenology*, para. 788; para. 805.

16. "Spirit is this movement of the Self which empties itself of itself and sinks itself into its substance . . ." para. 804.

17. See John Russon, *Reading Hegel's Phenomenology* (Bloomington: Indiana University Press, 2004), 21–22.

18. We are speaking inversely of an exclusion of the other through the internalization of all difference through sovereign representation.

19. Gadamer, *Hegel's Dialectic*, trans., Christopher Smith (New Haven, CT: Yale University Press), 74.

20. This is a point Rodolphe Gasché made at the meeting of the International Hermeneutisch Symposium in Freiburg, 2005.

21. Note that even if we happen to use a language of identity, this language does not require necessarily the dialectical imposition we find in Hegel or the Greeks.

22. "I said in my introduction that man is a yes. I will never stop reiterating that. . . . Man's behavior is not only reactional. And there is always resentment in a reaction. Nietzsche had already pointed that out in *The Will to Power*." *Black Skin White Masks*, 222. "And, through a private problem, we see the outline of the problem of Action. Placed in this world, in a situation, embarked, as Pascal would have it . . . , *Black Skin White Masks*, 229–30; "he who looks into my eyes for anything but a perpetual question will have to lose his sight; neither recognition nor hate" (29). All references refer to *Black Skin White Masks*, trans., Charles Lam Markmann (New York: Grove Press, 1967), and will be noted by page number only. In this case, 12. All references to the French edition come from *Peau noire, masques blancs* (Paris: Éditions du Seuil, 1952), the page number will follow after the English translation's pagination.

23. 12.

24. 60.

25. 9.

26. 29; Cf., on desalienation, 226. "I have ceaselessly strived to show the Negro that in a sense he makes himself abnormal; to show the white man that he is at once the perpetrator and the victim of a delusion. 225.

27. 228.

28. 38.

29. "*veritablement il s'agit de lâcher l'homme*," 9; French, 6.

30. "*de remettre l'homme a sa place*." 88; French, 71.

31. 232.

32. I should add that Fanon's encounter with Hegel occurs through the lectures of Hyppolite and Kojève in France and the influence of Aimé Césaire.

33. 30.

34. 227. Cf. Philip J. Kain, *Hegel and the Other* (Albany: State University of New York Press, 2005), 52–56. In his study Kain misses Fanon's point by explaining that Hegel's dialectic happens in terms of Kantian transcendental ethics.

35. 9.

36. 109.

37. 110.

38. 110.

39. 216–17.

40. 220.

41. 221.

42. 217.

43. 217.

44. 32.

45. In *Subjects of Desire*, Judith Butler argues that desire is fundamental to the movement of spirit and not subject to it. However, she also indicates that desire only occurs in concrete figurations. Indeed, she writes, "True subjectivities come to flourish only in communities that provide for reciprocal recognition, for we do not come to ourselves through work alone. . . ." (Judith Butler, *Subjects of Desire* (New York: Columbia University Press, 1987), 58; see also 46.)

46. 139.

47. I might add a narcissism that also figures nonexistence at the level of self-consciousness expected by both Fanon and Hegel.

48. See John Russon on the concrete sense of the dialectic: *The Self and Its Body in Hegel's* Phenomenology of Spirit (Toronto: University of Toronto Press, 1997), 72–75; and, in *Reading Hegel's Phenomenology*, chapter 15, "Absolute Knowing." (*Reading Hegel's Phenomenology* (Bloomington: Indiana University Press, 2004), 221–28.) In both cases Russon points to the necessity of a concrete determination in the dialectical movement, i.e., not only transcendental.

49. 9.

50. 111.

51. "There are times when the black man is locked into his body." 225.

52. 112.

53. "If there is an inferiority complex, it is the outcome of a double process: primarily, economic; subsequently, the internalization—or, better, the epidermalization—of this inferiority." 11.

54. 112.

55. "I do not trust fervor. Every time it has burst out somewhere it has brought fire, famine, misery. . . . And contempt for man. Fervor is the weapon of choice of the impotent." 9.

56. 120.

57. 299.

58. 18.

59. 229–30.

60. 229.

61. 229.

62. 229.

63. 229.

64. García Márquez, Gabriel, *Cien Años de Soledad,* 15ª edición (Madrid: Cátedra, 2004), 550.

65. García Márquez, Gabriel, *The Solitude of Latin America* (Nobel Lecture 1982).

66. García Márquez, Gabriel y Apuleyo Mendoza, Plinio, *El Olor de la Guayaba,* 5ª edición (Buenos Aires, Argentina: Editorial Sudamericana, 1996), 52.

67. Not to confuse literature with philosophy. For me their difference depends on the intensity and focus of the text, and not on the external form. But this is a point Aristotle already makes at the very beginning of his *Poetics*.

68. *El Olor,* 86.

69. *El Olor,* 87.

70. Speaking of those "desmesurada realidad" in his lecture the author says, "And if these difficulties . . . hinder us, it is understandable that the rational talents on this side of the world, exalted in the contemplation of their own cultures, should have found themselves without a valid means to interpret us. It is only natural that they insist on measuring us with the yardstick that they use for themselves. . . ." Nobel Lecture; Cf., *El Olor,* 51.

71. Michel Foucault, *The Order of Things* (New York: Vintage Books, 1994), xv–xxiv; *Les mots et les choses* (Paris: Gallimard, 1966), 9–16.

72. *El Olor,* 44.

73. *El Olor,* 44.

74. When Apuleyo observes that, "In *One Hundred Years of Solitude* the language has a brightness, a richness and profusion that is not found in your previous books . . ." García Márquez replies, "That is because I did not need it before." *El Olor,* 87.

75. With more direct relation to political, economic and social issues, García Márquez explains, "My conviction is that we have to invent our own solutions, in which we take as much advantage as possible of what those other continents have managed through long and hard histories, but without trying to copy them mechanically. . . ." *El Olor,* 147.

76. *El Olor,* 53.

Chapter 11

1. Galeano, Eduardo *Le Vene Aperte dell'America Latina* (Milano, Italia: Sperling & Kupfer, 1987.) My Translation.

2. Calvino, *Italo Lezioni Americane: sei proposte per il prossimo millennio* (Milano, Italia: Mondadori, 1993), 11. Quotes from this work are marked as LA. All translations are mine. The English Edition: Six Memos for the Next Millennium, trans., Patrick Creagh (New York: Vintage, 1996.)

3. One of the two papers with the highest circulation in Italy.

4. Pasolini's writings from this period are mainly gathered in two volumes: *Scritti Corsari* (Italy: Garzanti, Elefante ed., 2000); *Descrizioni di Descrizioni* (Milano, Italia: Garzanti, Elefante ed., 1996). Quotes from these works are marked "SC" and "DD," respectively.

5. SC.

6. Calvino, Italo *Le Città Invisibili* (Milano, Italia: Mondadori, 1993), Cronology, xviii. Quotes from this text are marked "CI."

7. CI., Presentazione, ix. From a lecture given in 1973 at the Graduate Writing Division of Columbia University, New York. Also published as "Italo Calvino On Invisible Cities," *Columbia*, #8, 1983, 37–42.

8. Ibid., x.

9. Pasolini, Pier Paolo, *Descrizioni di Descrizioni* (Milano, Italia: Garzanti, Gli Elefanti, 1996), 64.

10. LA., 65. Cf. Plato *Sophist*, 231B–236D.

11. LA., 7.

12. LA., 12.

13. LA., 16.

14. CI., Presentazione, xi.

15. CI., 74.

16. CI., Presentazione, ix.

17. Calvino, *Il Cavaliere Inesistente.*

18. Calvino, *Palomar.*

19. Calvino, *Il Barone Rampante.*

20. CI., 21.

21. We find this sensibility of thought in Aristotle and in Greek tragedy once we have considered the concrete and ephemeral character of political ideals, praxis, and ideologies.

22. LA., 16.

23. Calvino obscures the question of the relationship between poetry and thinking by speaking in this crucial passage of the poet-philosopher. Ibid.

24. LA., 43.

25. LA., 46.

26. LA., 50.

27. Comment by Claudia Baracchi in an earlier manuscript.

28. LA., 102.

29. Ibid.

30. LA., 110.

31. LA., 110.

32. LA., 128.

33. LA., 127.

34. Jacques Derrida, *Of Hospitality*, trans., Rachel Bowlby (Stanford, CA: Stanford University Press, 2000); *On Cosmopolitanism and Forgiveness*, trans., Mark Dooley and Michael Hughes (New York: Routledge, 2001); *Monolinguism of the Other or The Prosthesis of Origin*, trans., Patrick Mensah (Stanford, CA: Stanford University Press, 1998; *Politiques of Friendship*, trans., George Collins (New York: Verso, 2000); *Aporias*, trans., Thomas Dutoit (Stanford, CA: Stanford University Press, 1993). Alphonso Lingus, *The*

Community of Those Who Have Nothing in Common (Bloomington: Indiana University Press, 1994); *The Imperative* (Bloomington: Indiana University Press, 1998).

35. One of the characteristic of political ideologies, as well as that of the rhetoric of economic development, is that the affirmative repetition of the slogan is necessary for the perpetuation of belief; this repetition from the same essential need for sustaining an unchanging identity of calculative and analytical thought.

36. Comment by Claudia Baracchi in an earlier manuscript.

37. Edoardo Sanguineti, *Come si diventa materialisti storici?* (San Cesario di Lecce, Italy: Piero Manni, 2006).

38. Roberto Alperoli is the major of Castelnuovo.

Index